The U.S. Naval Academy

The U.S. Naval Academy

AN ILLUSTRATED HISTORY

BY JACK SWEETMAN

NAVAL INSTITUTE PRESS
Annapolis, Maryland

FOR DAD

Chapter-opening photographs

Page 2: Secretary of the Navy George Bancroft founded the Naval Academy. Courtesy: U.S. Naval History Division.

Page 18: An itinerant English artist, Charles Burton, painted this view of the officers' and faculty quarters along Buchanan Row around 1848. Courtesy: U.S. Naval Academy Museum.

Page 34: An exemplary character but an ineffectual disciplinarian, Commander George P. Upshur, who succeeded Buchanan as superintendent in 1847, found the midshipmen more than he could handle. This daguerreotype was made around 1851. Courtesy: U.S. Naval Academy Archives.

Page 54: Midshipmen practice light artillery drill in Touro Park, at Newport, Rhode Island, in 1863. Courtesy: U.S. Naval Academy Special Collections, Nimitz Library.

Page 82: Admiral David Dixon Porter was determined to make the Naval Academy a national institution rivaling West Point. Courtesy: U.S. Naval History Division.

Page 112: The Class of 1890, thirty-four strong, received its diplomas in an outdoor ceremony. Superintendent Sampson, wearing epaulets, stands in the middle ground at left. Courtesy: U.S. Naval Academy Special Collections, Nimitz Library.

Page 140: Midshipmen perform sail drill on the training ship *Severn*, around 1905. Courtesy: U.S. Naval Academy Museum.

Page 170: Color girl ceremony, 1921: Rear Admiral Archibald H. Scales presents the regimental colors to the color girl for transfer to the commander of the color company. Courtesy: U.S. Naval Academy Archives.

Page 194: In the rotunda of Bancroft Hall. Courtesy: U.S. Naval Academy Publications Office.

Page 214: Trident Scholar Edgar J. Enochs, '77, works on his project—an attempt to predict the effects of fatigue on pilot performance by monitoring brain waves. Courtesy: U.S. Naval Academy.

Contents

Foreword

The long-drawn-out and often turbulent genesis of our Naval Academy is a history long overdue to be told. Professor Sweetman has built this exciting and remarkable account with painstaking care to include not only how things evolved but why. Anyone interested in our navy will find it fascinating reading.

In the early days, development of fledgling U.S. naval officers who aspired to what is always the most important job in any navy, command of a man-of-war, was accomplished by "on-the-job" training. Professional skill and education, as well as personal standards, were largely dependent on the captains of the ships to which they were assigned. This was, at best, a variable base for such an exacting profession.

The deficiencies of such training resulted in years of widespread discussion and attempts to establish a shore-based school where "young gentlemen" could fit themselves for naval service.

Professor Sweetman helps us to understand the reluctance that for forty years obstructed the fulfillment of what would seem the obvious need.

Our young country was still groping its way, looking to older, more experienced nations for ways and means. The French and the British provided completely different systems. French midshipmen were educated in schools ashore, and emerged well-grounded in the theoretical aspects of the naval profession, and cultured as well. The British shipped in young boys and sent them to sea to learn what they could, sometimes with the help of a schoolmaster. To our interested officials, experienced senior naval officers and matter-of-fact congressmen alike, the choice was based on a purely practical concern. The British won their battles. The French did not. So the old hard-headed, backward pragmatists remained adamant in their opposition to the suggestions of many officers, schoolmasters, and secretaries of the navy. They believed in the basic necessity to win battles, and they did not want to abandon a system that had produced that result for one that had not yet demonstrated that it could.

Nevertheless, in the 1840s the United States had the "luck of a sailor." Remarkable Navy Secretary George Bancroft, a Ph.D. at age twenty, a workaholic, a disciplinarian, astute and persuasive, managed to bring into being a shore-based school on the Severn. Here, education was to be combined with practical training as well as the development of character. All this he accomplished without a single outside study, without advance authority or increase in funds, without even much opposition. But Secretary Bancroft's wisdom went even further. He had the good judgment to choose Commander Franklin Buchanan as the first superintendent. That courageous, experienced, successful naval officer was both demanding and understanding. He required strict compliance with the rules but he understood that the excessive energy of healthy young lads produces exuberance. He distinguished between pranks and willful insubordination.

The basic problems that confronted Commander Buchanan have confronted every succeeding superintendent and will always be present in a school that requires its graduates to have integrity, high personal standards, devotion to duty, self-discipline, professional knowledge, skill, and the wisdom to make portentous decisions under stress and with inadequate information.

One of these perennial problems is discipline. Some superintendents have been kindly, warm-hearted, slack disciplinarians. Each time such a man was at the helm, there was deterioration of morale, of standards, and of education, and the next superintendent had the difficult task of tautening a sloppy organization. Other superintendents have been martinets, with exactly the same results. People are different, but in an organization that demands a high order of accomplishment, running a taut ship is a necessity.

Change is inevitable in every area of planning and experience. Determining the proper mix of character-building, professional education, general education, and training will continue to be a battle of emphasis and a competition for time. But the basic long-term goal remains: to develop professional naval officers with all the attributes and knowledge they will need to win future battles at sea.

Professor Sweetman has created an outstanding book on an outstanding institution and the men who made it so.

Arleigh Burke

Arleigh Burke

Preface

When I came to teach at the Naval Academy, one of the first things I did was to go to the library to check out a history of the institution. Greatly to my surprise, I discovered that the most recent such work had appeared in 1900. Of course, many books had been published about the academy since that date—descriptions of life in the brigade of midshipmen, guides to its buildings and monuments, pictorials, and so forth—but no real history. It seemed to me that, after three-quarters of a century, it was time for another.

This book is the outgrowth of that reflection. It combines words and pictures to tell the story of the Naval Academy from its origins to the present. It is not a definitive history. That would require a volume several times this size. My aim has been to describe how a modest Naval School established, after years of struggle, in the obscurity of an unwanted army post grew to become a great national institution of unique and enduring significance. In view of that significance, I have also attempted to trace the relationship between the Naval Academy, the navy it serves, and the national policies both exist to support. Finally, I have tried to give some idea of what it was to be a midshipman in generations past.

The pictorial resources available presented an embarrassment of riches and the process of elimination was often agonizing. From the literally thousands of pictures examined, those chosen to appear here seem to me to show best the way and the look of life at the academy over the years. Three maps have been especially drawn to trace the expansion of the yard from its original 9 acres to its present 302 acres.

Interested readers will find the source of every quotation and statement of fact the book contains in the notes. All quotations are from primary sources; that is, they are the words of persons who witnessed what they relate. Contemporary accounts are indented. Those written long after the event are set in the text. All italics are original.

Acknowledgments

Many people contributed in many ways to the preparation of this book. There could have been no substitute for their assistance, and I am deeply grateful to them all.

Six former superintendents furnished invaluable accounts of their tours at the academy: Admiral James L. Holloway, Jr., USN (Ret.), Admiral Walter F. Boone, USN (Ret.), Rear Admiral John F. Davidson, USN (Ret.), Rear Admiral Charles C. Kirkpatrick, USN (Ret.), Vice Admiral Charles S. Minter, Jr., USN (Ret.), and Vice Admiral William P. Mack, USN (Ret.). Admirals Holloway, Davidson, Minter, and Mack also commented on their experiences as midshipmen.

Rear Admiral Robert W. McNitt, USN (Ret.), presently dean of admissions at the academy, discussed the academic reforms of the 1960s, in which he played an important part.

Numerous alumni recalled their years at the academy. I am especially indebted to: Captain James L. Anderson, USN (Ret.), Captain Edward L. Beach, USN (Ret.), Lieutenant Commander George L. Breeden II, USN, the late Lieutenant Commander John A. Brownell, USN, Admiral Arleigh A. Burke, USN (Ret.), Admiral Robert B. Carney, USN (Ret.), Vice Admiral Francis C. Denebrink, USN (Ret.), Mr. Richard B. Gilbert, Lieutenant Commander Dennis W. Glass, USN, Captain Christopher C. Johnson, USMC, Admiral David F. McDonald, USN (Ret.), Commander Joseph P. Norfleet, USN (Ret.), Mr. H. Ross Perot, Captain Roy C. Smith III, USNR (Ret.), and Mr. Charles M. Todorich.

Ensign John A. Bukaukas, USN, Lieutenant Frances C. Lane, USN, Lieutenant William J. Sabo, USN, and Mr. Todorich generously placed their unpublished papers regarding the history of the academy at my disposal. Rear Admiral James W. Kelly, CHC, USN (Ret.), allowed me to quote from his poem, "Johnny Talks with God."

The staffs of the Naval Academy Archives, the Naval Academy Museum, the Nimitz Library, the Naval Academy Public Affairs Office, the Naval Institute, the Naval History Division, the Library of Congress, the Maryland Hall of Records, the Maryland Historical Society, and the Museum of the Confederacy were as helpful as they were knowledgeable. Special thanks are due to Professor William W. Jeffries, Naval Academy archivist and director of the Naval Academy Museum; Mr. James W. Cheevers, curator of the Naval Academy Museum; Mrs. Jane H. Price and Miss Judy Gurrie of the Naval Academy Archives; Miss Alice S. Creighton, head of Special Collections, Nimitz Library, and her assistant, Miss Pamela Sherbert; Mrs. Patty M. Maddocks, director of the Naval Institute Library and Photographic Services; Mr. Charles S. Haberlein of the Naval History Division; and Mrs. Edmund Wordell of the Newport Historical Society, Newport, Rhode Island.

Valuable materials were also made available by Dr. John T. Mason, director of Oral History at the Naval Institute; Mr. Edward P. Wilson, Jr., Naval Academy Publications Officer; Mr. Thomas F. Bates, Sports Information Director, and Mrs. Rosemary Maersch, director of Sports Promotion, Naval Academy Athletic Association; Professor Anthony J. Rubino, of the Naval Academy Physical Education Department; Mr. Tom Marquardt, managing editor of Capital-Gazette Newspapers, Inc., Annapolis, Maryland; and Norm Goldberg.

My colleagues, past and present, in the History Department at the Naval Academy, most particularly Professor William M. Belote, Professor Paolo E. Coletta, Professors Emeritus Neville T. Kirk and E. B. Potter, Assistant Professor William Roberts, and Commander Gail W. Ward, USN, offered information and encouragement.

The manuscript benefited greatly from careful readings and perceptive comments by Professor Kirk, Mr. Paul Stillwell, Mr. Fred H. Rainbow, and Captain Roy C. Smith III (Chapters 9 and 10); my indefatigable editors at the Naval Institute, Mr. Jan Snouck-Hurgronje and Mrs. Mary Veronica Amoss; and my parents, Mr. and Mrs. Jack Sweetman, whose interest was an unfailing inspiration.

Mr. Jack E. Moore reproduced most of the photographs that appear in the book, and Mrs. Jackie Jones typed many of its pages.

By far my greatest debt, however, is to my wife, Gisela, whose cheerful and efficient assumption of every domestic responsibility gave me time to work on the book; who, while repeatedly disclaiming secretarial skills, just as repeatedly demonstrated them by typing all the draft and many of the finished chapters from a monumentally messy manuscript; and who was, overall, the perfect helpmate.

In all probability, there is no one among the persons named above, with the possible exception of my family members, who will agree with every interpretation and point of emphasis on the following pages, nor should they be considered accountable for them. The responsibility for the views expressed, as well as for any factual errors present, is mine alone.

The U.S. Naval Academy

CHAPTER ONE

The Struggle
for a Naval School

On September 13, 1842, the U.S. brig *Somers* set sail from the Brooklyn Navy Yard on one of the most fateful cruises in American naval history. For some years, progressive-minded officers had been advocating the introduction of a school ship for the training of naval apprentices— teen-aged volunteers, who, it was hoped, would be inspired to make the navy a career. This idea was to be put to the test by the voyage of the *Somers*. A trim little craft, 103 feet from stem to stern and 25 feet abeam, she carried a crew of 121, only four of whom were more than thirty years old: 5 officers, 7 midshipmen, 35 petty officers, seamen, and stewards, and 74 apprentice boys. Her captain was Commander Alexander Slidell Mackenzie, a mild-mannered, intellectual officer and amateur author whose friends included Washington Irving and Henry Wadsworth Longfellow. Described by a contemporary as "of medium height, with a fine head covered rather thinly by fine auburn hair, a high forehead, and of an amiable and pleasing rather than stern and commanding presence," he was a veteran of twenty-seven years' naval service. Among the *Somers*'s midshipmen was one with whom his name soon became linked in tragedy: nineteen-year-old Philip Spencer, the black-sheep son of Secretary of War John Canfield Spencer.

Everything went well on the outward leg of the voyage, across the North Atlantic to Madeira, Tenerife, and the west coast of Africa. Later, the officers recalled that upon leaving Madeira they detected a subtle change in the atmosphere aboard ship but it was nothing to cause alarm. On November 11, the *Somers* set out for home, shaping a southwesterly course to take on provisions at St. Thomas, in the Danish West Indies. She was still far at sea when, on the evening of November 26, Purser's Steward James W. Wales reported that he had been invited to join a mutiny being organized by Midshipman Spencer.

Young Spencer's plan, formed in association with Acting Boatswain's Mate Samuel Cromwell and Seaman Elisha Small, was to seize control of the *Somers*, murder her officers and loyal crewmen, and embark upon a career of piracy in the West Indies. Notes found in Spencer's possession confirmed the steward's report. Mackenzie thereupon placed Spencer under arrest. As the little *Somers* had no brig, Spencer was chained to the bulwarks on her quarterdeck. At once it became evident that the conspiracy was far advanced. The crew's attitude grew more threatening and, in the course of the next three days, Mackenzie arrested the six seamen most closely identified with Spencer's scheme. They, too, were put in irons on the quarterdeck.

When discipline continued to deteriorate, Mackenzie named seven of his officers to form a court of inquiry. Evidence taken from a number of the petty officers and older seamen caused its members to conclude that the situation in the *Somers* demanded immediate action. On December 1, they reported to Mackenzie that Spencer and his two chief confederates, Cromwell and Small, were guilty of a "determined attempt to commit a mutiny . . . of a most atrocious nature," and that owing to "the uncertainty as to what extent they are leagued with others still at large, [and] the impossibility of guarding against the contingencies which a day or an hour may bring forth, we are convinced that it would be impossible to carry them to the United States, and that the safety of [this vessel], the lives of ourselves and those committed to our charge require that they should be put to death."

Mackenzie concurred, and the three men were hanged at the yard-arm later that same day. Most inconveniently for those who later sought to condemn Mackenzie for his actions, during his arrest Spencer freely confessed that he had planned a mutiny, and not just in the *Somers*, but also on board both ships in which he served previously, the sloop of war *John Adams* and the frigate *Potomac*. "It seemed to be a mania with me," he declared. Informed that he was to be executed, he requested and received permission to give the command himself. To Lieutenant Guert Gansevoort, the *Somers*'s second-in-command, he said, "You can judge for yourself whether I die like a coward or a brave man." At the last moment, however, his nerve failed and he asked that Mackenzie give the order.

Small also admitted his complicity in the plot. In the last words which Mackenzie allowed him to address to his shipmates, he said, "I am no pirate. I never murdered anybody but I only said *I would*. Now see what words will do. Take warning by me." Cromwell died protesting that he was innocent.

To mark the solemnity of the proceedings, Mackenzie gave orders for the American flag to be hoisted at the same moment that the three men, black masks over their faces, were hauled aloft. He then addressed the ship's company, warning its members against the road that had led the conspirators to ruin and ending with a call for three cheers for the flag— "and," recalled Lieutenant Gansevoort, "hearty ones they were." The cloud that had settled over the *Somers* lifted, and she reached New York without further incident on December 14, 1842.

Sensational as these events were in themselves, the prominence of Midshipman Spencer's family made them even more so. Secretary of War Spencer, convinced that his son had been murdered by a jittery martinet, pressed to have Mackenzie indicted by a civil court. Although exonerated by a naval court of inquiry, Mackenzie himself requested trial by court-martial, foreseeing that only a full investigation of the circumstances surrounding the executions could clear his name. Charged with five offenses ranging from murder to conduct unbecoming an officer and a gentleman, he was acquitted on all counts.

The fact that the moving spirit in the *Somers* mutiny was a midshipman also called attention to the selection and training of naval officers. In this regard, as in many others, American practice was based on British precedent. In the Royal Navy, the term *midshipman*, originally used to designate an experienced seaman stationed amidships to relay orders fore

This contemporary print shows Midshipman Philip Spencer, Acting Boatswain's Mate Samuel Cromwell, and Seaman Elisha Small hanging from the yardarm of the brig *Somers*, two on the starboard side and one on the port, on the afternoon of December 1, 1842. The incident did much to promote interest in founding a naval academy. Courtesy: U.S. Naval Academy Museum.

and aft, emerged in the late seventeenth century as a rank for youths being trained to become officers. That training was essentially an apprenticeship. British midshipmen learned their profession in the school of experience. They went to sea at a tender age, usually from twelve to sixteen, and literally grew into officers. This was called "catching them young." A nod towards formal education was made in 1734, when schoolmasters were assigned to conduct classes aboard ship, but no one took their efforts very seriously. The Royal Navy was convinced that what counted was catching them young.

The French navy, in contrast, approached the problem of officer training by establishing schools at its shore establishments. The outcome of the numerous naval actions fought during the Anglo-French wars of the seventeenth and eighteenth centuries seemed to indicate that catching them young was the answer. Whereas the French system produced scientific officers who thoroughly understood the theoretical aspects of the naval profession, the British produced practical seamen who won battles.

It was, therefore, natural that the U.S. Navy chose to follow the British example. Appointed by the president or the secretary of the navy upon the recommendation of the members of Congress, midshipmen were sent directly aboard ship to learn by doing. The *Somers* mutiny cast the wisdom of this arrangement into doubt. Investigations into Mackenzie's conduct established that Philip Spencer was a confirmed troublemaker who had been sent into the navy in hopes that it would straighten him out. That there were disadvantages inherent in a system whereby an idle youth could be catapulted on board ship as a midshipman in the U.S. Navy, solely on the basis of political pull, had been dramatically demonstrated. The subject of officer education was heatedly debated in newspapers and magazines. Among the suggestions made for its improvement was the foundation of a naval academy.

The idea of an academy was by no means new. It had been proposed by John Paul Jones almost sixty years earlier. As practical a seaman as ever drew breath, Jones was also a self-made man who never missed an opportunity to add to his store of hard-won knowledge. During his sojourns in France before and after the cruise of the *Bonhomme Richard*, he was deeply impressed with the level of professional training in the French navy, then at a peak of efficiency. Writing in 1783, he recommended the organization of an academy at every American navy yard to teach young officers "the principles of mathematics and mechanics," and of a "fleet of evolution," each vessel with "a little academy on board," to conduct practical exercises.

Nothing came of his proposal. Once independence had been won, Congress abolished the Continental Navy. Its retention, so the argument ran, would be an unnecessary expense, a breeding ground for a new aristocracy, and a constant temptation to foreign adventures. A virtuous young republic, asking nothing of the outside world except the opportunity to trade in peace, had no need of a navy.

The depredations of the Barbary pirates soon exposed the fallacy of that line of reasoning. The outside world was not impressed by republican virtue. Without a navy to protect them, American merchantmen were easy game. Finally, on March 27, 1794, Congress reluctantly passed an act establishing the U.S. Navy. It was to consist of six frigates, to each of which the president was authorized to appoint an appropriate number of officers, including eight midshipmen.

The foundation of the navy revived the question of officer education. For a time the issue was associated with the idea of a military academy. Unlike the navy, the army had never been altogether abolished, and there had been talk of establishing such an academy ever since the Revolution. In 1799 Alexander Hamilton proposed a combined military educational system based on a "fundamental school" at West Point, New York, whose graduates would proceed to a specialized school, of which he envisioned three: one for engineers and artillery, another for infantry and cavalry, and a third for the navy. Endorsed by President John Adams, this plan was submitted to Congress by Secretary of War James McHenry the following year. It was not adopted, but in March 1802 Congress approved the establishment of a conventional military academy at West Point.

That was not the end of the combined academy concept, however. In 1808, Colonel Jonathan Williams, superintendent at West Point, proposed moving the military academy to Washington and appointing a professor to teach nautical astronomy and navigation. President Thomas

Petty officers and experienced seamen provided much of the informal instruction midshipmen received during their shipboard apprenticeship prior to the foundation of the Naval Academy. Here, Midshipman David Glasgow Farragut listens to a boatswain's mate discourse on the War of 1812. From James Barnes, *Midshipman Farragut*.

Jefferson forwarded Williams's report to Congress with the favorable comment: "Besides the advantage of placing [the academy] under the immediate eye of government, it may render its benefits common to the Naval Department." A bill to effect the transfer was introduced in the Senate but never came to a vote.

In the meantime, provision of a sort had been made for the education of midshipmen. Spelled out in the first book of naval regulations, issued under the personal auspices of President Adams in 1802, it was simply the adoption of the British practice of employing seagoing schoolmasters to conduct classes aboard ship. Since the U.S. Navy was not authorized to employ schoolmasters, the responsibility for acting as such was assigned to the ships' chaplains. "[The chaplain] shall perform the duty of a school-master," the regulation read; "and to that end he shall instruct the midshipmen . . . in writing, arithmetic, and navigation, and in whatsoever may contribute to render them proficients." Captains were enjoined to consider midshipmen "a class of officers, meriting in an especial degree, the fostering care of their government. They will see therefore, that the schoolmasters perform their duty towards them, by diligently and faithfully instructing them in those sciences appertaining to their department. . . ."

The inadequacy of this expedient is obvious. Granted that the average chaplain might be competent to teach English composition, his studies would hardly have prepared him to conduct classes in navigation. The desirability of improving the standard of instruction was implicitly recognized by Congress soon after the outbreak of the War of 1812, when the appropriation for the first American 74-gun ships of the line specified that a seagoing schoolmaster should be attached to each vessel. (On smaller vessels the chaplain continued to do double duty as a teacher.) By the end of the war fifteen such positions had been created.

Theoretically, this arrangement represented an ideal combination of education and training, of theory and practice. The reality was very different. In the first place, the provisions made for the schoolmasters were so poor that it proved difficult to attract able men. The only thing lower than the masters' salaries was their status. They were paid $25.00 a month, which was stopped between cruises, and aboard ship they were quartered with the warrant officers or, worse yet, their pupils. Over the years the schoolmasters' circumstances were gradually improved. They were accorded the title professor of mathematics. Their pay was increased until by 1835 it had reached the respectable sum of $100.00 a month; and in 1842 they were authorized to live and mess with lieutenants. But progressive as these measures were, they did not attack the fundamental defect of the schoolmaster system, which was the impossibility of conducting efficient instruction amid the distractions of service afloat. Writing from personal experience, the pioneer oceanographer Lieutenant Matthew Fontaine Maury explained:

> Under the present arrangement, the duties of the school-room . . . are subordinate to every other duty aboard ship. There the midshipman is practically taught to consider his attendance at school as the matter of least importance in his routine. . . . I have known a Captain, who forbade the Midshipmen to work out longitude, on the ground that it was a secret of the Captain and the Master; and, therefore, it was exceedingly officious, and unbecoming the character of gentlemen, for Midshipmen . . . to have anything to do with [it].

Enlightened captains such as Matthew Calbraith Perry took care that their midshipmen had time for study, but they were exceptions. The introduction in 1819 of a professional examination for promotion from midshipman to lieutenant brought no change in the state of affairs. For practical purposes, midshipmen were left to look after their education themselves. Some did an exemplary job of it. Maury, for example, would chalk problems in spherical trigonometry on round shot in the deck racks to work during his watches. The majority relied on luck and last-minute cramming.

In short, the provision of schoolmasters, seemingly a breakthrough in the professional education of the U.S. Navy, was actually a dead end. It did not establish an efficient system of instruction; and its mere existence enabled opponents of an academy to argue that no other was needed.

Still, the advantages of a permanent educational establishment ashore, free from the interruptions of sea duty, were too obvious to escape notice. Secretary of the Navy William Jones suggested "the expediency of providing . . . for . . . a naval academy" in a message to Congress in 1814, just as the schoolmaster system was going into effect, and Secretary Smith Thompson renewed the recommendation in 1822. Neither pressed the point, however. That was left to Thompson's successor, Samuel L. Southard.

An attorney by profession, Southard had served in Congress and sat on the bench of his native New Jersey. His familiarity with nautical affairs was so scanty that an acquaintance, upon learning of his appointment as secretary of the navy, asked if he could honestly say he knew a ship's bow from her stern. He nevertheless proved to be one of the most capable secretaries the navy ever had. Assuming office in September 1823, he soon became convinced that "the early education of most of our officers is very unequal to the character that they have subsequently to attain." Pointing to the contribution West Point had made to the military profession, he insisted, *Instruction is not less necessary to the Navy than to the Army.* In a special report to President James Monroe in January 1825 he explained that there could be nothing more conducive to "the discipline, efficiency and economy" of the navy than the foundation of an academy to educate its junior officers.

Between January 1824 and December 1827, Southard submitted no fewer than four recommendations to Congress for the foundation of such a school. From 1825 on, his efforts were supported by President John Quincy Adams, whose first State of the Union message asserted that "the want of a naval school of instruction, corresponding with the Military Academy at West Point . . . is felt with daily increasing aggravation." Together, the secretary and the president got action. Two bills calling for the creation of a naval academy were introduced in Congress in 1826, and in February 1827 a navy act whose provisions included the establishment of an academy passed the Senate after heated debate. The House voted 86 to 78 to strike out the portion relating to the academy, and the Senate accepted the amendment by a single vote, 22 to 21. This was the closest advocates of an academy ever came to achieving their object through legislative process.

The arguments that defeated Southard's campaign to establish an academy, and would prevail over similar efforts in the future, fell into two categories, ideological and practical. The former was rooted in the same prejudice that had resisted the foundation of the navy itself: that,

As secretary of the navy from 1823 until 1829, Samuel Southard campaigned tirelessly but unsuccessfully for the foundation of a naval academy. Courtesy: U.S. Naval History Division.

besides being a waste of public monies and a dangerous extension of federal power, there was something inherently aristocratic and hence un-American in such an institution. It was averred that the "glamor of a naval education," as a congressman from North Carolina put it, would "produce degeneracy and corruption of the public morality, and change our simple Republican habits." The practical argument held that it was absurd to think that naval officers could be prepared for their profession anywhere else than on board ship. This was a view supported by many senior officers. "You could no more educate sailors in a shore college," they snorted, "than you could teach ducks to swim in a garret."

Opponents of change were also wont to point out that American midshipmen had conducted themselves with distinction in every war in which the republic had been engaged. They led boarding parties; volunteered for dangerous missions; remained at their battle stations despite terrible wounds; and carried on with their duties in the face of direst peril. Their spirit was best exemplified, perhaps, by Midshipman James C. Jarvis in the Quasi-War with France. In command of the party in the maintop of the *Constellation* during her battle with the *Vengeance*, Jarvis was warned by a seaman that so much rigging had been shot away that the mast might topple at any moment. He replied, "If the mast goes, we go with it." That was exactly what happened, and the report of the sole survivor inspired a congressional resolution in praise of a young man "who gloriously preferred certain death to the abandonment of his post."

The gallantry Jarvis and others like him had displayed was adduced as proof that it would be folly to tamper with a system that produced midshipmen such as these. The flaw in this contention was that the issue was not whether midshipmen were as brave as they could be, but whether they were as well prepared for their profession.

Despite the virulence with which conservative opinion opposed the idea of education ashore, by 1827 two schools of sorts were already in operation. The first had been established in the frigate *Guerrière* at New York in 1821; the second, in the frigate *Java* at Norfolk a few years later. They were in no sense academies, however. Set up simply to prepare midshipmen for the lieutenant's examination, they offered little more than cram courses in navigation. Their staffs usually consisted of a single schoolmaster (or chaplain); attendance was voluntary; and outside class the midshipmen were left entirely to their own devices.

Southard's successor, Secretary John Branch, in his annual report of 1829, rather timorously reminded Congress of the schools' existence. He suggested that, "until some better system can be matured," Congress should clarify the schools' status by granting them legal authorization and enhance their utility by providing for them to teach foreign languages. Neither of these recommendations was adopted. Branch repeated them in vain the following year, and the schools continued as before. A breakthrough appeared imminent in 1832, when a board established to revise naval regulations proposed making attendance at available instruction compulsory for midshipmen on duty at the navy yards, but in the end this stipulation was dropped. The foundation of a third school, at Boston, in 1833, signified nothing more than an extension of existing arrangements.

Undaunted by past disappointments, progressive voices persisted in the advocacy of a naval academy. Lieutenant Maury deplored the lack of any real program for educating midshipmen in the prestigious pages of the *Southern Literary Messenger*. In April 1836 the officers and warrant officers of the *Constitution* and *Vandalia* petitioned Congress for "the establishment of a naval school," asserting that it could be funded from monies already allotted the schoolmaster system, "from which little or no benefit is derived." This petition furnished the basis for a bill reported a few weeks later by ex-Secretary Southard on behalf of the Senate Committee on Naval Affairs. The bill did not survive its second reading. Secretary James K. Paulding echoed Southard's arguments in his annual report of 1838. His recommendation met the usual rebuff. That he had expected nothing more is indicated by the fact that earlier in the year he had authorized the organization of another cram school, the navy's fourth, at the Philadelphia Naval Asylum, an old sailors' home. Paradoxically, in time to come this modest measure would prove a turning point in the long struggle for an academy.

That struggle now gained a new dimension. With the advent of steam power, the navy entered an age of technological revolution. The orders for its first three steam-driven vessels were placed in 1839. The educational implications were inescapable. A bright youngster might acquire an understanding of wind and sail by keeping his eye peeled, but he could hardly absorb the principles of steam engineering by scrutinizing a boiler. In 1841 Secretary of the Navy Abel P. Upshur informed Congress that the introduction of steamships into naval service made it necessary for officers to possess "a different order of scientific knowledge from that . . . heretofore . . . required." The best way of providing them with this

A one-year cram course to prepare midshipmen to pass the examination for promotion to lieutenant was established at the Philadelphia Naval Asylum in 1838. U.S. Naval Institute Collection.

knowledge would be by the institution of an academy, "with the . . . means of uniting theory and practice." Swayed by the logic of Upshur's presentation, for the second time the Senate approved a bill authorizing the establishment of a naval school. The promise raised by its passage was dashed when Congress adjourned before it reached the floor of the House. A similar recommendation by Upshur in December 1842 was ignored.

The news of the *Somers* mutiny sent a ripple of shock across the country that same month. At least briefly, the training of midshipmen became the object of widespread concern. Of the various reforms proposed at this time, the most important came from the professor at the Philadelphia Naval Asylum, twenty-three-year-old William Chauvenet. The most creative scholar ever to enter the schoolmaster system, Chauvenet was the son of a French veteran who emigrated to America after the fall of the First Empire. Graduating from Yale with high honors in 1840, young Chauvenet accepted an appointment as professor of mathematics in the navy in 1841. Originally assigned to the steam frigate USS *Mississippi*, he transferred to the Asylum School following the death of the professor there in April 1842.

Chauvenet was a born teacher. Many years later one of his former pupils, Rear Admiral Samuel R. Franklin, recalled that he had "the faculty of imparting what he knew to others in a higher degree than any man I have ever known." When Chauvenet took over the Asylum School this faculty was almost all he had to work with. Recitations were held in the basement and the educational resources on hand consisted of a worn-out circle of reflection and a small blackboard propped against the wall. With the enthusiastic support of the governor of the Naval Asylum, Commodore James Biddle, Chauvenet undertook a program of reform. Recitations were moved upstairs to a large, well-lighted room provided with blackboards and equipped with chronometers, sextants, and other instruments. Periods of instruction, which had been infrequent and informal, were regularly scheduled; a daily grade was assigned each student; and the approval of Secretary Upshur was obtained for the introduction of a far more stringent course in mathematics.

These improvements exhausted the possibilities under the existing system, which allowed midshipmen to spend no more than a single academic year (eight months) at the Asylum School. Chauvenet soon concluded that this was not long enough. In the winter of 1843-44, he developed a comprehensive plan to expand the school curriculum into a two-year program embracing all subjects necessary to a naval officer. If the Navy Department had the authority to send midshipmen to the Asylum School for one year, he reasoned, it must have the authority to send them there for two. Of course, a regular faculty would be required, but it could be formed by concentrating professors already in service at Philadelphia. In addition—and this was a revolutionary suggestion—interested naval officers might be assigned as instructors. Thus, at least in the beginning, the implementation of the program would not involve any extra expense. As Chauvenet explained later, "the first object was to initiate a *successful* course of study and then to ask Congress to support it."

This ingenious plan, approved by Secretary of the Navy David Henshaw, whom President John Tyler had appointed to office during a congressional recess the previous summer, was scheduled to go into effect in September 1844. Unfortunately, in January 1844, the Senate refused to confirm Henshaw's appointment. His successor, John Y. Mason, was persuaded that the navy could not spare midshipmen for two years ashore, and reversed the decision.

The rejection of Chauvenet's proposal put an end to the most promising start that had been made toward a naval academy to date. Still, the young professor's efforts had not been altogether in vain. The Asylum School had come to be recognized as by far the best in the navy's educational system. Its faculty was strengthened by the assignment of two more civilian professors and the first two officers ever detailed to teaching duties, Lieutenant James H. Ward and Passed Midshipman* Samuel L. Marcy; and plans were made to phase out the older schools and conduct all instruction ashore there.

Other attempts to promote the cause of an academy in 1844 fared no better. A bill calling for the provision of naval schools of instruction was unsuccessfully introduced in the Senate. The officers of the sloop of war USS *Vincennes* presented a petition to the same effect. Reporting on the condition of the navy, Commodore Charles Stewart recommended the establishment of a school to offer instruction in modern languages, international law, and steam engineering. Congress was not interested.

There, at the turn of the year 1844, the matter rested. Since 1814 the foundation of a naval academy had been advocated by seven secretaries of the navy and championed by a president. It had been the object of more than twenty bills, two of which had passed the Senate to die in the House. The advent of steam power and the *Somers* mutiny made the need for an academy more evident than ever. But the prospect that this need would be answered appeared just as remote.

The man who succeeded where everyone else had failed was appointed secretary of the navy by President James K. Polk on March 3, 1845. George Bancroft was an unusual combination of scholar and politician.

* A rank created in 1827 for midshipmen who had passed their examination for lieutenant but could not be promoted because there were no vacancies in the higher grade.

Left, Midshipman Stephen B. Luce in the midshipman's duty ("undress") uniform of the early 1840s. The straw hat was worn during the summer months and in the tropics. Courtesy: Newport Historical Society. Right, William Chauvenet, who took charge of the Philadelphia Naval Asylum School in 1842. Courtesy: U.S. Naval Academy Archives.

Born in Worcester, Massachusetts, in October 1800, the son of a Congregationalist minister, he entered Harvard at the age of thirteen. The power of his intellect so impressed his professors that upon his graduation they raised a fund to enable him to continue his studies in Germany, whose universities were the models of the world. At Göttingen, young Bancroft averaged five hours' sleep a night, devoting almost every waking hour to studies in theology, philosophy, ancient history, literature, Latin, Arabic, Hebrew, and Greek. Awarded the degree of doctor of philosophy a few weeks before his twentieth birthday, he remained abroad for another two years of study and travel in Germany, France, and Italy. He loved every minute. Nearing the end of his European sojourn, he confessed, "I cannot but wonder at my own happy destiny."

Following his return to America in the summer of 1822, Bancroft's happy destiny seemed to desert him. Once he ceased to be a prodigy, he had difficulty finding his place in the world. He had always intended to follow his father into the ministry. It soon became evident that he was not cut out for the cloth. Congregations found his sermons polished as marble, but less warm. An appointment as a Greek tutor at Harvard ended in disillusionment when his attempt to apply intensive German methods of instruction brought him into conflict with both students and faculty. Then he and another professor joined forces to found a German-style preparatory school called Round Hill, near Northampton, Massachusetts. A radical departure from American educational practice, Round Hill quickly achieved national prominence. After his initial enthusiasm had passed, however, Bancroft began to find the thought of spending his life hammering Greek grammar into adolescent heads oppressive. The deluge of schoolboy missiles of which his nearsightedness made him an opportune target doubtless added to his discontent.

Bancroft's fortune changed for the better between 1827 and 1831, when, in quick succession, he married a young lady of means; sold his share in Round Hill; developed an interest in politics; and conceived the idea of using the scholarly methods he had learned in Germany to write a great *History of the United States.* His new undertakings brought him both success and satisfaction. At the time of his appointment as secretary of the navy, he was the acknowledged chief of the Democratic party in Massachusetts and the publication of the first three (there would be ten) volumes of his *History* had placed him in the front rank of American historians.

Although he had no experience in naval affairs, Bancroft was open-minded, industrious, and astute. His tenure of office was distinguished by several important initiatives, including provisions for promoting officers on grounds of ability rather than strict seniority. He also proved a persuasive advocate of the navy's interests in the halls of Congress, securing larger appropriations than had any of his immediate predecessors. But by far the greatest of his contributions was the foundation of the Naval Academy.

No sooner had Bancroft entered on his duties than Chauvenet, confident that a scholar would appreciate the advantages of educating the navy's officers, renewed his proposal for a two-year course at the Naval Asylum. His memorandum made a strong impression. It convinced Bancroft that the existing system of officer education was inadequate; but he was too shrewd simply to dust off a plan that had already provoked opposition. The dismal record of his predecessors' attempts to establish an academy led Bancroft, historian that he was, to conclude it would be futile to meet congressional and professional opposition head on. If he were to make the academy idea a reality, he must avoid mobilizing its antagonists. First it would be necessary for him to gain the assent of the service. Then he would have to find a way to establish an academy without arousing Congress by a request for funds.

It took Bancroft only three months to mature his plans. Inquiry revealed the existence of an obsolete army post named Fort Severn at Annapolis, Maryland, where the Severn River flows into the Chesapeake Bay. Built in 1808 to command the approaches to the city harbor, the work had outlived its military value but was a promising site for a naval academy. That promise was enhanced by the fact that Chauvenet's enthusiastic young assistant at the Naval Asylum, Passed Midshipman Marcy, was a son of Secretary of War William L. Marcy. Undoubtedly in response to filial prompting, Secretary Marcy advised Bancroft that the army would not be sorry to see Fort Severn go. His cooperation raised the possibility that the physical facilities for an academy could be acquired free of charge.

Bancroft's solution to the problem of paying an academy's operating expenses followed the lines suggested by Chauvenet. The Navy Department budget for 1845 included $28,272 for "Instruction." This sum was the combined salaries of the twenty-five schoolmasters who were on active duty in 1844. The appropriation was not broken down into individual salaries, since the pay of seagoing instructors was stopped while they were between cruises ("on waiting orders"). As secretary of the navy, Bancroft had the authority to place whomever he wished on waiting orders. By exerting this authority to tacitly dispense with the services of most of the schoolmasters, he would be able to concentrate the best of them at an academy and apply the savings on the others' salaries to meet its operating expenses. He would not need to ask Congress for a cent.

Bancroft also took steps to disarm opposition within the navy itself. A five-member board composed of some of the service's most progressive senior officers, including Commodore Matthew C. Perry, was scheduled to meet in Philadelphia to examine the midshipmen completing the course at the Naval Asylum in June 1845. In a tactful letter of June 13, Bancroft requested the board's assistance in devising "a more efficient system of instruction for the young naval officers." Fort Severn had been recommended to him as a better location for a midshipmen's school than the Naval Asylum—"especially," he noted in an aside well calculated to win service support, "as a vessel could be stationed there to serve as a school in gunnery." He also suggested that it might be well to require all midshipmen ashore to attend the course of instruction.

The board replied with an enthusiastic letter of June 25, agreeing with every point Bancroft had made. There was even a hint that its members realized that he meant to do more than simply transfer the asylum course to Annapolis. "It may be remarked," they wrote, "that the Government already possesses all the necessary means for commencing at once a naval school, which may be enlarged and perfected at some future time."

The examining board's approval of the move could be counted on to discourage dissent from the navy's seniors. Next, Bancroft sought to enlist the support of its middle ranks. To that end, a board consisting of Commanders Samuel F. DuPont, William W. McKean, and Franklin Buchanan was constituted to review the proposed action. Its report was favorable. In anticipation of this outcome, Bancroft visited Annapolis to personally satisfy himself as to the suitability of Fort Severn for a naval school.

The last obstacle to the foundation of the academy had now been overcome. Bancroft's bureaucratic sleight of hand had reduced the problems that had baffled his predecessors to a matter of interdepartmental administration. The navy had been lined up. The Congress had been left out. On August 7, Bancroft directed Commander Buchanan to prepare a plan of organization for the new school. In his instructions, virtually the charter of the Naval Academy, Bancroft expressed the conviction that

the officers of the American Navy, if they gain but opportunity for scientific instruction, may make themselves as distinguished for culture as they have been for gallant conduct.

To this end it is proposed to collect the midshipmen who from time to time are on shore, and give them occupation . . . in the study of mathematics, nautical astronomy, theory of morals, international law, gunnery, use of steam, the Spanish and French languages, and other branches essential . . . to the accomplishment of a naval officer.

The effect of such employment cannot but be favorable to them and to the service. At present they are left, when waiting orders on shore, without steady occupation, young and exulting in the relief from the restraints of discipline on shipboard. In collecting them at Annapolis for the purposes of instruction, you will begin with the principle that a warrant in the Navy, far from being an excuse for licentious freedom, is to be held a pledge for subordination, industry, and regularity, for sobriety and assiduous devotion to duty. Far from consenting that the tone of discipline and morality should be less than at universities or colleges of our country, the President expects such supervision and arrangement as shall make of them an exemplary body of which the country may be proud.

The transfer of Fort Severn to the navy was officially effected on August 15, 1845. Buchanan was placed in command the same day. His plan of organization was approved by Bancroft two weeks later. The professors with whose services it was decided to dispense were placed on waiting orders and presently came to realize the necessity of seeking other employment. The professors selected for the school received orders to report to Annapolis, as did the midshipmen who were to compose their new classes. Buchanan declared the school open on October 10. A few days later an Annapolis newspaper, the *Maryland Republican*, reported that:

The school is being organized with all the rapidity consistent with methodical arrangement. The various buildings have been repaired and surprisingly improved, considering the small expenditure and the brief time allowed, especially the quarters allotted to the midshipmen. . . . About forty young gentlemen have already reported themselves, whose handsome appearance and gentlemanly deportment give a cheerful aspect to the streets of our quiet city.

The ducks were in the garret. The question now was whether they could be taught to swim.

CHAPTER TWO

The Navy Comes to Annapolis

None of Secretary Bancroft's provisions for the foundation of the Naval Academy proved wiser than his selection of its first superintendent. At forty-five, Commander Franklin Buchanan was a veteran of thirty years' service, nineteen of which were spent at sea. Of medium height, broad-shouldered, and ramrod straight, in his youth he was known as one of the strongest men in the navy. He was always known as one of the boldest. Once, while traveling on a civilian packet from Norfolk to Baltimore, he was threatened by a group of seamen bent on avenging what they considered injustices suffered at his hand on a recent cruise. Taking a sword cane from his cabin, he presented himself on deck. "There he stood," an eyewitness recalled, "with form erect, both hands resting on his cane; the expression of his countenance calm, resolute, and defiant. The seamen gathered around him and gave vent to their feelings in blasphemous oaths. . . . He stood in statuelike repose, not a word escaping his lips. For full five minutes or more he braved the tempest, but not a man dared lay the weight of his finger upon him. . . . [Then] he turned upon his heel, and passed down the stairway . . . into the after cabin and went to bed."

In his opening address to the entering midshipmen on October 18, 1845, Buchanan made it clear that the discipline he demanded on the quarterdeck would apply to the academy. He promised that "Every indulgence consistent with the rules and regulations of the institution, will be granted to those who merit it," but emphasized "the importance I attach to a strict compliance with all laws, orders and regulations." Following these remarks he read out eighteen articles comprising the "Rules and Regulations for the Internal Government of the Naval School." Article 17 summed up those pertaining to midshipmen, who were "not only required to abstain from all vicious, immoral or irregular conduct, but . . . to conduct themselves with the propriety and decorum of gentlemen." Events would reveal that he meant every word.

Buchanan's faculty numbered seven, four of whom came from the Philadelphia Naval Asylum. The latter included his executive officer, thirty-nine-year-old Lieutenant James H. Ward, whose lectures there were published as an *Elementary Course in Ordnance and Gunnery for Midshipmen*. Among the best-educated officers in the navy, he doubled as instructor in seamanship and gunnery. Following his Annapolis assignment he wrote a *Manual of Naval Tactics*, which was used as an academy text for two decades.

Commander Franklin Buchanan was the first superintendent of the U.S. Naval School, as it was originally called. A strict disciplinarian, he insisted that the school's standards should be second to none. This photograph was taken after his promotion to the rank of captain in 1855. Courtesy: Library of Congress.

Professor Chauvenet reported to the academy, of which he was virtually co-founder, to continue his classes in mathematics and navigation. With him came his assistant instructor in mathematics, Passed Midshipman Samuel L. Marcy. At age twenty-five they shared the distinction of being the youngest members of the staff. Described by a colleague as "modest, studious and very gentlemanly," Marcy was soon to wed an Annapolitan, Eliza Humphreys, daughter of the president of St. John's College. In recognition of his interest in the latest developments in naval science at home and abroad, he was assigned to three tours of duty at the academy between its foundation and the outbreak of the Civil War.

Natural philosophy, as the physical sciences were called, was taught by the Naval School's West Pointer, Professor Henry H. Lockwood. Born on a farm in Kent County, Delaware, thirty years before, he graduated from the Military Academy in the Class of 1836 and saw active service in the Second Seminole War. Army life had not proved to his taste, however, and in 1837 he resigned his commission and returned to Delaware to farm. Four years later, his brother, Naval Surgeon John A. Lockwood, convinced him that his abilities were lost behind a plow, and he applied to the navy for an appointment as professor of mathematics. On his first cruise he distinguished himself as adjutant of the naval landing party in the premature capture of Monterey, in what was then the Mexican province of California, by Commodore Thomas ap Catesby Jones in October 1842. In 1844 he joined the staff at the Naval Asylum, seconding

Left, Passed Midshipman Samuel L. Marcy, who was William Chauvenet's assistant at the Naval Asylum School and one of the academy's seven original faculty members. The son of Secretary of War William L. Marcy, he was instrumental in effecting the transfer of Fort Severn to the navy. He was a lieutenant when this photograph was made, some time around 1860. Courtesy: U.S. Naval Academy Archives. The academy's first executive officer, a position later designated commandant of midshipmen, was Lieutenant James H. Ward. Here, right, he is shown as a commander, on the eve of the Civil War. Courtesy: U.S. Naval Academy Archives.

Chauvenet in mathematics and navigation and Lieutenant Ward in gunnery. At Annapolis he became noted for his unpretentious hospitality, his love of long walks in the country, and the delight he took in his garden. Before many years had passed he acquired a small farm on the outskirts of the city. Quiet and unassuming, with deep religious convictions, he explained his philosophy in a letter to the future Mrs. Lockwood shortly after his arrival at the academy: "Wealth I never expect or particularly desire. A comfortable maintenance I intend to have—a cheerful content I propose as the goal of life." But as generations of midshipmen were to discover, Lockwood's homespun demeanor clothed a will of iron.

French was the responsibility of Professor Arsène Napoléon Alexandre Girault de St. Fargeau, whom it was inevitable the midshipmen would name Mr. Frog. Born in Troyes, France, in 1801, he emigrated to the United States in 1826 and became a naturalized citizen in 1833. He was the author of several French manuals and readers, one of which, not surprisingly, was adopted as an academy text. The only faculty member who came from outside the navy, he was recommended to Buchanan by "learned gentlemen in whom I have great confidence" and hired in Sep-

A West Point graduate, Class of 1836, Henry H. Lockwood, left, taught the midshipmen science and soldiering. During the Civil War, he served with distinction as a brevet brigadier general of U.S. Volunteers, and was photographed in the full-dress uniform of that rank. Courtesy: U.S. Naval Academy Archives. Professor Arsène Girault, right, gave instruction in French and Spanish. In this photograph, taken during the Civil War, he is wearing the uniform of the Corps of Mathematics, in which professors could be commissioned regardless of their fields. The five stripes on his sleeve indicate that he held the relative rank of commander. The corps' cap and shoulder device was a gold disc bearing, in silver, an Old English capital *P*. Courtesy: U.S. Naval Academy Archives.

tember 1845 "as temporary Agent of the Navy for teaching French" at $1,200 per annum. Three weeks after the commencement of classes Buchanan advised Secretary Bancroft that already Girault's "energy, zeal, and talent for teaching the French language, combined with his gentlemanly deportment, have gained for him the respect of all attached to the institution." Like the superintendent, Girault believed in a taut ship. When Midshipman David Ochiltree became insolent in his classroom,

This panoramic view of Annapolis, looking east from the cupola of the Maryland State House, was published in Baltimore in 1846. The Naval School is in the center background, below the flag. The first street at left, running directly from the circle to the waterfront, became Maryland Avenue. Courtesy: Maryland Historical Society.

Girault did not hesitate to deliver a sharp rebuke. Buchanan supported him fully, and Ochiltree was given an official reprimand.

Rounding out the faculty were Naval Surgeon John A. Lockwood, who taught chemistry and served as school physician; and Chaplain George Jones, a Yale graduate and long-time academy advocate, whose classes in "English branches" included English, history, and geography. The midshipmen called him "Slicky." Surgeon Lockwood was detached from the academy for sea duty in 1849 and retired as a fleet surgeon after the Civil War. Jones ceased teaching to become the academy's first full-time chaplain when that position was authorized in 1850. Leaving Annapolis in 1852 to accompany Commodore Perry's expedition to Japan, he returned to serve another tour as chaplain prior to his retirement in 1862.

These gentlemen found Annapolis a far cry from Philadelphia. The capital of Maryland since 1694, in colonial days it was a bustling port. The stately, Georgian mansions clustering its quiet streets testified to its erstwhile prosperity. Around the time of the Revolution, however, shipping began to go on up the bay to Baltimore, and Annapolis experienced a gradual eclipse. It was now a genteel backwater of some 3,000 inhabitants, the home of venerable St. John's College, rich in history, tradition, and little else. Naval Surgeon Edmund L. DuBarry, who had refused the appointment of school physician after visiting the city, described it as "the dullest and most horrible place in the U. States—it is very old, and I do not suppose a house has been built there in 40 years— the place is finished and will not improve." Indeed, the *National Intelligencer* reported that Secretary Bancroft's principal purpose in moving the naval school to "the healthy and secluded" location of Annapolis was to rescue midshipmen from "the temptations and distractions that necessarily connect with a large and populous city." As far back as 1826, the Maryland General Assembly had formally directed the federal government's attention to "the superior advantages . . . Annapolis . . . possesses as a situation for a naval academy." The landlords of Annapolis welcomed the coming of the school by raising rents.

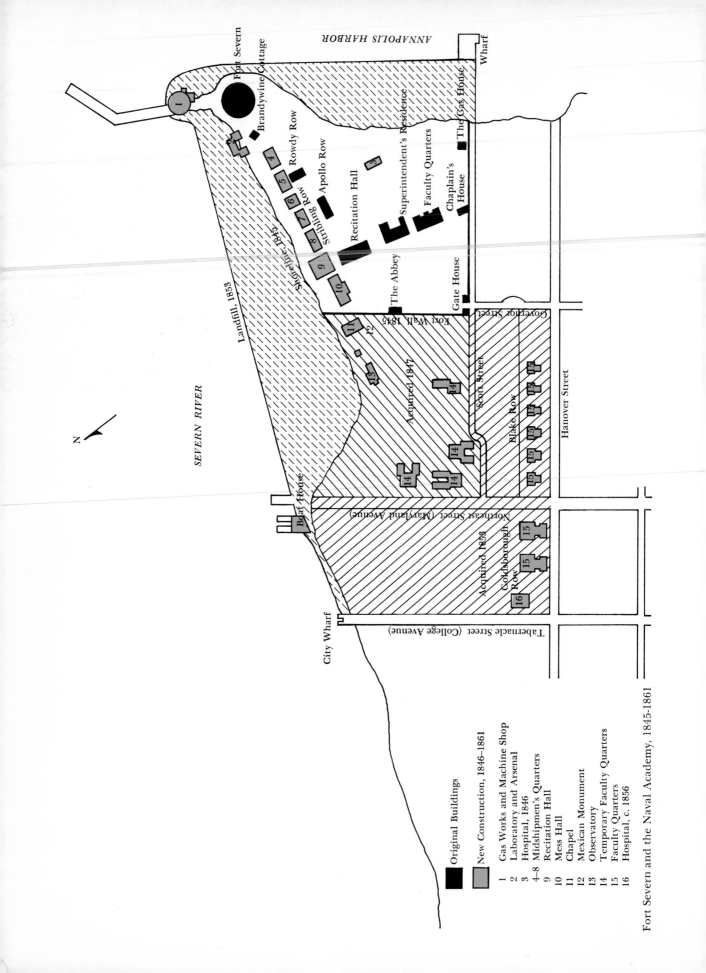

SEVERN RIVER

ANNAPOLIS HARBOR

N

Fort Severn
Brandywine Cottage
Rowdy Row
Apollo Row
Stribling Row
Recitation Hall
Superintendent's Residence
Faculty Quarters
Chaplain's House
The Gas House
Wharf

4
5
6
7
8
9
10

The Abbey
Gate House
Governor Street

Landfill, 1853
Shoreline, 1845

11
12
13
14
14
14
14

Fort Wall 1845
Acquired 1847
Scott Street
Blake Row
Hanover Street

Boat House
City Wharf

15
15
16

Northeast Street (Maryland Avenue)
Acquired 1853
Goldsborough Row
Tabernacle Street (College Avenue)

■ Original Buildings

▨ New Construction, 1846–1861

1 Gas Works and Machine Shop
2 Laboratory and Arsenal
3 Hospital, 1846
4–8 Midshipmen's Quarters
9 Recitation Hall
10 Mess Hall
11 Chapel
12 Mexican Monument
13 Observatory
14 Temporary Faculty Quarters
15 Faculty Quarters
16 Hospital, c. 1856

Fort Severn and the Naval Academy, 1845-1861

The gate house of Fort Severn is at right in this photograph taken for the album of the Class of 1861. The familiar cupola of the Maryland State House rises behind it. The imposing Georgian mansion at left is the colonial Government House, which was acquired by the academy in 1866. Courtesy: U.S. Naval Academy Archives.

Fort Severn stood on the eastern edge of town, at the tip of a wedge-shaped peninsula called Windmill Point, where the Severn River empties into Annapolis Harbor. It occupied approximately nine acres, open to the water but enclosed on its shore sides by two brick walls which met at a right angle at the southwest corner of the grounds. Authorized entry was by means of a masonry gate house at the end of Governor Street (today's Buchanan Road), close by the same corner. The fort itself, dating from 1808, occupied the very end of the peninsula. Circular in form, it consisted of a stone wall approximately 14 feet in height and 100 feet in diameter enclosing a brick magazine and an open gun platform. In 1845 it mounted ten guns.

Besides this work, there were seven buildings within the fort walls: the commandant's quarters, a row of officers' quarters, the quartermaster's office, a barracks, married officers' quarters, a hospital, and a bakery, plus small shops for the post sutler and blacksmith. Commander Buchanan took over the commandant's quarters, a handsome colonial mansion sometimes called the Dulany House, after the family from whom the government purchased the grounds for the fort. Already almost 100 years old, it served as the residence of the academy's superintendents until 1882. The officers' quarters, four pretty brick row houses built by the army in 1834, were assigned to the officers and faculty. They subsequently became known as Buchanan Row.

The use made of these buildings was compatible with their original character. The adaptation of the others was rough and ready. The barracks became the center of school life. Its second story was converted into

25

The Dulany House, almost a century old in 1845, served as the superintendent's residence until 1882. Courtesy: U.S. Naval Academy Archives.

classrooms, its first into a kitchen and mess hall. The remaining buildings were used to house the midshipmen, who, according to the fashion of the era, gave each of them a name. The bakery accommodated a group of youngsters who had come from a cruise in the frigate *Brandywine*. They christened it Brandywine Cottage. What had been the married officers' quarters was dubbed Apollo Row. A dilapidated frame structure whose warped doors and windows admitted both rain and snow, it was the least desirable of the dormitories. The residents regarded rain as the greater evil, because, they claimed, the temperature inside was never warm enough to melt snow. The blacksmith's shop was named the Gas House, in reference to the garrulity of its occupants. For similar reasons, the hospital became known as Rowdy Row. In contrast, the model behavior of the midshipmen billeted in the sutler's store caused it to be called The Abbey. This was presently proven a misnomer. An inspection inspired by the unnatural silence that prevailed at The Abbey every evening revealed that its inhabitants had tunneled through the wall abutting the rear of the building and "frenched out" to make merry in Annapolis.

The program established for the new school reflected the circumstances of its creation. Between 1840 and 1842, close to 200 midshipmen entered the navy, 136 in 1841 alone. When the school opened in 1845, these midshipmen, ranked according to the dates of their warrants, had almost completed the six years' service customary prior to taking their lieutenants' examination. To prepare for this examination, they were ordered to the academy for a year's instruction. Aged anywhere from eighteen to twenty-seven, they constituted the senior class and spent only one year at the academy. The junior class consisted of newly appointed acting midshipmen, aged thirteen to sixteen, who would pass through the new pre-commissioning program. Under this arrangement there were no "classes," per se, and midshipmen continued to be referred to as members of "dates" (those of their warrants), as they had been before.

Fifty-six midshipmen were ordered to the school for its opening session: forty-nine warranted midshipmen of the Dates of 1840 and 1841, and seven acting midshipmen of the Date of 1845. For some reason, the junior-senior terminology never took hold and the members of the two classes were referred to as oldsters and youngsters.

Buchanan's plan of August 1845, as amended and approved by Bancroft, specified that "every applicant . . . must be of good moral character . . . [and] free from all deformity . . . or infirmity of any kind which would disqualify him for performing the active and arduous duties of a sea life. He must be able to read and write well, and be familiar with geography and arithmetic." Students who were accepted were to spend a year at the academy, "subject to the exigencies of the service," during which time their progress would be closely monitored. Those who failed any of their semi-annual examinations would be, in the language of the day, "restored to their friends." The remainder would be sent to sea for a six months' probationary period, at the end of which those whose conduct was satisfactory would receive their midshipmen's warrants, effective as of the date of their acting appointments. Then, after two and one-half years' service afloat, they would return to the academy for a final year of studying for their lieutenants' exam.

In practice, things did not work so smoothly. The stipulation that midshipmen would be attached to the school "subject to the exigencies of the service" was not merely a sop to conservative opinion. Members of either the junior or the senior class were liable to be attached or detached at any point in the academic year. None of the Dates of 1840 through 1842 was ordered to the academy en masse, which was as well, since such numbers could not have been accommodated. Sections of the oversize Date of 1841 attended the academy every year from 1847 through 1850. But, on the whole, Buchanan's plan provided a framework for the operation of the academy in the early years of its existence.

The administration of the school was to some extent modeled after that of the Military Academy. An Academic Board, appointed by the superintendent from members of the faculty, was established to "decide on the merits of the midshipmen, report on the system of instruction, and suggest any . . . alterations which their experience may dictate." Provisions were made for there to be a Board of Visitors by adding to the existing duties of the Board of Examiners. In addition to conducting the annual lieutenants' examination, it was now "to inspect generally the management of the institution, and report to the Secretary of the Navy on its condition and the means of improving it." In time this new function entirely superseded the board's original purpose. Both these bodies were based on West Point practice. So was the requirement, which became a hallmark of academy education, that instructors keep themselves constantly informed of the progress of every student in their classes.

In one important area, however, the program for the Naval School completely ignored the West Point precedent. This was in regard to military training, of which none was prescribed. The midshipmen were not

The earliest known photograph of an academy midshipman is this battered tintype of nongraduate John Quincy Adams Crawford, Date of 1840. Midshipmen's rank was indicated by a pair of buff-colored cloth anchors sewn on the collar, one of which is visible above the lapel notch at left. The gold cap band, previously restricted to officers, was authorized for midshipmen in 1846. Courtesy: U.S. Naval History Division.

organized into any sort of formation; they were not drilled or mustered; they were not even required to wear uniform at all times. Except for the fact that they were subject to Buchanan's orders and to the laws of naval discipline, they might have been attending a civilian college.

The curriculum, which divided the midshipmen's day into five parts, was determined by the Academic Board. Classes commenced at 8:00 a.m. and continued, with an hour off for study, until noon. The period between 12:00 and 1:30 p.m. was allotted to "recreation and dinner." At 1:30 classes reconvened, and met without interruption for the next three hours. "Recreation and supper" occupied the time from 4:30 to 6:00 p.m. The evening hours were set aside for study. "Lights out" was at 10:00 p.m.

The amount of classroom time allocated to the various subjects was also decided by the Academic Board. The junior class was to receive thirty hours of instruction each week: five each in mathematics (including navigation), natural philosophy, French or Spanish, and a general course in ordnance, gunnery, and chemistry; and ten hours in English grammar and composition and geography. The senior class load was thirty-one hours: one in chemistry; two in ordnance, gunnery, and steam engineering; three in history and English composition; five each in mathematics and natural philosophy; and fifteen in French or Spanish. Every midshipman was required to recite in each subject daily, and his efforts were graded on a scale of 1 to 10. By modern standards, which require a midshipman to obtain permission to take more than twenty hours a week, these are staggering totals.

Another aspect of the curriculum that seems remarkable today is the number of hours devoted to Spanish or French. Professor Girault nonetheless experienced his share of the frustrations common to language instructors in English-speaking lands. Prior to the Board of Examiners' first visit to Annapolis, he carefully coached his star pupil, Midshipman William Nelson, Date of '40, to demonstrate a command of conversational French. Aware that their exertions had been all in vain, as the dreaded day approached Nelson memorized a medley of French phrases.

At the appointed hour, Girault and Nelson appeared before the Board of Examiners, among whose members was the redoubtable Commodore Matthew C. Perry.

"Mr. Nelson," Girault began, "which is your native state?"

Nelson did not understand a word. "Thank you," he replied, "I am very well."

Girault continued with a frown. "What cruise have you just completed?"

"I am about twenty-four years old."

Perceiving his student's strategy, Girault fired one question after another, certain that sooner or later Nelson would falter. But before the latter's store of phrases could be exhausted, Perry arose and brought the colloquy to a close by congratulating Girault on his pupil's proficiency.

The midshipmen were generally well behaved. Midshipman Edward Simpson, Date of '40, organized a sort of fraternity called the Spirits Club, which gathered at a tavern on Main Street every Saturday night to eat oysters and terrapin and drink whisky punch. The club was limited to nine members, all of excellent reputation, and enjoyed at least the tolerance of Commander Buchanan. Returning from their merrymaking one evening it occurred to the Spirits to collect the oil lamps from the city lamp posts and leave them in a pile in front of the gate house, but that was the worst of their transgressions. A more rambunctious group known as the Ballsegurs went in for collegiate pranks, such as tarring the clapper of the school bell and firing the morning gun at midnight.

Serious disciplinary problems did not arise until February 1846, when there was a sudden spate of them. On February 1, Midshipman Nones violated direct orders from Buchanan restricting him to the yard on account of academic deficiency. Reporting the incident to Secretary Bancroft as the first instance of "so flagrant an offence," Buchanan recommended that an example should be made. Bancroft agreed, and three days later Nones became the first midshipman to be dismissed from the school.

Later that same month, two midshipmen turned up dead drunk, and Surgeon Lockwood was summoned to nurse a third through a fit of delirium tremens. Buchanan responded with his customary vigor. To Bancroft he explained, "dissipation is the cause of all insubordination and misconduct in the navy, and will if countenanced by me under any circumstances at this School, ruin its usefulness to the Service, and seriously injure its character with the country." One of the offenders was dismissed and the other two received official reprimands. In his letter to the former, Secretary Bancroft observed tartly, "The School is not to be a hospital for incurables, but a school for selected young men." These somewhat draconian measures produced the desired effect, and only two other cases of drunkenness were reported during Buchanan's last twelve months as superintendent.

In academics no less than in conduct, Buchanan was determined that the school's standards should be second to none. He called attention to the need for expanding the little library that had been collected from the navy yards and ships, suggesting the establishment of an annual fund for the purchase of standard works "that the students and others may have frequent access to them." When Professor Lockwood reported his students' protests that his course text, Peschell's *Elements of Physics*, was too difficult, Buchanan replied:

> I cannot discover any good reason why "Peshels [sic] elements of physics" should not be retained as the text book of this School. The want of time to study the work analytically appears to be the only reason assigned by the Mid^n for wishing a more elementary substitute. . . . Professor Henry of Princeton College has adopted the work for his classes, and I do not know why the standard of education at Princeton should be superior to that at the Naval School.

At the same time, Buchanan drew a line between education and training, a difficult distinction that almost every successive superintendent has confronted in one form or another. As did most of the others, Buchanan decided that training must come first. Reviewing the school curriculum at the end of its first year of operation, he wrote:

> Natural Philosophy is a highly important branch of education to make an accomplished officer, but as the School was established with a view to make useful practical officers first, I wish that branch confined principally to Mechanics; to study should be made pleasant as well as useful to the mid^n and illustrated as far as possible by experiments.

Aware that his office involved important social obligations, Buchanan took care to foster good relations between the school and the city. He was no stranger to Annapolis, having married Anne Catherine Lloyd, daughter of one of its foremost families, in the Chase-Lloyd House on Maryland Avenue, not five minutes' walk from the school. From the beginning, midshipmen were readily received into Annapolitan society. The hospitality they enjoyed was repaid by a grand naval ball arranged by Midshipman Simpson's Spirits Club in the recitation hall on January 15, 1846. Guests came from as far away as Washington, Baltimore, and the Eastern Shore. Evidently a good time was had by all, as the journal of the officer of the day for January 16 notes: "No recitations today—All hands being employed repairing damage after the Ball." Repeated the year following, the academy ball became an annual event.

The Spirits also staged the academy's first theatrical, a production of Edward Bulwer-Lytton's lugubrious "Lady of Lyons." It was presented in an unused theatre on Duke of Gloucester Street. Immediately thereafter the theatre was demolished and a Presbyterian church erected in its place. In later years then-Admiral Simpson liked to point out, "thus, the Academy may claim credit for having spread religious influences in the community."

The outbreak of war with Mexico on May 13, 1846, electrified the school. On May 14, Buchanan volunteered for "immediate, active service at sea." Fifty-six midshipmen followed his example. Buchanan's request was denied. ("Were it not for the important business on which you are at present engaged," Bancroft assured him, "you would be among the first on whom the Department would call.") Acting Midshipmen John Adams, W. B. Hayes, and Thomas T. Houston had better luck. On May 20, they were ordered to the sloop of war *Dale*, which made them the first midshipmen ever to go from the academy to war. Another youngster and three oldsters received their orders between May 25 and June 2. The remaining members of both classes were required to finish the school term. However, the date of the oldsters' examination for lieutenant was moved forward four months, from September to June, and the forty-three midshipmen who passed it, all Date of '40, were able to join the fleet later that summer. In the event, the war lasted long enough for the members of the graduating class of 1847 to take part in its closing stages. A total of ninety alumni saw active duty in the course of the conflict.

The Mexican War also provided the occasion for the first of the academy's many monuments. Although the only graduate to lose his life in the war, Passed Midshipman William R. Thomas, Date of '41, succumbed to disease aboard ship off Veracruz, four other midshipmen died in the line of duty. Thomas B. Shubrick was decapitated by an enemy round shot while pointing a gun in the Naval Battery before Veracruz; Wingate Pillsbury drowned as he attempted to aid a seaman when a launch under his command capsized while chasing a Mexican coaster; and Henry R. Clemson and John R. Hynson went down in the ill-fated *Somers*, sunk by a sudden squall off Veracruz in December 1846. To commemorate these sacrifices, the midshipmen at the school took up a subscription for a memorial. A marble shaft supported by a rectangular base and four upright cannons, the Mexican Monument was erected in 1848.

In the meanwhile, the time had come for Secretary Bancroft to submit the navy's new budget to Congress. The fact that it included funds for a naval academy, which had been established without the approval of Congress, created a potentially prickly situation. Bancroft put the best possible face on the matter, noting that eleven of the twenty-two professors on the navy's payroll the previous year had been put "on waiting orders" and asking no more than "that you will continue to appropriate the same amount as formerly, but that it may be devoted specifically to this new system of instruction." On August 10, 1846, Congress acquiesced in his fait accompli, allocating $28,200 "for repairs, improvements, and instruction at Fort Severn, Annapolis, Md." Three days later, Bancroft directed Buchanan to make whatever "additions and alterations" the school buildings required to accommodate a student body of one hundred.

This was Bancroft's last service to the academy. On September 9, 1846, he left the Navy Department to accept the appointment of ambassador to the Court of St. James. Although he lived for forty-four more years, he visited the academy only once, in 1878. The prolix *History of the United States*, which he believed would be his monument, is unread today even by historians. His monument is the world's largest dormitory, Bancroft Hall, home of the brigade of midshipmen.

The new mess hall, completed in 1846, is shown at left in this print published that same year. The barracks building of Fort Severn, at right, was used for recitations. U.S. Naval Institute Collection.

The school commenced its second year of operation on October 12, 1846. By then Buchanan had the new construction well under way. The most important addition was a two-story, colonnaded, brick building erected adjacent to the recitation hall. Subsequently assigned to the department of seamanship, it originally housed the midshipmen's kitchen, mess hall, library, and lyceum. The library was organized by Professor Chauvenet; the lyceum by Chaplain Jones. The latter's holdings were greatly increased in February 1849, when President Polk ordered the navy's accumulation of captured enemy flags transferred to the Naval School. With them came the famous DONT GIVE UP THE SHIP flag flown by Commodore Oliver Hazard Perry at the battle of Lake Erie. These accessions formed the core of what became the Naval Academy Museum.

The autumn's work left the former barracks free to be used for classrooms. The faculty was delighted. Writing his wife, Professor Lockwood rejoiced:

Did I tell you that the mess-room and kitchen had been removed into the new building and that the old was being rapidly fixed up for academical purposes? One room will be devoted solely to me, where I may lecture, recite, experiment, study and do what I please. I'll invite you to take your knitting there sometime.

The school's second naval ball was held in the new building on January 21, 1847. Among the guests were Bancroft's successor, Secretary of the Navy John Y. Mason, and the naval committees of both the Senate and the House. Less than two weeks later, Buchanan renewed his request for active service. It was granted, and on March 16, he left Annapolis to assume command of the new sloop of war *Germantown*. The war had waited for him, and he arrived in Mexican waters in time to smell his share of gunsmoke on the expeditions up the Tuxpan and Tabasco rivers.

Buchanan's contribution to the school over whose birth he presided was immense. Much remained to be done before it deserved to be called an academy, but he had laid a solid foundation for the future. As early as January 1846 the *Nautical Magazine* noted:

> The appearance, order and studious habits of the midshipmen generally reflect the highest credit upon them, upon the institution, and upon the service of which they are members. . . . Aided by the zealous efforts of those having charge of the various branches of instruction, [the Superintendent] has already given to the institution a consolidated character which would render it difficult for an observer to detect traces of its recent origin.

Perhaps ducks could be taught to swim in a garret, after all.

CHAPTER THREE

Turbulent Times

It was providential that Buchanan had set the school on a firm footing. Otherwise, it might not have survived the administration of his successor, Commander George P. Upshur. A kindly, conscientious man who had been in the navy since 1815, Upshur was personally popular with the school staff. Within weeks of Upshur's arrival, Professor Lockwood was writing, "I see him often and am already far more intimate than I sh. have been with Capt. Buchanan in fifty years." Unfortunately, he proved incapable of controlling the midshipmen, and the strict discipline maintained by Buchanan dissolved. William Harwar Parker, Date of '41, put it charitably: "There have been stricter disciplinarians than Captain Upshur—but never a more honorable, high-toned gentleman. . . . If *example* counts for anything, we had it before us in him, and if we did not profit by it it was our own loss."

It was definitely their loss. A forceful executive officer might have made a difference, but Ward's replacement, Lieutenant Sidney Smith Lee, a brother of Robert E. Lee, was as ineffectual as Upshur. So their charges ran amok. Midshipmen whose averages entitled them to town liberty disdained to sign the liberty-book and frenched out simply for the fun of breaking regulations. A gang of twelve troublemakers called the Apostles once decked themselves out in bedsheets and stalked across Lieutenant Lee's garden on their way over the wall. Drinking clubs were formed with such suitably nocturnal names as the Crickets and the Owls. The Owls frequented a saloon kept by a German named Rosenthal. A number of their classmates did not even bother to go out of the yard for their parties. These revels were called reform banquets, an ironic reference to the Chartist movement, whose agitation for the reform of English politics was then at its peak. But, as Rear Admiral S. R. Franklin, Date of '41, confessed many years later, "There was no parallelism between what are called our 'reform banquets' and the Chartist meetings. . . . Every Saturday night . . . we assembled at the room of some choice spirit, where we were regaled with whisky and cigars, and crackers and cheese, and swapped yarns and sang songs until nearly midnight. . . . I happened one Sunday morning to be passing by a room where there had been a banquet the night before. Lieutenant Sidney Smith Lee . . . was passing at the same moment. He called my attention to this 'banquet-hall deserted,' and, raising his hands with an air of intense disgust, asked me if I had ever witnessed such a sight. Empty bottles were lying about the floor, half-smoked cigars were scattered in all directions, chairs were turned upsidedown, and everything in the room indicated that it had been the scene of rollicking dissipation. Lieutenant Lee was an amiable man, and, while he deplored the existence of such irregularities, he seemed powerless to prevent them."

Upshur acknowledged his own powerlessness following an evening excursion during which a group of midshipmen fell afoul of some toughs in town. "Word was passed to those inside [the school]," Admiral Franklin remembered, "and nearly the whole class, armed with pokers and other weapons which were near at hand, rushed out to the scene of action. However, by the time we reached there quiet had been restored and nothing more serious than a broken head or two resulted from the fray." The next morning Upshur mustered all hands and delivered a pathetic address, beginning with the words, "Raining as it was, and sick as I was, I was aroused from my bed . . ." and concluding with the plea, "I cannot govern you, young gentlemen: so if you will only govern yourselves, I shall be delighted."

This episode was among the incidents chronicled in the midshipmen's "Alphabet Song," a work whose anonymous authors, probably Owls, apparently intended to provide the Naval School with an equivalent of West Point's "Benny Haven." Its concluding stanza ran:

> U was old Upshur out in the rain
> V was the vagrants he could not restrain.
> W was the whisky made a bad mess.
> X was a symbol of math to guess.
> Y also helped torture the brain.
> Z is the zenith of glory to gain.

The chorus was equally infamous:

> "Oh middy, dear middy," old Chauvenet'd say,
> "I'll give to you ten if you solve this today."
> I winked and I blinked at old Chauvenet's shoe,
> And bilged like a middy when drunk ought to do.

No doubt the extent of the dissipation these verses celebrate was exaggerated. Serious, well-behaved students seldom figure in ribald songs. Drinking was a problem; but midshipmen who drank too much too often were unlikely to remain midshipmen. The failure rate of the midshipmen, Dates of 1840-1842, who attended the academy under Upshur was roughly 25 per cent. It must have included most of the midshipmen who winked and blinked at Chauvenet's shoe.

The midshipmen's misconduct did not end with dissipation. They also fought duels. This custom, although already extinct in civil society and strictly contrary to naval regulations, retained a certain chic among midshipmen. There had been rumors of duels, in which neither party succeeded in doing the other injury, during Buchanan's administration. Upshur's midshipmen were better shots. The first of their duels was fought between Walter W. Queen and Byrd A. Stevenson, both Date of '41, behind Fort Severn after the evening meal on May 4, 1848. Queen was hit just above the hip joint by a ball that penetrated to a depth of over six inches. His friends carried him to the Gas House and summoned Surgeon Lockwood, explaining that there had been an accident. Lockwood knew very well what had happened, and when he demanded, "What distance?" several of the onlookers blurted out, "Ten paces."

Dueling was an offense against which Upshur could not proceed without some embarrassment. As a passed midshipman he had attempted to resign from the navy in order to challenge his first lieutenant. Reporting the Queen-Stevenson incident to Secretary Mason, he commented that "Duelling, however reprehensible in itself, has hitherto been sanctioned by precedent and practice, among military men, as a necessary evil." What really upset him was that this particular duel had been fought within a few hundred yards of the office and residence of the school's commanding officer, "a fact which I think greatly aggravates the offence." Both combatants received official reprimands. Stevenson failed to graduate. Queen became a rear admiral.

The next duel took place scarcely a month later, on June 7, 1848, when Midshipman Francis G. Dallas, Date of '41, called out Midshipman John Gale, of the same date, for making what he considered "slanderous reports affecting my character . . . to a Lady whom I hoped . . . to make my wife." They met at the famous dueling field at Bladensburg, Maryland, where twenty-eight years earlier Commodore James Barron had mortally wounded Stephen Decatur. Dallas was hit in the right shoulder at the first fire and the physician in attendance intervened to halt the proceedings, although both principals desired a second shot.

This time the apparently epidemic nature of the offense provoked stern measures, and Gale and Dallas were dismissed. Whether because their punishment served as a deterrent or because their classmates were simply more sensible, midshipmen did not fight any more duels.

Another problem revolved around Professor Lockwood. It was precipitated when the Academic Board recommended adding infantry and light artillery drill to the school curriculum. In that era, naval officers were often called on to lead ships' landing parties into action ashore; a smattering of small-unit tactics would therefore be a valuable addition to their professional education. Moreover, reasoned the board, "[The drill] would not occupy more than half an hour daily, would be a healthy exercise, and would tend to the military character of the school." As a West Point graduate, Lockwood was a natural candidate for drillmaster. A battery of brass six-pounders was obtained from the army, and in February 1848 Lockwood embarked upon his additional duties with an enthusiasm equaled only by the midshipmen's disgust. Drilling was something done by soldiers, and their attitude towards that genus was summed up by the maxim, "A messmate before a shipmate, a shipmate before a stranger, a stranger before a dog, but a dog before a sojer."

The midshipmen were not backward in making their feelings known. They dubbed Lockwood "The Shore Warrior," called his drill periods "pig driving," and did their best to make the description apt, milling around in contrived confusion and finally shuffling through the movements in a parody of a military manner. They also resorted to sabotage, dismantling the guns and throwing the linchpins into the Severn.

The climax came on St. Patrick's Day 1848, when members of the Date of '41 hanged Lockwood in effigy from the academy flagstaff. This was too much, even for Upshur, and the culprits were court-martialed for disrespect to a superior officer. Their counsel brought the proceedings to a halt by showing that Lockwood was not an officer, superior or otherwise; he was merely a civilian employed by the Navy Department. The success of this strategy was short-lived. New charges were framed, on

The oldest existing photograph of the battalion on parade shows the
midshipmen formed up in front of Fort Severn in 1860. Professor Lockwood
is in the right foreground, holding his sword across his knees. Courtesy:
U.S. Naval Academy Archives.

which the accused midshipmen were duly convicted, but their first line
of defense had stung Lockwood into action. Together with Chauvenet,
he protested that, without authority over their students, the professors
would be in an impossible position. The point was well taken, and the
professors were given equivalent rank as commissioned officers, which
had the incidental effect of increasing their pay by $400 a year. The
midshipmen grumbled that at that rate Lockwood could afford to be
strung up annually.

The outcome of this affair compelled the midshipmen to concede that
there was no escaping Lockwood's drills. That did not mean they felt
obliged to take them seriously. The professor had a stutter, and the
midshipmen never overlooked the opportunities it offered to enliven the
proceedings. During artillery drill one day Lockwood started the battalion towards the Severn. As the head of the column neared the water's
edge, he prepared to give the order to "Halt!" What came out was
"Haw-haw-haw!" Without breaking step, the midshipmen marched over
the embankment and into the river, dragging their little cannons behind
them. By the time Lockwood managed to enunciate the command, the
boys on the dragropes were waist-deep in the water.

But the last laugh did not always belong to the midshipmen. On a
subsequent occasion Lockwood's infirmity asserted itself under identical
circumstances. The Severn did not appear as inviting as it had earlier,
however, and the battalion quietly came to a halt of its own accord.
When Lockwood had regained control of his tongue, he exclaimed,
"Wh-why d-don't you do it?"

But while ill-disciplined midshipmen plagued the present, important
plans were being made for the future. Late in 1849 the Academic Board
proposed a sweeping reform of the entire academy program. Its report
was reviewed by a committee whose members included Superintendent
Upshur, Commander Buchanan, Professor Chauvenet, and Army Captain
Henry Brewerton, superintendent at West Point. The recommendations
that emerged were put into force on July 1, 1850. With their adoption
the academy began to assume its modern form.

An acting midshipman gazes coolly out of a woodcut published in 1853. The anchor devices on his cap and lapels had been authorized for midshipmen a year earlier. Courtesy: U.S. Naval Academy Special Collections, Nimitz Library.

The new regulations extended the course of study to a full four years. It was still interrupted by sea duty, however. Upon entering the navy, an acting midshipman spent two years ashore at Annapolis. Then he was sent to sea for three years, receiving his midshipman's warrant after the first six months, just as before. Following this period he returned for a final two years at the academy, at the conclusion of which he took his lieutenant's examination. The faculty was organized into six departments: naval tactics and seamanship; mathematics; the sciences; gunnery and infantry tactics; ethics and English; and modern languages. To measure the midshipmen's progress, a numerical grade scale was established, ranging downwards from 4.0, with 2.5 as the minimum passing mark. The function of the Academic Board remained the same. In recognition of the significance of these changes, the Naval School was officially renamed the U.S. Naval Academy.

A comprehensive disciplinary system, similar to that in effect at the Military Academy, was also introduced. Previously, a midshipman's demerits were debited against his academic average. This procedure affected his class standing and could, if it pulled his average down far enough, cost him liberty privileges; but its impact was at best indirect. Under the new system, demerits were administered independently of academics. Although they were factored into the determination of final class standing, they served primarily as the measure of a midshipman's conduct. Anyone accumulating 200 demerits in the course of a year was automatically dismissed. In addition to the imposition of demerits, a series of graduated punishments, beginning with confinement to the yard and climaxing with dismissal, was established for various offenses.

The regulations also gave the institution a distinctly military character. Midshipmen were required to wear uniform at all times while attached to the academy. Mandatory formations were introduced. The student body was organized, man-o'-war fashion, into gun crews, which changed into companies for infantry drill, and a hierarchy of midshipmen officers was established. Each gun crew was headed by a first captain, who was drawn from the first class, and a second captain, from either the first or second class. On parade, Professor Lockwood continued to command the battalion, as it was constituted, but he was seconded by an adjutant and an assistant adjutant, the highest ranking midshipmen officers.

Simultaneously, Owls, Crickets, and other midshipmen clubs were abolished by a blanket prohibition of "all combinations under any pretext whatsoever." Dueling, the possession of firearms, playing cards, "spirituous, vinous, fermented or other intoxicating drinks," tobacco "in any shape," cooking in rooms, contracting unauthorized debts, and matrimony were expressly forbidden. No one, including officers and professors, was to go outside the academy walls without the permission of the superintendent. The position of executive officer was renamed commandant of midshipmen and its incumbent gradually came to be charged with direct responsibility for the behavior of the battalion.

Commander Upshur completed his tour at the academy the same month that these regulations, which might have saved him so much grief, went into effect. He was succeeded by Commander Cornelius K. Stribling, a fifty-year-old South Carolinian who entered the navy during the War of 1812. As a lieutenant, he distinguished himself while in command of a sloop of war on the West India Station by capturing one of the last pirate ships to be taken by the U.S. Navy.

There was a distinct improvement in the discipline of the academy during Stribling's superintendency. Midshipmen continued to make their share and more of mischief. They were unruly in quarters, playing such pranks as setting pails of water atop doors to douse duty officers and extinguishing the gas lights throughout an entire building by blowing vigorously into a burner. They frenched out to drink in Annapolis. They loaded the morning gun with bricks. When a French frigate came up the bay, the first class was ordered to make ready to salute her by removing the window sashes that had been fitted into the embrasures of Fort Severn. They obeyed the order but, unnoticed by the officers, placed them directly under the muzzles of the guns, where the concussion shattered all 136 panes. These were the sort of pranks and practices to be expected of a high-spirited, collegiate population. None approached the insolent outrages that occurred under the previous administration. Years later, Stribling recalled, "There was nothing connected with the Academy, which gave me so much anxiety, as the

The Naval School was given a military character and renamed the Naval Academy during the superintendency of Commander Cornelius K. Stribling, shown here following his promotion to captain. Courtesy: U.S. Naval Academy Archives.

discipline of the students. So many boys just released from parental restraint, and a number of young men with the experience gained by associating . . . with older men; to be subjected to the same rules, was a problem of doubtful solution. The attempt was made, and that it succeeded at all, is to me a source of unceasing thankfulness."

The final reorganization of the academy program was carried out under Commander Stribling. Throughout their terms as superintendent Buchanan and Upshur made repeated requests for a practice ship to be attached to the academy, as had been foreseen at its foundation. The

41

"Target Practice from the Naval Battery" is the title of this woodcut. While an officer spots the fall of shot through his telescope, an imperturbable waterman continues tonging oysters. Courtesy: U.S. Naval Academy Archives.

ship did not materialize until 1851, when the midshipmen were able to undertake a coastal cruise in the government steamer *John Hancock*. At New York, they transferred to the *Preble*, a third-class sailing sloop of war which was officially assigned to the academy. This experiment proved so successful that service circles which hitherto had insisted on getting the midshipmen to sea early, even at the cost of interrupting their education, became satisfied that annual summer cruises would serve the purpose. Accordingly, in July 1851 the Academic Board recommended that the midshipmen's four years at the academy should run consecutively. Endorsed by a board of officers, which, as usual, included Commander Buchanan, the proposal was approved by Secretary of the Navy William A. Graham on November 15, 1851. Midshipmen who had entered the navy before January 1851 were to complete the old program. Their successors were to remain acting midshipmen throughout their academy career, receiving midshipman warrants upon graduation. It was also stipulated that, in the future, warrants would be awarded only to academy graduates. This provision established the academy as the navy's sole source of line officers. It was to remain so, with wartime exceptions, for the next seventy years.

Official designations of the four new classes followed West Point terminology. Midshipmen were identified as fourth classmen, not fresh-

Fort Severn as it appeared in the 1850s, after being roofed in. Courtesy:
U.S. Naval Academy Archives.

men; third classmen, not sophomores; second classmen, not juniors; and
first classmen, not seniors. Informally, fourth classmen became known as
plebes, another West Pointism. Third classmen were called youngsters
and second classmen oldsters, the old Naval School names for acting and
warranted midshipmen. The custom of classifying midshipmen according
to the dates of their warrants was dropped, and they were identified as
members of the class in which they graduated.

Major improvements were also made to the academy's physical plant.
An extensive construction program, which continued throughout Stribling's superintendency, was undertaken in 1850. Fort Severn was closed
to the weather by a wooden wall, which turned its embrasures into gun-
ports, and a conical roof crowned with the inevitable cupola. A combined
laboratory and armory was built between it and the Severn. Five two-
and three-story brick dormitories were laid out backing up to the river on
a line between the fort and the Seamanship Building. This subsequently
became known as Stribling Row. The Seamanship Building itself was
enlarged. A chapel in Greek revival style, complete with four Ionic
columns, went up on its left, and a granite-coped, three-story Recitation
Hall on its right. To the west of the chapel, ground was broken for a
small observatory. Both the chapel and the observatory stood outside the
original confines of Fort Severn. The land had been acquired in 1847,

The dormitories along Stribling Row housed the midshipmen from 1853 to 1869. The quality of construction was not good, and the back wall of one building fell out during study hours one evening. Courtesy: U.S. Naval History Division.

The chapel, Seamanship Building, and Recitation Hall, seen here from left to right, were the first buildings erected following the transfer of Fort Severn to the navy. Courtesy: U.S. Naval Academy Special Collections, Nimitz Library.

when Commander Upshur was authorized to purchase four large lots, amounting to twelve acres, adjacent to the southwestern wall of the post between Scott Street and the Severn River. Their acquisition extended the academy grounds to Northeast Street, as Maryland Avenue was then called.

A second addition was made under Stribling in 1853. It involved three separate transactions, forming an L-shaped plot bounded by Tabernacle (now College Avenue), Hanover, and Governor streets. These additions, thirty-three acres altogether, almost quadrupled the extent of the grounds. They also provided fill for a seawall, the beginning of the academy's gradual advance into the Severn.

Meanwhile, by an act of August 31, 1852, appointments to the academy had come under the control of Congress. Until then they had been made by the president, supposedly in proportion to the populations of the states and territories. Under the new law, appointing authority was assigned exclusively to the members of the House of Representatives. This act furnished the basis for all subsequent legislation. Soon thereafter, a few appointments-at-large were restored to the president; later, the secretary of the navy was empowered to appoint a limited number of enlisted men from the fleet; and ultimately the congressional authority was extended to the Senate.

In November 1853 Commander Louis M. Goldsborough relieved Commander Stribling to become the academy's fourth superintendent. A burly giant, standing six-feet-four-inches tall and weighing close to 300 pounds, to a half-grown midshipman he looked "as tall as a sequoia and as large as a mountain." His booming voice and bluff manner were as imposing as his bulk. Admiral S. R. Franklin, who, as a lieutenant, taught at the academy under Goldsborough, recalled that "he would almost frighten a subordinate out of his wits, but he was *au fond* an exceedingly kind-hearted man. His bark was a great deal worse than his bite." The midshipmen referred to him as Goldberry.

The academy made steady progress during Goldsborough's four years at its helm. By the time he took over, the teaching staff had grown to twelve civilians and six officers. Courses were made more demanding; the curriculum was revised; and the number of academic departments was raised to nine by separating navigation from mathematics, dividing modern languages into its French and Spanish components, and establishing a department of mechanical drawing, sketching, and perspective. This last was made the responsibility of Professor Edward Seager, a versatile gentleman who doubled as fencing master, or "Instructor in the Art of Defence," drilling the midshipmen by gun crews once weekly.

The first graduation exercise, for six members of an accelerated section of the Date of 1851, was held on June 10, 1854. It was a simple ceremony. Students, faculty, and the Board of Examiners assembled in the new chapel at noon. Following a prayer by the chaplain, Commander Goldsborough delivered a brief address and presented the certificates of graduation. The last midshipmen who entered the navy under the old system, most of them of the Date of 1850, were graduated in 1856. The academy received its first presidential visit that same year, when President Franklin Pierce attended one of the midshipmen's naval balls.

By then, summer cruise had become a regular feature of the program of instruction. The *Preble* had made the academy's first foreign cruise, to the West Indies and Madeira, in 1852 and sailed even farther, to the

Commander Louis M. Goldsborough's gargantuan size and salty manner awed the midshipmen, but he usually took a lenient view of their misdeeds. Improvements in the curriculum during his administration caused conservatives to complain that he was introducing "a damned sight too much science into the institution." Here, he appears as a rear admiral, wearing the shoulder straps prescribed for that rank in January 1864. Courtesy: U.S. Naval Academy Archives.

northern coast of Spain, in 1853. The cruise arrangements had yet to be perfected, however. In the opinion of an officer who accompanied the cruise of 1855, a coasting voyage to Maine: "Proper provision for . . . [the] well-being of the Midshipmen was not then made, and the poor boys had a very hard time of it. They were ill-fed, and were not well cared for." All cruises between 1853 and 1858 were made in the *Preble*

Inside Fort Severn, midshipmen fence under an officer's watchful eye while, at rear, others go through gunnery drill. Courtesy: U.S. Naval Academy Special Collections, Nimitz Library.

except that of 1856, when she was replaced by the *Plymouth*, another, somewhat larger sloop which became the academy's practice ship in 1859.

The chapel and observatory, the last of the buildings begun under Commander Stribling, were completed in 1854. Steam heat and gas light had come to the academy a year earlier, when the necessary plants were built on the point behind Fort Severn. The new dormitories were opened to occupancy between 1851 and 1853. They contained a total of ninety-eight double rooms, each fifteen feet square and furnished with one iron bedstead and one bureau per occupant. Midshipmen purchased everything else according to highly specific regulations, which stipulated that roommates would share, among other articles, a looking glass, wash-basin, slop bucket, and broom.

During Goldsborough's superintendency, a hospital and two faculty quarters were built in the northwest corner of the yard, along what became known as Goldsborough Row, and the science building was enlarged. It soon became evident that the construction of the quarters, at least, left a great deal to be desired. Rear Admiral Edmund O. Matthews, Date of '51, related that one night while he and his classmates were studying in their rooms, they "suddenly heard a rumbling sound, the lights were extinguished, and there was a crash and a rush of cold air.

This view of the academy from Annapolis Harbor appeared in *Ballou's Pictorial Drawing Room Companion* for December 1855. Fort Severn is at right center. The buildings to its left are the superintendent's residence and the officers' and faculty quarters along Buchanan Row. The small, two-story building between them and the seawall is the hospital. Courtesy: U.S. Naval Academy Special Collections, Nimitz Library.

One wall of the building had fallen out, leaving the rooms towards the water exposed. Fortunately the floor beams did not rest on this wall, else the admiral would not have been left to tell the story. As it was, he found himself sitting on a shelf in the open air."

Discipline remained loose. An unpopular assistant professor of chemistry, William R. Hopkins, whom the midshipmen called Bull Pup, was locked in a glass case in his laboratory, and long-suffering Professor Lockwood's drills were sabotaged at every opportunity. One evening the professor forgot to return his battery to the safety of the armory. The morning sun revealed disassembled guns, carriages, wheels, and limbers strewn across the grass in a scene reminiscent of a deserted battlefield. Another contretemps occurred while Lockwood was conducting artillery drill. After past experiences, he had begun to have his commands given by bugle but the bugler was ill one day and he had to shout them out.

The battalion was pulling its six-pounders forward by half-batteries (two guns at a time) in the direction of the superintendent's residence, firing blank charges at each halt. At the critical moment, Lockwood began to stutter. Gleefully, the midshipmen rushed the last half-battery into position, the muzzles of its guns almost touching the board fence behind the superintendent's garden. Ignoring Lockwood's frantic gesticulations, they fired, and the superintendent's fence disappeared in a cloud of kindling.

The persistence of such antics owed a great deal to the forbearance of the staff. As a midshipman who entered the academy in 1856 recalled, "A general good-humored tolerance . . . characterized the relations of the officers and students. . . . While the ones were in duty bound to enforce academic regulations, which the others felt an equal obligation to disregard, it was a kind of game. . . . [The officers], I think, had an unacknowledged feeling that . . . some relaxation of strict official correctness must be endured. Larking, sometimes uproarious, met with personal sympathy, if official condemnation. Nor did we mind being detected by what we regarded as fair means. . . . The exceptional man, who inspected at unaccustomed hours . . . who came upon us unawares, was apt to be credited with rather unofficer-like ideas."

Commander Goldsborough shared the attitude that boys will be boys. Members of the Academic Board who came to him to complain of what he considered a midshipman's traditional transgressions met with brusque brush-offs. But his patience was not unbounded. Its limits were exceeded one night in 1854, when a pair of amateur arsonists eliminated one of the academy's outbuildings. The next day Goldsborough stormed up as the battalion was leaving formation, called an immediate halt, and delivered an impassioned oration based on the article of war that prescribed the penalty of death for "any person in the Navy, who shall maliciously set on fire, or otherwise destroy, any government property not then in the possession of an enemy, pirate or rebel." The force of his remarks moved one of the miscreants, Midshipman John S. Barnes, '54, to immortalize them in the following lines:

> Young gentlemen assembled!—
>   It makes no matter where—
> I only want to speak to you,
>   So hear me where you are.
>
> Some vile incendiary
>   Last night was prowling round,
> Who set fire to our round-house
>   And burned it to the ground.
>
> I'll read the Naval Law;
>   The man who dares to burn
> A round-house—not the Enemy's—
>   A traitor's fate shall learn.
>
> And if a man there be,
>   Who does this traitor know,
> And keep it to himself,
>   He shall suffer death also!
>
> 'Tis well, then, to tell, then,
>   Who did this grievous ill;
> And, d—n me, I will hang him,
>   So help me God! I will!

confidence of President Theodore Roosevelt, honorary degrees from Oxford, Cambridge, Harvard, and Yale, and a handsome income to augment his navy retirement.

On his appointment to the academy, at the age of sixteen, Mahan had already completed two years at Columbia College. Learning that under existing regulations an appointee could enter any class for which he was academically qualified, he decided to aim for the third. Today the procedure through which a midshipman may satisfy course requirements by examination is called *validation*. Mahan validated his entire fourth-class year and went directly into the youngster class, thus becoming the only midshipman ever to pass through the academy without being a plebe. A number of wartime classes have been graduated in three years or less, but the time saved has come from the top, not the bottom, of the curriculum. Their members all had a plebe year.

Mahan thoroughly enjoyed his first two years at the academy. He liked his classmates, who do not seem to have resented his sudden appearance in their midst. He was pleased to discover that he could make excellent grades without trying, which left his study periods free for the romantic novels he devoured. In the end they undid him and he graduated number two. He loved cruise, despite occasional bouts of seasickness, declaring, "Life at sea, so far as I have experienced it, is the most happy, careless & entrancing life that there is." Like many precocious youths more comfortable in the company of adults than of his peers, he spent delightful evenings as a guest in the homes of his officers and professors. His father was personally acquainted with both Superintendent Goldsborough and the commandant of midshipmen, Lieutenant Thomas T. Craven. His mother was a houseguest of the Cravens when she visited Annapolis, and Alfred developed a crush on the commandant's daughter, Nannie.

The trouble came his first-class year, when Mahan was given the two stripes of a first captain. It had already become a tradition that a midshipman never put a member of his own class on report. Mahan did not think that this was an honorable tradition. He asked his father for his opinion, and the colonel did not think so, either. That settled it. Mahan began reporting first classmen. A few faithful friends sympathized with his stand, but most of his classmates were outraged. They retaliated by putting him "in Coventry." That is, they ceased to acknowledge his existence —a procedure that was ruled unconstitutional at West Point, where it was called "The Silence," over a century later. When academy authorities questioned his classmates about the matter, the midshipmen insisted it had nothing to do with the fact that Mahan had put them on report; it was because they found him anti-social.

Mahan persisted in his lonely course, convinced of its rectitude, but the rejection it brought him undoubtedly contributed to the aloofness with which he armored his feelings thereafter. For the rest of his life he was careful to keep mankind at arm's length. But when it came time for him to write his memoirs, Mahan made no complaints of his academy days. He liked to remember the tolerance the officers had shown for midshipmen escapades and the pleasures of the academy's social life. "Not only on Saturdays and holidays," he wrote, "but every day, and at all hours not positively allotted to study or drills, the midshipmen might visit the houses of the officers and professors to which they had entrance . . . and, of all the humanizing and harmonizing influences under which [they] came, none exceeded that of the quiet gentlefolk, of modest means, with whom they mingled thus freely." He did not mention that he had been put in Coventry.

One point upon which Mahan agreed with Dewey was the efficiency of the education he received. "The Academy constituted for us an atmosphere perfectly accordant with the life for which we were intended," he declared; "and an educational institution has no higher function to discharge than this."

As the Board of Visitors concluded its annual report for 1857, the academy could no longer be considered an experiment. The ducks had learned to swim.

CHAPTER FOUR

Midshipmen in Blue and Grey

Dewey and Mahan received their certificates of graduation from Captain George S. Blake, who had succeeded Commander Goldsborough to become the academy's fifth superintendent in September 1857. A portly, dignified, old gentleman who had spent much of his long career in the Coast Survey, he became noted for a habit of placing his hand on his stomach and declaring, "I can lay my hand upon my heart, and say I never wronged a midshipman!" He made it a point to personally answer all letters from the parents of his charges, turning out an average of 1,000 replies a year throughout the eight years of his superintendency.

Blake was fortunate to be seconded by a series of exceptionally able commandants of midshipmen. The first was Commander Thomas T. Craven, the only officer ever to serve two tours in that capacity (1851-55 and 1858-60). His major contribution was the improvement of the organization of summer cruise. Having commanded the rather haphazard cruises of 1851-54, he returned to the academy in 1858 with plans to establish a shipboard routine that would provide each midshipman with the broadest possible experience. Craven described his system in his report of the cruise of 1860:

> At an early period in the cruise the first class were put in charge of the deck, and performed all the duties of lieutenants in charge of the watch. They have also been carefully instructed in the use of the sextant . . . and in ascertaining the longitude and latitude by Bowditch's, Chauvenet's and other methods. They became familiar, so soon, with their work, that I was enabled, in a short month, to call upon any of this class to take observations for latitude or longitude by the sun, moon, or stars, and to feel the most perfect confidence in the correctness of their work. They were all taught practical seamanship. During a pretty smart gale, one of our topsails was split, and the occasion was taken advantage of, to practice in shifting topsails. . . . In short, they were instructed in every branch of seamanship, from heaving the lead, steering, reefing and furling, making and taking in sail, up to the most intricate evolution.

Although the midshipmen steadfastly resisted the administration's efforts to wean them from the evils of alcohol and tobacco, discipline continued to improve. The first officially approved midshipmen's association, the Lawrence Literary Society, was organized in 1858. Ironically, the major incident of the period was an exaggerated expression of an attitude that the academy authorities were beginning to promote: that the midshipmen should govern themselves. It was precipitated by Midshipman

The academy's little band posed beside the Severn in the summer of 1860.
Courtesy: U.S. Naval History Division.

Henry D. Foote, '61, a chronic malefactor whose classmates had informally approached the administration to recommend his dismissal. In April 1859, Foote burst into Professor Lockwood's quarters in a state of intoxication and, finding the professor absent, beat his Negro maid over the head with a stick until blood flowed. In view of the obvious gravity of this offence, it would seem that his peers might have reasoned that his days in their midst were numbered and waited for justice to take its course. Instead, they chose to act. A party of six midshipmen apprehended Foote in his room one evening, forced him to carry his mattress to the secluded shoreline behind Fort Severn, and there tarred and feathered him. The outcome was that Foote was dismissed for his assault on Lockwood's maid, and the vigilantes were dismissed for their assault on Foote. Unlike him, however, they were subsequently offered the opportunity of returning to the academy, and several went on to graduate with their class.

By 1859, the faculty had grown to number fourteen civilians and almost as many officers. It suffered a great loss that year with the resignation of Professor Chauvenet. Offered the chair of astronomy and natural philosophy at Yale College and a similar position at Washington University in St. Louis, he accepted the latter, thus ending eighteen years' outstanding service to the cause of naval education. In the words of Lieutenant William H. Parker, who had been both his pupil and his colleague, "he was the life of the naval school." Appointed chancellor of Washington University in 1862, Chauvenet became a founder and vice-president of the National Academy of Sciences and published several mathematical treatises which, by the time of his death in December 1870, had brought him worldwide renown.

The increase in the faculty was a consequence of the academy's steadily expanding enrollment. The institutional bursting-point was reached in October 1859, when the midshipmen reporting for the commencement of the academic year outnumbered the accommodations available on

Stribling Row. The problem was solved by converting the sloop *Plymouth* into a school ship for the fourth class. The midshipmen were lodged on her berth deck; gas and steam lines were run out from shore; and all except four guns were removed from her main deck, which was enclosed to form a study and recitation room. Apart from some overcrowding, the experiment was adjudged a success and the decision was made to replace the *Plymouth* the following year with the frigate *Constitution*, the famous "Old Ironsides" of the War of 1812. Not only was she a considerably more commodious vessel, but it was felt that her historical associations "must, undoubtedly, exercise a salutary influence on the minds of the pupils." The commencement of classes in October 1860 found a total of 281 midshipmen in attendance.

Construction had become a large part of the academy scene. Between 1859 and 1861 the houses in the southwest corner of the yard, on the land acquired in 1847, were demolished, and six two-story, brick quarters were built backing up to Hanover Street to form what became known as Blake Row. Three more permanent additions to the yard were made around the same time. The first came in March 1858, when Commodore Matthew Perry's widow, carrying out his expressed wish, presented the academy with a huge, patinaed bronze bell that had been given to Perry by the regent of the Loo Choo (Ryukyu) Islands during the former's expedition to Japan. Later discovered to date from 1456, it became known as the Japanese Bell.

The Herndon Monument, a massive shaft of Quincy granite, was erected in 1859. It commemorates Commander William Louis Herndon, who went down with the mail steamer *Central America* in a storm off Cape Hatteras in September 1857. After making every possible effort to save the ship, Herndon left the quarterdeck long enough to don his full-dress uniform, in which he returned to his post to meet a seaman's death.

The Tripoli Monument, the most elaborate in the yard, was moved there from the national capitol grounds in November 1860. Commissioned by the officers of the Mediterranean squadron in 1806, it was executed by the Italian sculptor Micali, of Leghorn, to honor the memory of the six American naval officers killed in action during the War with Tripoli. British soldiers knocked the hands off the female figures at the base of the monument during the scorching of Washington in 1814, but the damage had long since been repaired.

A few months prior to the monument's appearance, Commander Craven was relieved as commandant of midshipmen by Lieutenant Christopher R. P. Rodgers. A son of Commodore George Washington Rodgers and nephew of Commodores John Rodgers and Oliver H. and Matthew C. Perry, the new commandant awed the midshipmen by his knightly manner and noble ideals. Sometimes called the Chesterfield of the Navy, to them he appeared the "embodiment of dignity and elegance." It was his inspiration to draw a sharp distinction in status between the four classes, culminating in the elevation of the first class into a sort of aristocracy, granted special privileges and charged with special responsibilities.

Around the same time, outstanding students of all classes were granted visible recognition. For some years, the *Navy Register* had printed a star behind the names of the top five members of every graduating class. Under Blake, all midshipmen maintaining an overall academic average of at least

Lieutenant Christopher R.P. Rodgers, commandant of midshipmen in 1861, impressed the midshipmen as the ideal naval officer. He returned to the academy to serve as superintendent from 1874 to 1878 and again in 1881. Courtesy: U.S. Naval Academy Special Collections, Nimitz Library.

85 per cent were authorized to wear a five-pointed gilt star on their collars. It is still worn today.

At this point, the development of the academy was interrupted by events over which its administration had no control. The presidential campaign of 1860 brought the decades-old differences between the North and the South to a head. To the South, the election of Abraham Lincoln signified the defeat of its long struggle to retain a balance of power in the national government. Charles E. Clark, '64, recalled years later that, "Ever since my class entered the academy in September [1860], the growing unrest and trouble of the country had been disturbing the equilibrium of our little world. There was much wrangling and many arguments between the boys, but no real quarrelling. In the general sense of upheaval, no one—this was especially true of the Northerners—felt certain enough of the ground under his feet to take an assured position. In fact, the youngsters at the Academy were in about as bad a muddle as the country at large."

The situation soon acquired a tragic clarity. Convinced that it had become impossible to preserve either the doctrine of states' rights or the institution of slavery within the framework of the Union, the South

capture the *Constitution* that night. Every conceivable preparation was made to resist the attack, and the schooner *Rainbow* was sent out into the Chesapeake to reconnoiter. Early the next morning she returned to the academy to report that a large steamer was standing down the bay. It seemed as though the moment had come. Blake ordered the drummers to beat the assembly; every gun that would bear was trained on the unknown vessel; and Lieutenant Edmund O. Matthews was sent off in a boat to ascertain her purpose.

Matthews returned with good news. The steamer was the ferryboat *Maryland*, commandeered by General Benjamin F. Butler to carry his Eighth Massachusetts Infantry to Annapolis. Her appearance in the bay was fortuitous. Butler's regiment was aboard train at Philadelphia, en route to Washington, when the rioting broke out in Baltimore. Learning that the Gunpowder and Bush Creek railway bridges to Baltimore had been burned on the night of the 19th, Butler detrained at Perryville, Maryland, and seized the ferry, with the intention of reaching Annapolis by water and proceeding overland to the capital.

Blake lost no time in boarding the *Maryland* to confer with Butler. According to the latter, Blake burst into tears upon learning that the troops were to land at Annapolis. "Thank God! Thank God!" he exclaimed. "Won't you save the *Constitution*?"

Thinking he meant the document, Butler replied, "Yes, that is just what I am here for."

"Are those your orders? Then the old ship is safe."

Realizing that they had been talking at cross-purposes, Butler explained, "I have no orders. I am carrying on war now on my own hook; I cut loose from orders when I left Philadelphia. What do you want me to do to save the *Constitution*?"

"I want some sailormen, for I have no sailors; I want to get her out, and get her afloat."

Butler was happy to oblige. His regiment contained a number of Marblehead fishermen. While his crack company, the Salem Zouaves, took over security of the *Constitution*, the fishermen were placed at Lieutenant Rodgers's disposal. Rodgers had them transfer the *Constitution*'s upper-deck guns to the *Maryland*, lightening the old frigate's draft, after which the ferry towed her out of her berth. Scarcely had she slipped her moorings than she swung back into the mud. Laboriously refloated, she began her voyage down the Severn. Off Greenbury Point Light, she went aground again. Putting out kedge anchors, Rodgers had just pulled her into deep water when a sudden squall drove her back on the shoal. Night and the tide were falling fast and a report that obstructions were being placed in the outer channel revived the apprehension that an attempt would be made on the ship, after all.

But everything came right. A passing steamer hauled the *Constitution* into a deep anchorage and the obstructions proved to have been the figment of someone's imagination. Her upper-deck guns were brought back on board and, on the morning of April 22, she stood ready to cover the landing of Butler's troops.

Exactly how that was to be accomplished was not clear. In process of getting the *Constitution* afloat, the *Maryland* herself had run hard aground. The problem was solved when the steamer *Boston* arrived from Philadelphia with the Seventh New York Regiment on board. Ignoring the protests of Maryland Governor Thomas Hicks that the appearance of

A "special artist" for *Frank Leslie's Illustrated Newspaper* sketched the army encampment on the academy grounds in April 1861. It is easy to see why Captain Blake decided that it would be impossible to continue classes there. Courtesy: U.S. Naval History Division.

Northern troops would push the state over the brink into secession, Butler browbeat the New Yorkers' reluctant commander into landing his men at the academy wharf. The *Boston* then ferried Butler's own regiment ashore.

Both regiments were quartered in the yard. The first classmen gave up their rooms to the officers of the Seventh New York, in appreciation of which its colonel entertained them by putting the regiment through its paces. Not wanting to be outshone by soldiers, the midshipmen asked Professor Lockwood how they could return the compliment. He must have savored the moment. His answer was to have them demonstrate their detested light artillery drill at double time. The New Yorkers were impressed.

The academy became an armed camp. When the first two regiments bivouacked there proceeded to Washington, three others arrived to take their place. Recognizing the impracticality of resuming classes under these conditions, Captain Blake wrote Secretary Welles on April 24 to suggest the immediate transfer of the school to some more tranquil setting. One which occurred to him was Fort Adams, an unused army post at Newport, Rhode Island.

Blake had already resolved to get both the midshipmen and the *Constitution* out of harm's way, by using the latter to carry the former to temporary refuge in New York. At roll call that same morning the midshipmen were ordered to assemble at the academy wharf, where a steamer would carry them out to the *Constitution*. As the drums beat formation, twenty Southern midshipmen who were awaiting acknowledgment of their resignations fell in with their classmates for the last time. They would not be making the trip north. Earlier, the Class of 1861 had literally passed a peacepipe, from which even the nonsmokers had taken a puff, and promised to remain friends though divided.

When the battalion was mustered, the academy band played "Hail Columbia" and "The Star-Spangled Banner." Then Lieutenant Rodgers stepped forward. As a fourth classman remembered: "The wharf was crowded and there was some confusion . . . but when . . . Rodgers came down the long line, and paused opposite its center, all were hushed, for it had been said that he meant to give us a farewell address. Looking at the row of boyish faces turned expectantly towards him, and at the flag floating above their heads, he raised his arm, and pointing to it, began, 'Be true to the flag,' and then broke down completely. I am sure many others were in tears; I know I was."

A moment later, the soldiers who had been looking on shattered the solemnity of the occasion by bursting into the ranks of midshipmen to comfort them with bear hugs and exclamations of "Never mind! You'll be coming back, boys! We'll see that you get your school again!"

The *Constitution* sailed on April 26. Secretary Welles approved the transfer of the academy to Fort Adams on the 27th, and the steamer *Baltic* was detailed to transport the officers, instructors, and their families, together with the library and as much academic apparatus as she could carry, to the new location. The two ships reached Newport within two hours of one another on May 9. Captain Blake remained to tie up loose ends in Annapolis, so it fell to Lieutenant Rodgers to get the academy back into operation. Efficient as always, he was able to reconvene classes on May 13.

The following four years were among the most difficult in the history of the academy. Between 1861 and 1865 the number of vessels in commission in the U.S. Navy increased from 42 to 641. To meet the insatiable demand for officers created by this unprecedented expansion, thousands of volunteers were commissioned from the merchant marine, and the standards of the academy were sacrificed to the goal of turning out the maximum number of midshipmen in the minimum amount of time. Ten members—exactly half—of the Class of 1861 were ordered to active duty the day the battalion left Annapolis. The remainder of that class and the Classes of 1862 and 1863 received their orders a few days after they arrived in Newport. These detachments, which added 112 officers to the fleet, left only the 76 members of the plebe class at the academy. Before the end of May the proposal had been made to send it out, too. Fortunately, Lieutenant Rodgers succeeded in averting such action by vigorously protesting that it would "virtually destroy the academy and undo the work of years."

The selection of Fort Adams as a temporary home for the academy was soon revealed to have been a mistake. Its cramped and fetid masonry casemates were not fit for long-term occupancy. When the Class of 1865 reported in July 1861, a record-breaking 203 strong, it was lodged on board the *Constitution*, and at the approach of winter the academy took a one-year lease on the Atlantic House, a hotel in downtown Newport. An imposing, four-story building with a Parthenon-style pediment supported by six massive columns, it stood on the corner of Pelham and

During its four years at Newport, Rhode Island, the academy was quartered in the Atlantic House. Note the cannon on the porch. Courtesy: U.S. Naval Academy Special Collections, Nimitz Library.

Touro streets, facing Touro Park. The ground floor was appropriated for the officers' quarters and mess; classes were held on the second story; upper-class midshipmen were jammed into the third and fourth. Perry's DONT GIVE UP THE SHIP flag was hung in the main hall. In the absence of a wall or other boundary, the academy yard was defined as the "enclosures of the Atlantic House and Touro Park," beyond which midshipmen were not to pass except on liberty. The fourth class remained in the *Constitution*, which was tied up on the town side of Goat Island. In October 1862 she was joined by another wooden frigate, the *Santee*. A pork-barrel project laid down in 1820 but not launched until 1861, the *Santee* was to remain with the academy an even fifty years.

Life in these floating dormitories was grim. Park Benjamin, who reported aboard in 1863, believed that, "Nothing could have been more desolate than the outlook to the 'plebe' whose first experience brought him to these school-ships. During the day he sat and studied at one of the desks, long rows of which extended up and down the gun-deck, and occasionally marched ashore to the windy recitation rooms, where he contracted bad colds along with a knowledge of arithmetic. The commissary department was always more or less out of gear, and the meals eaten in the blackness of the berth-deck by the light of a few ill-smelling oil lamps were wretched. . . . The midshipmen all slept in hammocks, and, for the first fortnight, punctuated the still hours of the night with stunning thuds on the deck, as they continued . . . to discover . . . different ways they could fall out of them."

A midshipman, apparently, executed this pen-and-ink drawing of the schoolroom on the gun deck of the *Constitution* during the academy's sojourn at Newport. Courtesy: U.S. Naval Academy Special Collections, Nimitz Library.

Caspar F. Goodrich, '65, a member of the only class ever to pass through the Naval Academy without spending a day at Annapolis, recalled the lack of sanitary arrangements: "There were no shower-baths—only a week-end tub was obtainable. For washing, we stood four, five or six deep waiting our turn at the few bowls put up below. Nor would those behind us tolerate any undue lingering over our hasty toilet. Each midshipman had a small locker on the berth deck into which he put his clothing. Since he had to hang his wet towel on a hook inside the door, all his belongings shared the towel's dampness. . . . It was amusing to note the horror depicted on a newcomer's face, as he realized the conditions confronting him."

In the meanwhile, at Annapolis the academy yard had been converted into an army post. The city's strategic position on the inland waterway and the fact that it had a direct rail link with Washington made it a center of martial activity as troops and supplies poured in from Northern coastal cities. Placed in command of a hurriedly constituted Department of Annapolis, Butler extended the railroad to the academy waterfront and put up a row of huge storehouses along the shore of the Severn. But once it became clear that Maryland and its rail lines to the north were secure, the importance of the locality lessened. Butler moved on to infamy as the "Beast of New Orleans," and Annapolis assumed the status of a secondary base of supply.

Another period of activity opened in October 1861, when the city was chosen as the port of embarkation for an expedition against the

A wartime photograph shows hospital tents on the academy's parade ground.
Courtesy: U.S. Naval Academy Special Collections, Nimitz Library.

coast of North Carolina. A joint army-navy operation, its commanders were General Ambrose E. Burnside and former superintendent L. M. Goldsborough, now promoted to the newly created rank of flag officer. More than 30,000 men were assembled in the academy yard, on the campus of St. John's College, and just outside the city at camps Parole and Richmond. With the expedition's departure in February 1862, Annapolis reverted to its rear-area routine.

That spring Secretary Welles decided it was time for the midshipmen to return to Annapolis and asked the War Department to relinquish the academy's facilities. His request was denied on grounds of military necessity. An army hospital was established in the yard, and Annapolis settled down to a quiet war. A final flurry of excitement occurred in the summer of 1864, when the alarm aroused by General Jubal Early's raid into Maryland led the local authorities to entrench Annapolis and barricade the yard, but the Confederates did not come anywhere near.

At Newport the academy soon began to lose cohesion. Lieutenant Rodgers was ordered to sea shortly after its arrival there, and succeeding commandants of midshipmen were replaced on the average of once a year throughout the conflict. The turnover in officer instructors was equally drastic. None wanted an academy assignment in wartime. Before long the faculty consisted almost solely of civilians, not all of whom proved suited for their posts. The consequent confusion was aggravated by the detachment of the upper classes and the size of the war-swollen plebe classes, each as large as the entire battalion had been a few years before. Part of the Class of 1864 was ordered to active duty in May 1863; the remainder was called in September, and the entire Class of 1865 was graduated in November 1864. The lack of upper-class models for incoming midshipmen was keenly felt. Private-school boys introduced hazing, an alien practice that bedeviled academy authorities for a century thereafter. In one celebrated incident Midshipman Thomas G. Welles, '67, a son of the secretary of the navy, was thrown overboard from the *Santee* and towed back and forth by a rope tied around his waist. He resigned. Considering that there was no athletic program—Captain Blake thought sports undignified—or any other approved outlet for adolescent energies, it is a wonder even greater outrages did not occur.

There was also a decline in academic standards. Admission requirements were lowered to little more than literacy. Of the 10,000 books that were carried to Newport, only 1,000 were unpacked. A few premature graduates performed so poorly in the fleet that they were returned to the academy to try again. Charles Sigsbee, '64, recalled that "I don't think I averaged three-quarters of an hour of study per day. Brighter students may have found it still easier. . . . I learned all my geometry between dismissal from breakfast and study hours, and that was about twenty minutes; I got through all right, too. The Academy was, in those days, very slipshod."

Difficulties and deficiencies notwithstanding, the academy continued to provide the preponderance of its graduates with an adequate professional education. Captain James G. Goodenough, Royal Navy, who visited Newport in February 1864, was highly impressed. Recording his impressions in his diary, he wrote, "This college is more advanced than our [Royal Naval College] Britannia. . . . If application and study are of any use, I'm afraid that these people will have very superior men to ourselves in their navy. They are working harder and more intelligently for it than we are. . . . But the boys don't seem to get exercise enough. I can't make out that they have any games, or outdoor amusement, either."

The Newport plebes enjoyed one advantage over their predecessors, however. They were full-fledged midshipmen from the moment they entered the academy. Congress abolished the rating of acting midshipman by an act of July 21, 1862. It was inspired by the prisoner-of-war cartel with the Confederacy, which specified that a midshipman had an exchange value of seven ordinary seamen but was vague regarding such amorphous beings as "acting midshipmen on probation," the undergraduates' official designation. The same act eliminated the rank of passed midshipman and created that of ensign, as which midshipmen were to be commissioned immediately upon graduation. The Class of 1863 was the only one to benefit from this provision. The following year the Navy Department managed to have the application of the law modified to require graduates to serve at least one year as midshipmen prior to being commissioned.

The practice cruises out of Newport were probably the most exciting ever made, since they involved the possibility that the cruise ship would encounter one of the Confederate raiders. Shortly after the move north, Lieutenant Rodgers proposed conducting the summer cruise of 1861 off the Confederate coast. "Our lads did not falter when in hourly expectation of an attack at Annapolis," he declared, "and I think we would pledge ourselves that the Government would find the practice ship an efficient cruiser." Captain Blake vetoed the idea, and that year there was no cruise at all.

Midshipman Charles Sigsbee chose to be photographed as a scholar, although in later years he declared that he got through the academy without studying more than three-quarters of an hour a day. He was captain of the *Maine* when she was blown up in Havana Harbor in 1898. Courtesy: U.S. Naval Academy Archives.

Cruises resumed in 1862, when the sloops of war *John Adams* and *Marion* exercised in coastal waters, with orders to overhaul and identify every vessel they met. The midshipmen had great fun, but all the ships they saw were friendly. In the course of her cruise, the *John Adams* visited the Union bases at Yorktown, Virginia, and Port Royal, South Carolina, giving her midshipmen a close-up view of campaign-support activities.

A consummate seaman, Stephen B. Luce left a life-long impression on the midshipmen who served under him during the practice cruises of 1862 and 1863. This photograph was taken shortly before he was promoted to lieutenant commander in the summer of 1862. Courtesy: U.S. Naval Academy Special Collections, Nimitz Library.

The *Marion* was commanded by one of the most exceptional officers ever to serve at the academy, Lieutenant Commander Stephen B. Luce, Date of '41, who later founded the Naval War College. A master of the profession to which they aspired, Luce was idolized by the midshipmen. Decades later one of them recalled "the universal admiration of his outstanding qualities. . . . In knowledge of and authority in that now lost art, Seamanship, he was without rival in our own, or possibly any, Navy. . . .

The schooner-yacht *America* was assigned to the academy in 1862. Courtesy: U.S. Naval History Division.

Luce's spare, trim figure, side whiskers, clean-cut features, immaculately neat attire and officer-like bearing are unforgettable, as is his ringing, melodious tenor voice . . . which could be heard above the soughing of the wind in the rigging, the shaking of the canvas and the rattle of the running gear. . . . To hear it inspired every soul on board."

First assigned to the academy from 1860 to 1861, Luce was recalled, against his will, to become head of the Department of Seamanship in January 1862. Upon assuming his new duty he was shocked to discover that there was no standard text on the subject. As a stop-gap solution, he cut up and combined sections of the various works in use at the academy and gave them to a Newport printer. The result was immediately recognized as the midshipmen's bible. Repeatedly revised, Luce's *Seamanship* remained the academy text for the next forty years.

Three vessels were used for the cruise of 1863, the *Marion*, the schooner-yacht *America*, and the sloop of war *Macedonian*. The first two skirted the northeastern seaboard. The *America* was the famous ocean racer that beat fourteen vessels of the Royal Yacht Squadron to win the One Hundred Guineas Cup, later renamed the America's Cup, in 1851. Subsequently sold to an English yachtsman, at the outbreak of the war

Lieutenant Alfred Thayer Mahan sat for this portrait while serving at the academy in 1862. Courtesy: U.S. Naval Academy Archives.

she was purchased by the Confederate government for use as a blockade-runner. Scuttled in a tributary of the St. John's River when Union forces cut her off from the sea, she was raised and, after brief service with the South Atlantic Blockading Squadron, presented to the Naval Academy. She remained at the academy until 1873, in which year Secretary of the Navy George M. Robeson arbitrarily ordered her sold, over the protest of academy authorities, for a fraction of her worth.

The *Macedonian*, with Luce in command, crossed the North Atlantic. Her officers included Lieutenants W. T. Sampson and Alfred T. Mahan. Midshipman Charles E. Clark found Mahan's manner "rather apt to make others feel that they had better keep their distance." That was what it was supposed to do; but Clark discovered that Mahan was not as stern as he seemed. Watching his classmates leave ship on a foreign liberty to which he was not entitled, Clark was amazed when "Lieutenant Mahan, seeing me standing near the rail, said with a friendly nod, 'Don't forget to be back by sunset,' and as I could not logically return without having gone, I waited for no further encouragement."

Upon reaching Plymouth, England, Luce received an urgent warning from the American ambassador, Charles S. Adams, that a Confederate cruiser was believed to be in the area. The response was scarcely what the ambassador expected. Instead of making for home, Luce disguised the *Macedonian* as a Spanish merchantman and prowled the Bay of Biscay in hopes of luring a raider under his guns.

Later it was learned that no Confederate cruiser was in European waters at that time. There were a number of Confederate officers, most of them blockade-runners, on the Continent, however. On liberty in Paris, Luce's midshipmen encountered several of their former classmates. "We . . . would gladly have renewed acquaintances," one of the Northern boys wrote, "but their senior officer and our captain objected to our associating in any way. . . . We felt it a trifle hard."

Among the *Macedonian*'s midshipmen was the first foreign national and first member of royalty to attend the academy. He was Pierre d'Orléans, Duc de Penthièvre, a son of Admiral Prince de Joinville and grandson of King Louis Philippe, the last Orléans to occupy the throne of France (1830-1848). Persona non grata in his homeland under the Second Empire, he was admitted to the academy in 1860 on the understanding that his family would defray the expense of his education. His acceptance was not entirely unprecedented. A handful of Brazilian and German midshipmen had been given training on U.S. naval vessels in the 1840s; but no foreign student had been enrolled at the academy.

The young duke was a favorite with his classmates, who called him Pete. One of them recalled: "If d'Orléans felt himself a prince in exile, it was never obvious. He neither asked nor expected any different treatment from that given to the other midshipmen. . . . That he heartily enjoyed the feeling of being just a boy among other boys was very clearly shown . . . during our second practice cruise. While we were in England, d'Orléans was given leave, with permission to rejoin the ship at Lisbon, where he was to visit some of his royal relatives. On our arrival in that port, the King of Portugal, attended by a large retinue, came on board, bringing d'Orléans with him. Pete broke away from his party as soon as he could, and was on his way forward, when he noticed a classmate standing near the mainmast, gazing at royalty, which was making its way along the quarterdeck. As a gentle means of attracting his friend's attention, Pete dealt him a vigorous kick in the rear, and then fled. There was at once a wild pursuit up one gangway and down the other. D'Orléans could easily have escaped by taking refuge with his party upon the quarterdeck, but instead he chose to be caught just where the mauling he received could be seen to the best advantage by the king and the scandalized courtiers."

It was in the course of this cruise that Luce issued the order:

At sea, August 14th [1863]

It has been observed that during church service a number of Midshipmen instead of rising at the proper times remain seated. This is not proper in any point of view. Those who belong to the Episcopal Church should conform to the rules of their own Church as a matter of religious duty. Those who belong to other Churches should out of respect for the Christian religion and deference to the Church they attend, follow the customs of that Church for the time being.

Those who are so unfortunate as to belong to no Church whatever should remember that it is but the part of a well bred gentleman to show respect for Religion, and when attending service, evince at least an outward regard for the sacred exercise.

The academy's first foreign student was a grandson of King Louis Philippe:
Pierre d'Orléans, Duc de Penthièvre. Popular with his classmates, who called
him Pete, he relished the democracy of midshipman life. Courtesy: U.S. Naval
History Division.

The summer cruise of 1864 was the first in which the academy's practice ships sailed as a squadron, which consisted of the *Marion, Macedonian, America,* and the steam gunboat *Marblehead.* They had just
begun a series of exercises in Long Island Sound when a revenue cutter
dashed out from New London with a report that the CSS *Florida* had
burned a merchantman off Cape Henry the previous night. Commandant
of Midshipmen Donald McNeill Fairfax deployed the academy squadron
to intercept the raider if she should proceed north along the coast. The
Marblehead was sent to patrol Nantucket South Shoal and the *Mace-*

The academy's ships lie off Goat Island, with the rooftops of Newport in the background; from left to right, the frigates *Santee* and *Constitution*, in which plebes were quartered, and the sloop of war *Macedonian*. Courtesy: U.S. Naval Academy Museum.

donian, Marion, and *America,* the latter two in company, cruised off Block Island. The *Macedonian* beat to quarters one morning at the approach of a low, grey steamer everyone assumed was the *Florida* but proved to be a captured blockade-runner on her way north. The *Florida* never appeared, and the remainder of the cruise passed without incident.

Relative to numbers engaged, the war that raged during the academy's years at Newport was the bloodiest Americans have ever fought. Alumni in blue and grey took part in almost every naval action in it. Up to and including the Class of 1860, the academy graduated a total of 410 midshipmen. At least 67 were already dead by the outbreak of war, a grim indicator of the mortality of mid-nineteenth-century naval life. Of the remainder, 174 held true to the Old Flag; 72 took their stand under the Stars and Bars. What part, if any, the other 97 played in the conflict is unknown. Twenty-three of the 114 members of the Class of 1861 and the prematurely graduated Classes of 1862 and 1863 went South when Virginia joined the Confederacy. The graduating Class of 1864 was the first to be wholly Unionist; 21 of its original members had already become midshipmen, CSN. At war's end, the academy's graduates numbered 659; 400 of them had served on the side of the North, 95 on that of the South.

No academy graduate reached the rank of captain in either navy. Both navies included too many officers whose seniority predated the foundation of the academy. A number of alumni commanded ships, however. Perhaps the most outstanding of these was James I. Waddell, Date of '41, lieutenant-commanding the CSS *Shenandoah,* the commerce-raider that destroyed the New England whaling fleet, capturing thirty-eight vessels and inflicting damages officially calculated at $1,361,983.00.

Two graduates became major generals in the Union army: Samuel P. Carter and William Nelson, both Date of '40. Lincoln reportedly referred to them as his web-foot generals. Nelson was shot to death in 1862 by a subordinate whom he had slapped in the face. Carter returned to the navy after the war, served as commandant of midshipmen at the Naval Academy from 1870 to 1873, and was promoted rear admiral on the retired list in 1882, which made him the only officer of the U.S. armed forces ever entitled to two different sets of stars.

Other academy men distinguished themselves in subordinate positions. At the age of twenty-three, George Dewey served as executive officer of the USS *Mississippi* at the Battle of New Orleans and was cited for heroism in the action in which she was sunk off Port Hudson. Later assigned to the same position in the steam sloop *Monongahela*, for a time flagship of Admiral David Glasgow Farragut, he never forgot the day the admiral looked up from an order he was writing and inquired, "Now, how the devil do you spell Apalachicola? Some of these educated young fellows from Annapolis must know." John McIntosh Kell, Date of '41, was executive officer in Captain Raphael Semmes's *Alabama*, the greatest of all the Confederate cruisers. At the Battle of Roanoke Island in February 1862, seventeen-year-old Midshipman Benjamin H. Porter, '63, commanded a battery of naval howitzers "with a degree of skill and daring," to quote the official report, "which not only contributed largely to the success of the day, but won the admiration of all who witnessed the display."

Probably the most gallant naval exploit of the war was performed by Lieutenant William B. Cushing, '61, who resigned from the academy to avoid dismissal midway through his first-class year. This was the destruction of the Confederate ram *Albemarle*, which he approached under cover of darkness in a steam launch with a spar torpedo protruding from her bow. A year later, he spent six hours in a skiff marking the channel to Fort Fisher under heavy fire. Recalled by an instructor as "rather a delicate-looking youth," he brought his troubled academy career to an end by a cartoon of his Spanish instructor, Professor Edward A. Roget. His academic obituary read: "Aptitude for study: good. Habits of study: irregular. General conduct: bad. Aptitude for Naval Service: not good."

Twenty-three academy graduates were killed in action or died of wounds in the course of the conflict, sixteen fighting for the Union and five for the Confederacy. A list of the battles in which they fell forms an outline of the naval history of the war: Hampton Roads, New Orleans, Port Hudson, Yazoo Pass, Mobile Bay, Fort Fisher. Hardest hit was the Class of 1863, which lost eight of its fifty-five members, five in blue and three in grey.

Former members of the academy's faculty and staff also distinguished themselves in the war. None won greater laurels than its first superintendent, Franklin Buchanan, one of those who cast their lots with the South. The years since the Mexican War had been good ones for "Old Buck." A Confederate officer assigned to his staff recalled that "at 62 years he was a strikingly handsome old man; clean-shaved, ruddy complexion with a very healthy hue . . . high forehead, fringed with snow-white hair, thin close lips, steel-blue eyes; and projecting conspicuously . . . his wonderful aquiline nose. . . . When full of fight he had a peculiarity of drawing down the corners of his mouth until the thin line between his lips formed a perfect arch around his chin." On March 8, 1862, he commanded the ironclad *Virginia* (ex-USS *Merrimac*) in the attack on the Union blockading squadron at Hampton Roads, Virginia, ramming and sinking the frigate *Cumberland*, 30 guns, and forcing the frigate *Congress*, 50, to surrender. A serious leg wound received late in the action kept him ashore when the *Virginia* went out for her epic duel with the *Monitor* the next morning. Promoted to the rank of admiral, the first in the Confederate Navy, he was subsequently placed in command of the naval defenses of Mobile Bay. At the climax of the battle there on August 5, 1864, he took his flagship, the ironclad *Tennessee*, into the midst of the Union fleet, single-handedly engaging three monitors and fourteen wooden men-of-war at point-blank range for more than an hour before, badly wounded and informed that the ship could no longer be fought, he authorized his flag captain to surrender.

Commander James H. Ward, Buchanan's commandant of midshipmen, gained the lamentable distinction of becoming the first Union naval officer killed in action. At the outbreak of war, he organized the Potomac Flotilla, a force established to keep the river open to Washington. On June 27, 1861, he was picked off by an enemy sharpshooter during an engagement with Confederate forces on shore at Mathias Point.

Another of the original faculty, Lieutenant Commander Samuel L. Marcy, gave his life for the Union six months later. In command of the USS *Vincennes* on blockade duty off the mouth of the Mississippi, he took his ship's boat close inshore to shell a beached blockade-runner. The boat's howitzer sheared its mounting and Marcy was crushed by the recoil.

Professor Lockwood also went to war; but not in the navy. Although almost a quarter-century had passed since he left the army, the frustrating years he spent teaching midshipmen to soldier had kept his hand in. Offering his services to the governor of his native Delaware in May 1861, he was commissioned colonel and appointed to raise the First Delaware Infantry. Soon thereafter named Brigadier General, U.S. Volunteers, he led a brigade at the Battle of Gettysburg and later commanded a corps area whose boundaries included the city of Annapolis.

Meanwhile, the Confederacy took steps to form its own naval academy, a testimonial to the acceptance the academy idea had gained in the sixteen years since Bancroft had sequestered Fort Severn. In December 1861 the Confederate Congress approved an act providing "that some form of education be established for midshipmen." A few months later, in the spring of 1862, another act was passed specifically authorizing a naval academy to be attended by 106 acting midshipmen appointed by members of Congress and President Jefferson Davis. The "site" selected for the academy was the CSS *Patrick Henry*, a passenger steamer turned gunboat anchored in the James River at Drewry's Bluff, seven miles below Richmond. Cabins were built ashore to house personnel who could not be accommodated on board ship. Lieutenant William H. Parker, the loyal secessionist, was appointed superintendent. Commander John M. Brooke, Date of '41, was detailed to supervise the development of the course of instruction.

The problems Brooke and Parker faced in organizing an academy under the chaotic conditions prevailing in the war-torn Confederacy were aggravated by the refusal of Congress to appropriate supplementary funds to expand the facilities ashore. Eventually they settled on a split session, somewhat similar to that employed at Annapolis in its early years, which provided that the midshipmen would rotate between shipboard or seacoast duty assignments and terms at the academy. Those absent from the academy were expected to pursue independent studies and take semi-annual examinations prepared at the academy and administered by designated officers. The final plans for the school, submitted to Secretary of the Navy Stephen R. Mallory in July 1863, were closely modeled after those of the U.S. Naval Academy.

Lieutenant William Harwar Parker was head of the Department of Seamanship at the outbreak of the Civil War. He "went South" and was subsequently appointed superintendent of the Confederate States Naval Academy. From J.T. Scharf, *History of the Confederate States Navy*.

Classes opened on the *Patrick Henry* in October 1863, with 52 of the Confederacy's 106 acting midshipmen in attendance. Recitations were held in two rooms between the paddle boxes on her hurricane deck. The ship herself provided facilities for practical exercises. Infantry and artillery drills were held ashore at Drewry's Bluff. Superintendent Parker's first commandant of midshipmen was Lieutenant Wilburn B. Hall, who edged out Mahan to graduate Number One in the Annapolis Class of 1859. The staff consisted of six officer instructors, six civilian professors, two assistant surgeons, a paymaster, an assistant engineer, a boatswain, a gunner, and a sailmaker.

Confederate authorities considered the program a success from the start. Superintendent Parker was delighted with the quality and behavior of his midshipmen, and soon Secretary Mallory advised President Davis that "the satisfactory progress already made by the several classes gives assurance that the Navy may look to this school for well-instructed and skilful officers." Two classes were graduated: the first, of twenty-six members, six of whom had resigned from the Annapolis Classes of 1863 and 1864, in August 1864; the second, of which only fragmentary records remain, in December.

The education of the midshipmen in the *Patrick Henry* was a great deal more eventful than that received by their counterparts at Newport. Drewry's Bluff was the strongpoint of the Confederate line on the James River, and Union ironclads regularly pushed upstream to test its defenses. Three of the school ship's original ten guns were landed to reinforce the batteries there, and when enemy ships appeared the midshipmen

The CSS *Patrick Henry*, home of the Confederate Naval Academy. Her curious-looking foremast was rigged to provide sail training for the midshipmen. U.S. Naval Institute Collection.

were sometimes rushed ashore to help man them. Midshipman James M. Morgan, CSN (ex-USNA '64), thought his alma mater "the most realistic war college which ever existed. . . . On top of [the recitation] rooms were posted signalmen who from daylight to dark wigwagged to, and received messages from the batteries. The scenes in the recitation rooms were frequently exciting and interesting. The guns on shore roared and the shells burst, and the professor would placidly give out the problem to the youngster at the blackboard, to be interrupted by the report of some gun which his practiced ear told him was a newcomer in the fray. He would begin by saying 'If x—y— One moment, Mr. Blank. Would you kindly step outside and find out for me which battery it is that has opened with that Brooke gun?' The information obtained the recitation would be resumed, only to be again interrupted by a message from the captain that a certain battery was short of officers and a couple of midshipmen were wanted. It was useless to call for volunteers; every midshipman clamored for permission to go."

The Confederate midshipmen also participated in minelaying operations and the activities of the James River Squadron. Occasionally they took part in distant operations. In the winter of 1863 ten of them joined in a combined assault on the Union position at New Bern, North Carolina. The attack miscarried, but the boat party to which the midshipmen belonged surprised the Union gunboat *Underwriter* and captured her in hand-to-hand fighting. During the struggle seventeen-year-old Midshipman Palmer Saunders, CSN, was killed by a cutlass blow that split his head open to his shoulders. In May 1864 the entire battalion was ordered into action when a Union landing at Bermuda Hundred threatened Richmond from the rear. Two details were rushed ashore to strengthen the Drewry's Bluff batteries and three others were assigned to the gunboats of the James River Squadron. Later that summer, parties of midshipmen took part in two coastal operations in North Carolina.

Volunteers for these expeditions were so numerous that the instructors solved the problem by accepting them on the basis of class standing—perhaps the only instance in history when academic excellence was rewarded by combat duty. Reporting to Secretary Mallory, Commander Brooke summed up the midshipmen's record with the words, "Though but from 14 to 18 years of age, they eagerly seek every opportunity presented for engaging in hazardous enterprises; and those who are sent on them uniformly exhibit good discipline, conduct and courage."

Danger was not the only extracurricular acquaintance of the *Patrick Henry*'s midshipmen. They became familiar with hardship as well. Midshipman Morgan recalled that "the James River furnished a capital article of chills and fever—not malaria, but the good old-fashioned kind with the shivers which made the teeth chatter and burning fever to follow. On an average about one half of the midshipmen went through this disagreeable experience every other day. No one was allowed to go on the sick list on account of chills and fever; one was, however, allowed to lie down on the bare deck while the chill was on, but had to return to duty as soon as the paroxysm was over." Morgan and his classmates shared the hunger that became the companion of the Southern fighting man. "The menu offered little variety," he wrote. "If it was not a tiny lump of fat, it was a shaving of fresh meat as tough as the hide which had once covered it, with a piece of hardtack and a tin cup of hot water colored by chicory or grains of burned corn, ground up, and brevetted *coffee*. But no one kicked about the food, as it was as good if not better than the poor soldiers in the trenches received."

Despite the perils and privations that were an integral part of the educational experience at the Confederate Naval Academy, the South's leading families did not hesitate to enroll their sons. Among its alumni were nephews of President Davis and General Robert E. Lee and the sons of Secretary Mallory; Captain (later Admiral) Raphael Semmes of the *Alabama*; and General John C. Breckinridge, the Democratic candidate in the presidential election of 1860 and the last Confederate secretary of war.

There were around seventy midshipmen at the academy at the beginning of April 1865, when Grant finally punched through Lee's lines. It was their finest hour. On April 2, as the Confederate government prepared to evacuate Richmond, Superintendent Parker was informed that his midshipmen had been chosen to guard the train carrying the Confederate treasury—$500,000 in gold and silver bullion.

Sixty midshipmen under Parker's personal command boarded the train south at six o'clock that evening. Ten others, under Lieutenant J. W. Billups, the assistant professor of seamanship, remained behind to scuttle the *Patrick Henry*. That melancholy mission accomplished, they were captured as they attempted to rejoin the main body.

For the following month the midshipmen moved steadily south, transferring the treasure from railway cars to wagons, while Parker searched for a Confederate authority to whom it could be relinquished. It was the pursuit of a dying dream. For a few days the column acted as escort to Mrs. Davis, the president's wife. The midshipmen's conduct was magnificent. "Foot-sore and ragged as they had become by that time," Parker related, "no murmur escaped them and they never faltered."

Finally, on May 2, Parker located the Confederacy's fugitive government at Abbeville, South Carolina. The acting-secretary of the treasury

James Morris Morgan, '64, was one of the many Southern-born members of the Classes of 1861 through 1864 who resigned from the academy to take their stand in Dixie. This photograph, taken in 1863, shows him in the undress uniform of a Confederate midshipman. From J.M. Morgan, *Recollections of a Rebel Reefer.*

directed him to turn the treasure over to the commander of President Davis's escort, and Secretary Mallory granted the midshipmen leave from which they were never recalled.

Twelve years later, a man approached Parker in the lobby of a Baltimore hotel. Seeing that Parker did not recognize him, he said, "I am Lieutenant Billups of the rear guard."

"Report!" said William Harwar Parker.

The end of the war meant the end of the naval careers of the officers who went South. Some found positions in the British and American merchant marine. Most entered new occupations ashore. Both Admiral Buchanan and Lieutenant Parker served terms as president of Maryland Agricultural College (later the University of Maryland). Buchanan died at his home near St. Michaels, on the Eastern Shore of Maryland, in May 1874. Parker was subsequently appointed U.S. consul at Bahía, Brazil. The *Shenandoah*'s James I. Waddell reentered naval service of a sort in the early 1880s as commander of the Maryland state forces in the Chesapeake Bay oyster war. John McIntosh Kell became adjutant of the state of Georgia. Julian M. Spencer, '61, late Lieutenant, CSN, returned to Annapolis and served for many years as the academy librarian.

Still others became soldiers of fortune. Between 1870 and 1875, six academy graduates, all Confederate navy lieutenants, took service in Egypt, whose progressive Khedive Ismail recruited several dozen Civil War veterans to act as advisers to his armed forces. Beverly Kennon, Date of '46, was commissioned colonel of ordnance and charged with rebuilding the coastal fortifications of Alexandria. He designed a network of underground forts with disappearing guns, but financial cutbacks caused the project to be shelved and he resigned in disgust. The one battery he completed was the only Egyptian position to survive the British naval bombardment of 1882.

Major William P. A. Campbell, Date of '47, was attached to the staff of the most famous of Ismail's foreign officers, British General Charles G. "Chinese" Gordon; he died in Khartoum in 1874. William H. Ward, Date of '49, became a lieutenant colonel of marines and was detailed as interpreter for General William Tecumseh Sherman when the latter visited Egypt in 1872. Charles Iverson Graves, '57, an instructor at the Confederate Naval Academy, probably made the most of his years in Egypt. Commissioned lieutenant colonel in the Egyptian army, he was decorated by the khedive for his work in surveying the wild territory around the entrance to the Gulf of Aden. When the financial crisis of 1878 forced Ismail to discharge the Americans, the thrifty Graves returned to Georgia with savings sufficient to pay off the mortgage on his farm, where he lived out a happy life.

Wilburn B. Hall, first commandant of midshipmen at the Confederate Naval Academy, held a series of staff appointments in Cairo. Alexander Macomb Mason, '62, soldiered in Chile and Cuba before accepting an Egyptian lieutenant colonelcy. He spent eight adventurous years in khedival uniform, exploring the savage wastes of the Sudan, serving under Chinese Gordon as deputy governor of the Equatorial Province and making the first circumnavigation of the Albert Nyanza. A seventh academy alumnus, James Morris Morgan, successively Midshipman USN and CSN, was made a lieutenant colonel at age twenty-four. Finding Egypt infuriatingly unlike America, he returned home after two hectic years.

The saddest of such cases was that of Lieutenant Joseph Fry, Date of '41. Temperamentally unsuited for a business career, for years after the war he barely managed to eke out an existence for his wife and seven children. Finally, in 1873, he made a desperate decision. In Cuba, revolution had broken out against Spanish rule. Approached by Cuban agents, Fry accepted command of the *Virginius,* an American-registered steamer being used to run guns to the rebels. A Spanish warship captured her on his first voyage. At Santiago, Fry and his crew were tried as pirates by a military court and, despite the presumed protection of the American flag, condemned to death. His bearing greatly impressed the Spanish officers. In a last letter to his wife he wrote: "The President of the court-martial asked me the favor of embracing me at parting, and clasped me to his heart. I have shaken hands with each of my judges; and the secretary of the court and interpreter have promised me, as a special favor, to attend my execution. . . . It is curious to see how I make friends." He and fifty-two companions were cut down by a firing squad the next afternoon. Their execution was one of the milestones on the way to the Spanish-American War.

CHAPTER FIVE

"Porter's Dancing Academy"

Despite the efforts of various communities to entice the academy to settle with them, Secretary Welles's determination to restore it to Annapolis never wavered throughout the four and one-half years of war. The Newport City Council represented the advantages that would accrue if the school were permanently located on an island in neighboring Narragansett Bay. Perth Amboy, New Jersey, countered with a claim that it possessed a morally superior environment. The Board of Visitors recommended abolishing the academy, as constituted, and setting up seven separate schools to be filled by competitive examinations. Welles fended off all such proposals and in May 1864 Congress passed an act providing for the academy to return to Annapolis before October 1865. Following the Confederate collapse in the spring of that year, the army moved out of the yard. It left it a wreck.

A graphic description of the state of the academy buildings and grounds near the war's end was given in an anguished letter, signed "Graduate," printed in the *Army and Navy Journal* of October 22, 1864:

> My eyes were struck by the view of a number of hospital tents occupying the grounds once held sacred from the footprints of anyone. Around these tents were trodden innumerable footpaths, marring the beauty of the grounds. Next came an unsightly board fence dividing the upper from the lower grounds; then came roads and pathways, made on pavements and grass plots, the crossing of which once subjected a student to demerits. . . . The fine buildings I found occupied in various ways. Most of them are used as hospitals, while other portions are given up as sutler-shops, where lager-beer, etc., is dispensed. The fine old quarters of the Superintendent are used as a billiard saloon. What a transformation from their once legitimate use. Within the enclosure is also a barber-shop, tailor-shop, photograph gallery, etc. Thousands of dollars will be required to restore this valuable institution to its original condition.

But the abuse of its physical facilities was the least of the damage the academy suffered in the course of the war. Far more serious was the deterioration that occurred in its administration, academic standards and, most important of all, morale. Restoring its vitality was the greatest challenge faced by any superintendent since Buchanan. Old Captain Blake was obviously not equal to the task. The new superintendent would have to be more than a good officer; he would have to be a great one. Welles's choice was unerring. On September 9, 1865, Rear Admiral David Dixon Porter became the academy's sixth superintendent.

Broad-shouldered and barrel-chested, with a bristling black beard, Porter stood only five feet seven inches but gave the impression of being a much larger man. At fifty-two, he had enjoyed the most picturesque career of any officer in the navy. A son of Commodore David Porter of War of 1812 fame, he went to sea as a midshipman in the Mexican Navy, then commanded by his father, in 1826. A year later he assisted his cousin, Captain Henry Porter, in quelling a mutiny aboard ship, and in 1828 participated in a bloody action between the Mexican brig *Guerrero*, 22 guns, and the Spanish frigate *Lealtad*, 64. The little *Guerrero* was pounded into submission, and fifteen-year-old David Dixon spent the following year on board a Spanish prison ship in Havana Harbor. Appointed a midshipman in the U.S. Navy in February 1829, he soon became known as one of its ablest officers. During the Mexican War he served as first lieutenant of the steam gunboat *Spitfire* and distinguished himself in a series of exploits that included the capture of a Mexican fort with a naval landing party of sixty-eight men. Between 1849 and 1853, as captain of a succession of mail steamers, he habitually broke the existing speed records on the routes he traveled.

Despite his outstanding record, at the start of the Civil War Porter was a lieutenant with twenty years in grade. A year and one-half later he was an acting rear admiral, and that was just the beginning. Although, as a popular hero, he was overshadowed by his foster brother, Admiral Farragut, at war's end he was the only naval officer who had received congressional votes of thanks on four separate occasions. In 1866, when the rank of admiral was created for Farragut, Porter was made the navy's vice admiral.

Porter's interest in the academy dated back to the spring of 1862, when his son Carlisle failed out of it. Writing Assistant Secretary of the Navy Gustavus V. Fox, he declared: "I would ask nothing better after this war than to have command of the Naval Academy, and get the right sort of officers into the Navy. A new era should be instituted." In 1865 he had his chance, and the qualities he brought to the task guaranteed success. Ambitious, egocentric, and vengeful of any slight, real or imagined, he was also a superb leader, dynamic, intelligent, and innovative. At the academy his life-long determination to have anything with which he was associated be the best was reinforced by his conviction that war with one or more European power was imminent—a war in which he was confident that he would hold the principal naval command. The midshipmen he turned out would be his subordinates. He wanted them to be first-rate.

By the time classes reconvened in October 1865, the grounds had been restored to a semblance of their former beauty. Upper classmen found them "a welcome substitute for the prim little Newport square and the dusty desert of Goat Island." But Porter realized that the yard, however beautified, was no longer adequate to its purpose. Stribling Row had been built to house 198 midshipmen; wartime legislation had increased the academy's authorized complement to 566. The fourth class could be quartered in the *Constitution*, but that was only a partial solution. If, as Porter proposed, the Naval Academy was to become a great national institution rivaling West Point, it would have to expand.

Expand it did. Cultivating the political contacts he had made during the war, Porter was able to obtain appropriations for a major program of acquisition and construction. His first addition was the Maryland Government House and its four acres of grounds fronting on Annapolis

A bird's-eye view shows Annapolis and the Naval Academy as they appeared shortly after the Civil War. Courtesy: The Mariners Museum, Newport News, Virginia.

Harbor between Hanover Street and the academy, which were purchased from the state for $25,000 in August 1866. The rambling colonial mansion, which had served as the residence of the governors of Maryland for almost a century, was enclosed within the yard. Its wings and numerous outbuildings were razed and a row of officers' quarters and a guest house for the Board of Visitors were built backing up to Hanover Street. The academy library was transferred from Seamanship Hall to the first floor of the mansion itself and the superintendent's offices were established on the second.

The following year Porter persuaded the trustees of St. John's College to sell the pie-shaped, ten-acre parcel called the College Lot on Graveyard (later Dorsey, now College) Creek. This purchase reflected either prescience or sheer acquisitiveness on his part, as it was removed from the yard and could be of no value unless the intervening properties were obtained. Finally, in November 1868, he bought Strawberry Hill, a sixty-seven-acre tract on the opposite shore of College Creek. On it he built a huge, dovecote-Victorian hospital, popularly known as Porter's Folly, in ominous proximity to which he laid out the Naval Academy Cemetery.

Concurrently with these transactions, Porter launched an extensive construction program on the existing grounds. The first postwar project, a new armory adjacent to Fort Severn, was completed late in 1865. A hall for the newly established Department of Steam Enginery followed in 1866. A new, brick chapel was ready in 1868, after which the old one was converted into a lyceum. The "Daguerrean gallery" (photographic studio), subsequently enlarged into a chemistry laboratory, was finished the same year. A science building and the midshipmen's New Quarters were completed in 1869.

The latter was by far the most imposing of Porter's additions to the yard. Four red-brick stories high, with an illuminated clock tower and

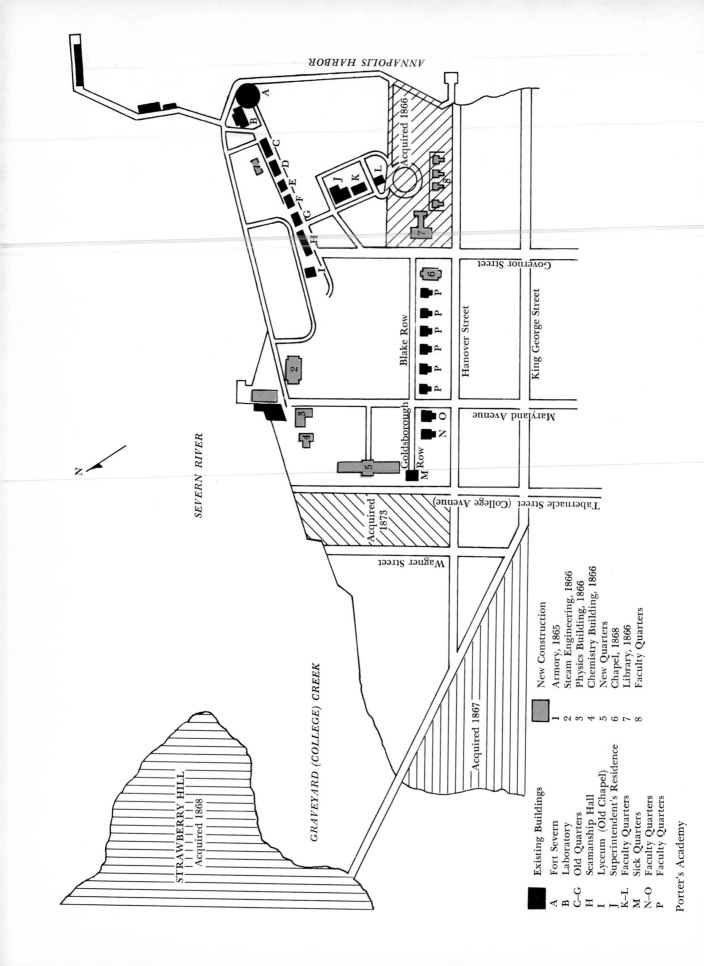

ANNAPOLIS HARBOR

Acquired 1866

A

B

C

D

E

F

G

H

I

J
K
L

7

8

Governor Street

Blake Row

6

P
P
P
P
P
P
P

Hanover Street

King George Street

2

3

4

5

Goldsborough

M Row

N O

N

Maryland Avenue

Tabernacle Street (College Avenue)

Acquired 1873

Wagner Street

SEVERN RIVER

N

GRAVEYARD (COLLEGE) CREEK

Acquired 1867

STRAWBERRY HILL
Acquired 1868

New Construction

1   Armory, 1865
2   Steam Engineering, 1866
3   Physics Building, 1866
4   Chemistry Building, 1866
5   New Quarters
6   Chapel, 1868
7   Library, 1866
8   Faculty Quarters

Existing Buildings

A   Fort Severn
B   Laboratory
C–G   Old Quarters
H   Seamanship Hall
I   Lyceum (Old Chapel)
J   Superintendent's Residence
K–L   Faculty Quarters
M   Sick Quarters
N–O   Faculty Quarters
P   Faculty Quarters

Porter's Academy

This photograph of the yard was taken in 1870 from the cupola of the New Quarters. It shows, from left to right, the Physics Building, the Steam Building, the gas works, the Armory, part of Fort Severn, Stribling Row, Recitation Hall, the Seamanship Building, the lyceum (former chapel), the superintendent's residence, and Buchanan Row. None survive. Courtesy: U.S. Naval Academy Special Collections, Nimitz Library.

an iron veranda extending across all 293 feet of its face, its architecture reminded an alumnus of "an ugly factory." The ground floor contained offices, reception and recitation rooms, and a mess hall. Midshipmen were accommodated, two to a room, on the upper stories. The kitchen, laundry, steam room, and bathrooms were in the basement. The baths boasted running water, which had come to the academy with the completion of the Annapolis waterworks in 1867. Midshipmen were required to make use of them at least once a week. The dormitories along Stribling Row, henceforth known as the Old Quarters, were occasionally used to quarter a class when the strength of the battalion exceeded the capacity of the New Quarters.

The figurehead of an Indian warrior, which became known as Tecumseh, was set up beside the lyceum in 1866. Salvaged from the 74-gun line-of-battle ship *Delaware*, one of those burned to prevent their seizure by the Confederates at Norfolk in 1861, it really represents Chief Tamanend, a peaceful Delaware who befriended the early settlers. But Tamanend never caught the midshipmen's fancy, and at various times they referred to him as Powhatan, King Philip, and even Old Sebree, after a supposed resemblance to Midshipman Uriel Sebree, '67. Eventually, they settled on Tecumseh, the name of the Shawnee chieftain who ravaged the American frontier in the War of 1812. From the first, however, the midshipmen made a pretence of believing that the stern-visaged warrior possessed supernatural powers and they adopted him as a patron saint.

The change in the academy's outward appearance was matched by the reform of its academic program. Porter's first concern was with his faculty. At war's end it consisted of twenty-nine civilians, seven of whom were department heads, and ten officers, only one of whom, the commandant of midshipmen, was a department head. As Secretary Welles had some-

The New Quarters housed the battalion of midshipmen from 1869 to 1904.
The Tripoli Monument is in the right foreground. Courtesy: U.S. Naval Academy
Special Collections, Nimitz Library.

what ruefully foreseen, Porter ransacked the navy for bright young officers to redress the balance. At the close of his first year as superintendent, the civilian faculty had been reduced to twenty-five, including five department heads, and the officer component had been increased to thirty-one, including four department heads.

The latter comprised perhaps the most outstanding group of officer instructors any superintendent ever assembled. Lieutenant Commander Luce was called back to serve a third tour at the academy, this time as commandant of midshipmen. Among his assistants was Lieutenant Commander Winfield S. Schley, '60, later to become the controversial hero of the Spanish-American War. The teaching staff included no less than three future superintendents: Lieutenant Commander Francis M. Ramsay, Date of '50, head of the Department of Gunnery; Lieutenant Commander Robert L. Phythian, '56, head of the Department of Navigation; and Lieutenant W. T. Sampson, instructor in physics. Lieutenant George Dewey was detailed to the Department of Discipline in 1867. Of the original faculty, only Lockwood and Girault returned to Annapolis. Girault retired in February 1866. Lockwood resumed his place as head of the Department of Natural and Experimental Philosophy and remained until 1869, when he was ordered to the Washington Naval Observatory. He retired with the staff rank of commodore in 1874 and died at the age of eighty-five in December 1899.

The epitome of undergraduate elegance, two midshipmen study in the Victorian comfort of their room in the New Quarters. Courtesy: U.S. Naval History Division.

Porter's guiding idea in revising the academy curriculum was to make its professional portions more practical, up to date, and attractive. The possibility of opposition from the Academic Board was forestalled by his announcement that the superintendent had three votes. Porter also introduced the practice, followed for almost a century, of having instructors rotate between classes every month. Mathematics requirements were simplified and integral calculus was dropped. The faculty was warned against being unduly dogmatic in its presentations, "so that when [the midshipmen] have arrived at maturer years, and had more experience, they may be better able to judge for themselves, without following in the ruts of their instructors." A 13-inch mortar was mounted on the seawall, and the *Santee* was transformed into a gunnery ship from which broadsides were fired into the bay, rattling glass in the nearby physics and chemistry buildings. The double-turreted monitor *Tonawanda* (later renamed *Amphitrite*) and a Confederate "David" torpedo boat were attached to the academy. The Department of Seamanship fitted out a hall with large-scale, working models of sailing ships on which to instruct the midshipmen. Gunnery set up a similar model room in the lyceum. Several practice ships were moored in the Severn and every Saturday the midshipmen were drilled in duties aloft. When distinguished visitors came to the academy, Porter would send the midshipmen into the shrouds to amaze his guests by demonstrations of their proficiency.

The spar deck of the *Santee* in 1870. Courtesy: U.S. Naval Academy Special Collections, Nimitz Library.

Ironically, Porter's only failure occurred in the most ambitious of his innovations, the Department of Steam Enginery. The experience of the Civil War had caused Secretary Welles to conclude that academy graduates should be able to function as both line officers and engineers. To this end, steam engineering (as the department was later named) was removed from Natural and Experimental Philosophy and constituted as a separate department under Chief Engineer W. W. W. Wood, whom the midshipmen quantified as W_4O_2D. Appropriate blocks of academic time were set aside for instruction, and during the summer cruise of 1866 the midshipmen alternated watches on deck and in the engine room.

The program was not a success. The midshipmen showed no interest in the courses, and their engineering performance on cruise was so unsatisfactory that the experiment was abandoned. Steam stayed in the curriculum, but the academy made no pretense of qualifying the midshipmen as engineers. Instead, recourse was had to the curious expedient of introducing a special two-year course for engineers only. This arrangement remained in force until 1874.

The attempt to promote steam engineering came close to costing Porter more than disappointment. It almost cost him his life. At the end of the war the steam launch that Cushing used to sink the *Albemarle* went to the academy. In 1867 Porter and Chief Engineer Eben Hoyt, Wood's successor, decided to rig her out as a miniature brig, in the hope

Ordnance of all sorts and sizes, as well as the flag Commodore Oliver Hazard Perry flew at the Battle of Lake Erie, were displayed in the Gunnery Model Room in the lyceum. Courtesy: U.S. Naval Academy Special Collections, Nimitz Library.

of enticing the midshipmen to take an interest in her machinery. As the time for her trial voyage approached, Hoyt invited the superintendent to come along to handle the sails while he tended the engine. Porter planned to go but he was feeling unwell that day. His indisposition was providential. The boat's boiler exploded, killing or fatally injuring everyone aboard. This tragic incident did nothing to further the cause of steam engineering at the academy.

Despite the practical emphasis of Porter's reforms, conservative circles in the navy feared that the balance between education and training had been loaded in favor of the former. In its report for 1866, the Board of Visitors recommended reducing instruction in physics, history, mechanics, astronomy, English composition, and law to occasional lectures. Fortunately, better judgment prevailed and this antediluvian document was relegated to the limbo it deserved.

Of all Porter's accomplishments, however, none were so important as those that built midshipman morale. His policies showed clearly that he remembered what it was like to be young. Discipline was restored, but midshipmen were allowed to work off demerits by performing guard duty during free time—a mixed blessing for succeeding generations. Other punishments reflected Porter's sense of poetic justice. When the man who

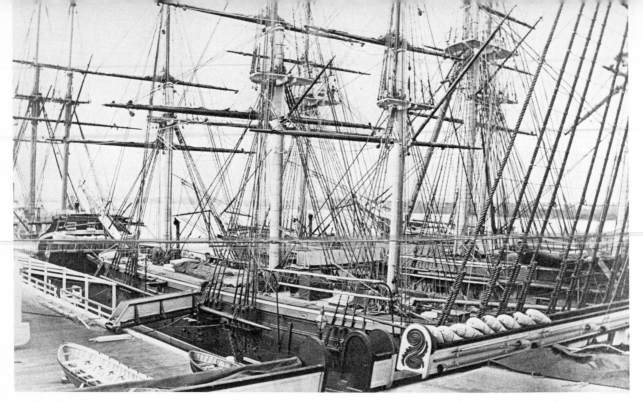

The rigging of practice ships tied up at Santee Wharf creates an abstract geometric design. Taken from on board the *Constitution*, the photograph shows, left to right, the *Santee, Marion, Dale,* and *Macedonian*. Courtesy: U.S. Naval Academy Special Collections, Nimitz Library.

Training aid turned death-trap, the launch that sank the *Albemarle* was fitted out as a miniature, steam-and-sail brig in an attempt to interest midshipmen in engineering. Her explosion produced the opposite effect. Courtesy: U.S. Naval Academy Archives.

Dress parade: the Naval Academy band, which came into its own under Porter,
and the battalion of midshipmen, 1869. Courtesy: U.S. Naval History Division.

First captains wore a double diamond without any stripes, second captains a single diamond.

In fall and spring, dress parade was held every fair evening. The ceremony became popular with the midshipmen, whose pleasure in their own smart turn-out was increased by the participation of the academy's newly resplendent band. Since its foundation by Commander Stribling in 1853, the band had been small and nondescript. Porter enlarged it and outfitted its members in blue uniforms with red facings and gold piping. Its drum major was still more impressively attired in a costume crowned by an enormous bearskin cap. He was known as Old Denver, whose double duty as chief watchman made him the midshipmen's nocturnal nemesis. But they forgave him when he raised his huge baton and the band struck up a stirring air, stepping off, as a member of the Class of '67 recalled, "in a way that aroused the delighted admiration of every youngster in the battalion."

One of the great lessons of the Civil War was the necessity of interservice cooperation. To promote good relations between the academies, in 1868 Porter and General Grant arranged for the summer cruise to call at West Point. The midshipmen had their first meeting with their counterparts in the corps of cadets. In addition to exchanging visits between ship and shore, the two student bodies held a drill competition, in which the midshipmen had the satisfaction of being judged more proficient in performing the manual of arms than the West Pointers.

With Porter's encouragement, social activities were resumed. Mrs. Porter set an example for wives in the yard by inviting midshipmen to tea. Hops, "believed to have a very refining influence upon the young gentlemen," were held monthly in the gymnasium of Fort Severn. Over their heads a star-spangled, sky-blue ceiling was adorned with a scroll inscribed *Dieu et les dames.* Early each January the first class gave a formal ball, which was followed six weeks later by a second-class dress

In full rig, Old Denver, drum major of the academy band, could have passed for a refugee from the Grande Armée. He also served as chief watchman. Courtesy: U.S. Naval Academy Archives.

The Naval Academy Ball of January 1869. Courtesy: U.S. Naval Academy
Special Collections, Nimitz Library.

hop. These were grand affairs attended by cabinet officers, members of
Congress, foreign dignitaries and, on one occasion, President Grant. Inevitably, there were those who felt Porter was going too far. Sly references
were made to "Porter's Dancing Academy," and former Superintendent
Goldsborough quipped, "In my time we educated the head. Now, by
Neptune, they educate the heels!" The foundation of June Week was
laid by the introduction of impressive graduation exercises, in which
distinguished personalities were invited to participate. The graduating
class of 1867 was honored by the presence of Secretary Welles and Admiral
Farragut, and in 1869 Porter persuaded his friend Grant, the new president, to present the midshipmen with their diplomas.

School spirit soared. "There were midshipmen . . . at the Academy
who had been disciplined the year before by Blake for daring to play
cricket in Touro Park," recalled Park Benjamin, who was one of them.
"It was hard for them to appreciate the full extent of the changes which
had taken place about them, and that amusements were now to be
encouraged." They were quick to make the adjustment. A musical club
and minstrel troop were formed. Midshipman Samuel W. Very, '66, was
excused from minor duties to manage their activities and to construct an
instrument of his own invention, based on the harmonium, which he
called a humstrum. On the other hand, Midshipman Robert Means
Thompson, '68, "who plays so abominably on the fish horn" was notified
that he would oblige Porter "by going outside the limits when he wants
to practice, or he will find himself coming out 'the little end of the
horn.'" Benjamin organized a theatre group whose productions could not

President Grant presents diplomas to the Class of 1869, with his friend Porter
at his side. Courtesy: U.S. Naval Academy Special Collections, Nimitz Library.

have been received more enthusiastically if the players had come from
Drury Lane. His class, 1867, became the first to identify itself by its
graduation year and to adopt a crest, which he designed, and class colors.

Benjamin also produced the first publication illustrating midshipman life, a volume of humorous drawings he called *Shakings*. It came
near to being suppressed on the grounds that it violated a regulation
forbidding the unauthorized dissemination of information regarding the
academy. In the end, only the sketch of Admiral Porter's encounter with
the cadet-lieutenant commander was censored. Years later, Benjamin
explained: "Unlike many of the 'class books' which have since been issued
. . . *Shakings* was not designed to perpetuate events or individuals, but
simply to show without caricature the actual life of the midshipman . . .
and of that life as it was . . . its pictures are accurate."

As superintendent, Porter prided himself that, in contrast to his predecessor, he could not be bothered with "writing to the mama's." He made

Midshipman George W. Mentz, '70, portrays a maiden enamored of the sailor played by Midshipman Nicholas L. Roosevelt, '68, in the earliest known photograph of an academy theatrical. Courtesy: U.S. Naval Academy Archives.

an exception in the case of Mrs. Mary Anne Yorke, of Providence, Rhode Island, whose letter elicited the following reply:

> Your note addressed to me as Rev. D. D. Porter, Chaplain of the Naval Academy, requesting that your son be permitted to attend the Catholic Church in Annapolis is received. Whilst being neither a Reverend nor a Chaplain, but only a plain seaman, and Admiral, and Superintendent of the Naval Academy, I can readily understand and acquiesce in your wish.

In the spring of 1869 President Grant called on Porter to revitalize the administration of the Navy Department. The admiral continued to reside in Annapolis, but the center of his activity shifted from the academy to Washington, and in December he was officially detached. Behind him he left what was, to all intents and purposes, a new naval academy, an institution that he had raised from its Civil War nadir to an unprecedented peak of efficiency. Following Farragut's death in August

A leader of the Class of 1867, Park Benjamin put on an uncharacteristically solemn expression for his graduation picture. Courtesy: U.S. Naval Academy Special Collections, Nimitz Library.

Arrival of the future Admirals of our Navy.

First Night in (?) a Hammock.

Great-gun Exercise.—"Ready!"

Furling Sail.—"Keep fast that tricing-line!"

"Who let go that after-fall?"

Going to morning "Formation."

Howitzer Exercise.— "Forward into line! Left oblique!"

An Evening Party disturbed.

Love Lane.

The Hop.

Park Benjamin's *Shakings*, the first midshipman publication, consisted of a series of humorous sketches of academy life. Courtesy: U.S. Naval Academy Special Collections, Nimitz Library.

1870, Porter became the navy's second admiral, in which capacity he served until his demise in February 1891; but nothing he did during those twenty years proved as lasting as what he accomplished on the banks of the Severn.

One sign of the prestige the academy had gained came, curiously enough, from Japan. When, in 1853, Commodore Perry's visit jolted that country out of its historic isolation, perceptive Japanese recognized that from a material standpoint their civilization had fallen centuries behind that of the Western World. The consequent civil strife having culminated in the restoration of imperial authority in 1868, the young Emperor Mitsuhito launched a crash program of modernization. Foreign experts were recruited to introduce Western technology and methods to Japan and selected young Japanese were sent to study at schools abroad. Among the first institutions to which the Japanese government applied for permission to enroll students was the Naval Academy. By a joint resolution of July 1868, Congress acceded to the request "provided that no expense shall thereby accrue to the United States," and the first Japanese midshipman, Jiunzo Matsumura, entered the academy in 1869.

There seems to be an unwritten law governing the selection of the academy's superintendents, which decrees that reformers will be followed by conservatives. Porter's successor was another Civil War hero, Commodore John L. Worden, who was in command of the *Monitor* when she met the *Merrimac*. He bore the scars of the battle. Powder grains driven under his skin by a direct hit on the eye slit of the *Monitor*'s conning tower left his cheeks permanently smudged.

Despite his identification with ironclad technology, Worden's mindset remained that of the days of wooden ships and iron men. In his opinion, never secret, the midshipmen at Annapolis would have been much better off afloat. Lieutenant George Dewey happened to be in the superintendent's office one day when Worden was interviewing a midshipman charged with a disciplinary offense.

Suddenly, Worden exclaimed, "Where you ought to be, young man, is not ashore in a landsman's school but right on board ship, where you would learn the business of being a seaman in the same hard school that I learned it."

This repetition of Worden's well-known views sent a smile flickering across the offender's face.

"Don't you grin at me," Worden barked, "or I will throw you out of the window!"

At that point, Dewey was unable to keep from smiling. "The Admiral caught me at it, too," he related. "For a minute I did not know but he might try to throw me out of the window. However, he controlled his temper and said nothing."

As superintendent, Worden saw his task to be that of keeping the academy steady on the course Porter had plotted. He made no significant changes in its organization or curriculum and the only notable addition to its grounds during his administration came with the purchase in 1873 of the district known as Lockwoodsville, a four-acre shantytown behind the New Quarters. That was the year in which the battalion made its national debut, marching in Grant's second inaugural parade. It was also the year in which the *America* was removed from the academy; the *Constitution* had been detached in 1871. The latter's place was taken by

Blunt-spoken Admiral John L. Worden, the hero of the *Monitor*, succeeded Porter as superintendent in 1869. He made no secret of his belief that midshipmen would be better off afloat. Courtesy: U.S. Naval Academy Archives.

the frigate *Constellation*, an almost equally illustrious septuagenarian, on which the midshipmen made every summer cruise until 1894.

Worden's task was not an easy one. The Naval Academy is a mirror of the navy, and since the Civil War the navy had fallen on hard times. The war over, America lost interest in its armed forces. In 1865 the navy was the largest in the world; by the time Worden began his tour at the academy, ruthless demobilization followed by barebones budgets had reduced it to one of the smallest. The decline was reflected in the law of July 15, 1870, which changed the status of the Naval Academy midshipmen to "cadet-midshipmen," and that of the two-year students to "cadet-engineers." Under its provisions, academy graduates did not become full-fledged midshipmen until after they had completed the four-year course, performed a regular tour of sea duty, and returned to Annapolis to take a "graduating examination." Even then, they were not eligible for promotion to ensign until a vacancy occurred in that rank. Three years later, the hitherto indefinite term of the midshipmen's probationary sea duty was set at two years. The underlying difficulty was that the graduates who entered the navy during the Civil War were clogging its constricted, postwar promotion channels. The top twelve graduates of the Class of 1868, for example, had made lieutenant by 1872, but were destined to remain lieutenants until 1893.

The academy was also confronted with its first hazing problem. The practice, introduced at Newport, continued under Porter, but no one had been injured and congressional attention had not been attracted. Under Worden things took a turn for the worse. Hazing was carried out by the third class. The indignities to which its members subjected fourth class-men ranged from mildly absurd to really brutal. A plebe might be compelled to eat soap or drink ink; he might be thrown through a transom; shaved with a blunt instrument; ordered to make a face, to stand on his head, or to climb his wardrobe and from its top recite "Mary had a little lamb" over and over again; pitched into the Severn; bounced in a blanket; or made into a sandwich, that is, laid between two or more mattresses upon which third classmen trod.

In 1870 the plebes turned on their tormentors, whom they greatly outnumbered, and defeated them in a battle royal on the plebe floor of the New Quarters. That ended hazing for that year. Once they became third classmen, however, they gleefully revived the practice against which they had rebelled. Their actions upheld the academy axiom that the plebes who were most resentful of being hazed became the most ruthless hazers. Outraged parents wrote the authorities protesting the abuse of their sons, and eleven of the offenders were dismissed.

The next major outbreak occurred in the spring of 1874. Worden took stern action, dismissing the ringleaders and canceling summer leave for the entire third class. Congress reacted also. Peppered by parental complaints, in June the legislators passed what became known as the Hazing Law. This act decreed that hazing of any type or degree was a court-martial offence and gave the superintendent authority to dismiss any midshipmen found guilty thereof. Aside from abbreviating some of their careers, its principal impact on the midshipmen was to increase the spice of indulging in a practice whose imprudence was already among its chief attractions. As Congress after Congress and superintendent after superintendent discovered to their annoyance and chagrin, the act did not inhibit hazing.

Another explosive situation arose with the admission of the academy's first black midshipman, James Conyers, in September 1872. Appointed by a Reconstruction congressman from South Carolina, his appearance hit the yard like a bombshell. Most of the officers, Civil War veterans, had fought in the war that emancipated Conyers's people, but they never expected emancipation to come so far so fast. In the words of Lieutenant Robley Evans: "The place was in an uproar at once, and the excitement among all classes was intense. As I walked along the row of officers' quarters, all the coloured servants were at the front gates discussing the news. When I reached my own quarters, my dining-room boy, a small, copper-coloured imp, with his eyes sticking out of his head, said to me, 'My Lord, Mr. Evans, a nigger done enter the Naval Academy!' That was

It was all done with mirrors: Midshipman Albert A. Michelson paints a self-portrait. Courtesy: U.S. Naval Academy Museum.

what we were all feeling, though we expressed ourselves somewhat differently."

The officers' prime concern was to protect Conyers from the third class, whom they feared might carry his hazing to an extreme. They were fairly successful, although great alarm was felt when he was found to be missing from his bed one raw, winter evening. Eventually he was discovered in a treetop in a remote corner of the yard, clad only in his nightshirt, barking like a dog. Punitive action was made impossible by Conyers's stalwart refusal to identify his hazers. Found deficient in mathematics and French, he resigned at the start of his third-class year in November 1873.

A second black midshipman, Alonzo C. McClennan, also from South Carolina, was appointed to the academy that same year. He resigned on account of academic difficulties in 1874. The class that entered the academy that September included a third black, Henry E. Baker, Jr., who was

The Class of 1874, plus a little boy, assembled at the Herndon Monument for a group photograph. Bradley A. Fiske stands second from right in the top row. U.S. Naval Institute Collection.

dismissed for disciplinary offenses two months later. Sixty years were to pass before there was another black midshipman.

Worden's classes included two distinguished scientists: Albert A. Michelson, '73, the first American to win the Nobel Prize, and Bradley A. Fiske, '74, inventor of the stadimeter, the naval telescopic gunsight, and numerous other items of naval technology. The son of Polish immigrants, reared in Western mining towns, Michelson was something of a rarity at the academy, most of whose students came from genteel, though rarely wealthy, backgrounds. Fiske, whose father was an Episcopal clergyman, was more typical.

Ironically enough, Michelson and Fiske got into a fight. Fiske took exception to the way Michelson, a first captain, spoke to him on parade one day and sent him a challenge. Unknown to Fiske, Michelson took a serious interest in his first-class boxing lessons. "The details of the fight were very carefully arranged," Fiske wrote; "in fact the arranging of the details took longer than the fight itself. That I did not have the slightest chance became evident in about one minute; but I hammered away the best I could until the referees saw that I couldn't see out of either eye and declared the fight was finished. I was put on the sick list by the surgeon 'for contusions,' and I stayed on the sick list for eight days."

Michelson had the reputation of making the best grades with the least study of any man in his class. The time saved he devoted to a variety of private interests, which already included scientific experiments. In a graduating class of twenty-nine, he ranked first in optics and acoustics, second in mathematics, heat and climatology, third in statistics, and twenty-fifth in seamanship. Admiral Worden handed him his diploma with the words: "If in the future, you'll give less attention to scientific matters and more to your naval gunnery, there might come a time when you would know enough to be some service to your country."

After two years' sea duty, Michelson was assigned to the academy as an instructor in physics and chemistry. While preparing to teach an advanced physics course, he was surprised to learn that only three men had ever attempted to determine the speed of light by a terrestrial measurement. He decided to demonstrate the best of their methods to his class. Augmenting the equipment available at the academy with a borrowed heliostat and a mirror he bought for ten dollars, Michelson was able to refine the procedure until he obtained the most precise measurement ever made. (Today the line of sight along which he conducted these experiments, then the seawall, is marked by bronze discs in the plaza between Michelson and Chauvenet halls.) Offered the first chair of physics at the Case School of Applied Science in Cleveland in 1882, Michelson reluctantly resigned his commission to pursue a scientific career. His Nobel Prize, for physics, was awarded in 1907. But he never lost his love for the navy. Although he was sixty-five when the United States entered World War One, he volunteered for active duty and was gratified to be attached to the Bureau of Ordnance with the rank of lieutenant commander, U.S. Naval Reserve.

Among Michelson's Annapolis colleagues was Professor James Russell Soley, a naval historian who became the only civilian faculty member ever to move to an executive position in the Navy Department. Head of the Department of English Studies, History, and Law from 1873 to 1882, in the latter year Soley was called to Washington to serve as Navy Department librarian and to organize the Naval War Records Office. When the office of Assistant Secretary of the Navy was revived in 1890, President Benjamin Harrison appointed him its first holder.

Despite the pitiful condition to which the navy had been reduced by the seventies—at the opening of the decade it had only fifty-two ships in full commission—the level of professional interest among its officers was high. On the evening of October 9, 1873, fifteen officers of the academy staff met in the Science Building to establish a society for the discussion of matters of naval concern. The result was the U.S. Naval Institute, an organization dedicated to "the advancement of professional, literary, and scientific knowledge in the Navy." The institute soon became and has remained the open forum of American naval opinion. In 1874, to reach members unable to attend its monthly meetings at the academy, it commenced publication of *The Papers and Proceedings of the United States Naval Institute*. Among the early contributors to the *Proceedings* was Commander Alfred T. Mahan, who served his final tour at the academy as head of the Ordnance Department, 1877-1880.

The battalion practices light artillery drill, about 1875. Courtesy: U.S. Naval Academy Special Collections, Nimitz Library.

In September 1874 Worden was succeeded by Rear Admiral C. R. P. Rodgers. The commandant of midshipmen in 1861, Rodgers embarked upon his duties with the aspiration of building on his predecessors' work to bring the academy to a new standard of excellence. In February 1874 Congress abolished the two-year engineering program and provided for the annual appointment of twenty-five cadet-engineers to a four-year course. Rodgers took special interest in the development of the curriculum. In their third- and fourth-class years, the engineers were given many courses in common with the midshipmen, but while the latter received instruction in seamanship and other subjects relevant to the duties of line officers, the engineers were taught blacksmithing, carpentry, boiler-making, foundry work, and engine-building. They also made their summer cruises separately, on small steamers which visited navy yards and shipbuilders. As first and second classmen, they took advanced technical courses conducted by a newly established Department of Mechanics and Applied Mathematics. As a final test of their proficiency they were required to design and build a steam engine, from raw materials to finished product. This was the first course in mechanical engineering in the United States,

Cadet-engineers of the Class of 1882 took their "coaling clothes"—and presumably a bag of coal dust to begrime their faces—to the photographer's studio for a class portrait. Courtesy: U.S. Naval Academy Archives.

and civilian colleges and universities actively sought its graduates to establish similar programs of their own.

Rodgers also revised the midshipmen's curriculum, concentrating professional subjects in the first- and second-class years, and adding upper-level electives in mathematics, mechanics, physics, and chemistry—a revolutionary change, at which the usual outcry went up from service conservatives. He applied the Hazing Law in a determined attempt to stamp out the practice once and for all. When Secretary of the Navy Richard W. Thompson questioned the authority of the Academic Board to recommend the dismissal of midshipmen for bad conduct, Rodgers replied with such vigor that Thompson quietly let the matter drop.

Rodgers left the academy in July 1878. The success of his administration received international recognition at the Paris Universal Exposition in October of that year, when the Naval Academy was awarded the Diplôme de Médaille d'Or for "the best system of education in the United States." Rodgers himself was not completely satisfied with the result of his efforts; but idealists seldom are. He had not, as he had hoped to do, inspired the midshipmen to adopt a more decorous mode of con-

"Decatur Nelson Jones his name
Reports at library."

Entrance

"I wish that I knew," groans Plebe,
"What 'tis you want me to du!"

Trials

"A wicked scrape were the middies in,
It might be labeled 'orgie'-nal sin."

Pleasures

"Washington beauties there, by the score,
Vie with the belles of Baltimore."

Graduation

These views, a sort of pilgrim's progress, appeared in *Fag Ends from the Naval Academy*, a commercial publication based on midshipman contributions, in 1877. Courtesy: U.S. Naval Academy Special Collections, Nimitz Library.

duct. The pages of *Fag Ends from the Naval Academy*, a commercial publication of 1877 based largely on midshipman contributions, show that they remained as mischievous as ever. Considering the grim circumstances of the American naval profession, it was remarkable that Rodgers was able to accomplish all that he did.

The new superintendent was Commodore Foxhall Parker. A sick man when he took the post, Parker died during June Week 1879, not quite a year after his appointment, and was succeeded by Rear Admiral George B. Balch. It was widely rumored that Secretary Thompson selected both in the belief they would prove more amenable than Rodgers to his desire to reduce the number of dismissals from the academy by curtailing the authority of the Academic Board. The conduct of their superintendencies suggests there was something to the rumor. Although Parker died too soon to leave a mark on the academy, he viewed the Academic Board as an unnecessary adjunct to business best decided between the secretary and the superintendent. Balch relinquished the presidency of the board to the commandant of midshipmen. A fine old sea dog with a splendid war record, "Papa" Balch allowed the midshipmen to wrap him around their little fingers. Fondly remembered as a "fatherly old gentleman," he became a forgiving figurehead. The midshipmen were happy but discipline was lax.

The great advance in officer education during this period was made outside the academy walls. Cadet-Engineer Francis T. Bowles, '79, set it in motion by requesting leave from the academy to take the advanced course in shipbuilding at the Royal Naval College at Greenwich, England. Secretary Thompson not only approved his request but authorized a classmate, Cadet-Engineer Richard Gatewood, to accompany him. In the following years, the Navy Department usually sent two or more of the leading graduates of each class to study naval architecture in England or France. Upon their return home they were assigned to the Corps of Naval Constructors. This informal postgraduate program continued for almost a quarter-century, by which time, due largely to the efforts of the men who passed through it, American naval technology had become the equal of any in the world.

The battalion of midshipmen made two trips to Washington under Balch: the first, to participate in the dedication of the Farragut Monument, and the second to march in President James A. Garfield's inaugural parade. Garfield returned the visit in June Week 1881 and became the first president to address the battalion. Less than a month later, he was assassinated. By that time, the academy had begun to feel the need of a strong hand at the helm.

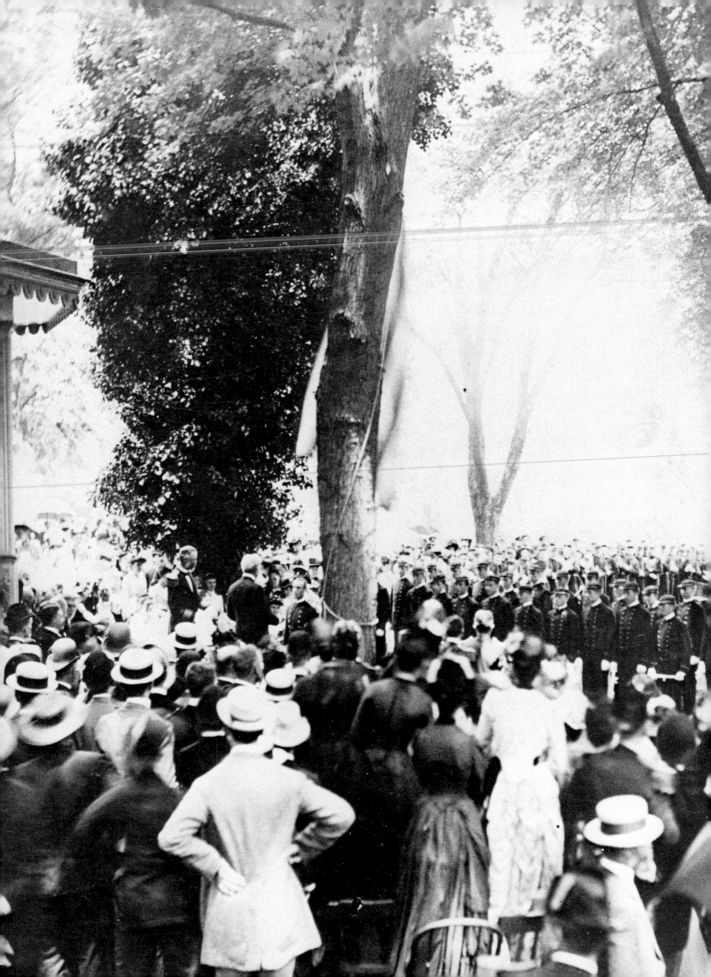

Midshipmen study in their room in the New Quarters. This photograph was
taken for the Naval Academy's exhibit at the Chicago World's Fair in 1893, but
it could have been made at any time between 1880 and 1905. Courtesy:
U.S. Naval Academy Special Collections, Nimitz Library.

boards" to work out the answers. This practice became increasingly controversial with the passage of time.

Meanwhile, the officer promotion problem had progressed from bad
to worse. The hump created by the big Civil War classes continued to
obstruct promotion, and the annual influx to the fleet of the academy's
graduating classes only increased the congestion. By the beginning of the
1880s, there was one officer for every four enlisted men, and it was taking
Annapolis graduates as long as eight years to make ensign. "Thus," wrote
Park Benjamin, who resigned rather than continue to endure it, "the
unfortunate cadet midshipman, regardless of his years and his attainments and his diploma, found himself performing the same little round
of duties and entrusted with no more responsibility than was his grand-
father (if he came of a naval family) at the age of twelve. He lived in
the steerage and shared the tin wash-basin with half a dozen others, some
of them men with wives and offspring, jammed his clothes into a pigeon-

"Manning the boards," as in this math class, was a daily feature of midshipman life. Courtesy: U.S. Naval Academy Special Collections, Nimitz Library.

hole locker, meekly stood watch on the forecastle, alternated with the messenger boys in exercising his highly educated legs to carry messages, and occasionally got up at 5 a.m. to take the stewards ashore in the market boat." This was the period in which a character in a play by Oscar Wilde contradicted a young lady's lament that America had neither ruins nor curiosities by referring her to its navy and its manners. Admiral Rodgers had several times suggested either reducing the academy's intake of plebes or holding a competitive examination for admission to the second class, but his counsel was ignored.

Finally, Congress advanced a surgical solution. On August 5, 1882, it passed a Personnel Act stipulating that the number of officers annually commissioned in the line, the Engineer Corps, and the Marine Corps could be no greater than the number of vacancies that had occurred in the preceding year. Appointments were to be made on the basis of class standing. Graduates whose services were not required would receive their diplomas, a year's severance pay ($950), and the good wishes of their government. This legislation was resented most deeply by the members of the classes that had entered between 1877 and 1881, upon whom its effects fell ex post facto. To young men who had spent six years of their lives preparing for a naval career, the inequity appeared all the greater in that no serious effort was made to cut back on admissions to the academy.

The act also attempted to ease the friction that existed between line officers and engineers. Apparently in hopes of nipping their differences in the bud, it abolished the titles of "cadet-midshipman" and "cadet-engineer," and substituted the all-embracing term "naval cadet." This pleased no one.

The single positive feature of the act was that it contained the first official notice that academy graduates could enter the Marine Corps. This provision took effect a year later, when ten members of the Class of 1881 opted for the corps upon the completion of their probationary sea duty. Between 1883 and 1897 a total of fifty graduates became Marines, five of whom served consecutive terms as commandant, heading the corps from 1914 through 1936: George Barnett, '81; John A. Lejeune, '88; Wendell C. Neville, '90; Ben H. Fuller, '89; and John H. Russell, '92. The years when these men led the corps were the ones in which it identified the amphibious mission and developed the doctrine it employed with such success in World War Two. The naval background and associations of its commandants undoubtedly contributed to these developments.

Otherwise, the implementation of this act was devastating. Of the sixty-three graduates of the Class of 1881 who had already joined the fleet for their two-year probationary period, only twenty-two were retained. Of the thirty-seven graduates of the Class of 1882, twenty-one were discharged or resigned under the shadow of the act. The retention figure for the Class of 1883 was thirteen of fifty-four; for the Class of 1884, twenty-nine of forty-six; for 1885, twelve of thirty-six; for 1886, thirteen of twenty-five; and for 1887, thirty-one of forty-four. Later legislation restored the discharged engineers and allowed the naval cadets to take Marine commissions, but only one, R. H. Jackson, '87, was ever accepted into the navy line. Some of those discharged made successful careers in the army and the Coast Guard; many of the others were given temporary commissions in the navy during the Spanish-American War. One of those who went into the army, Second Lieutenant Harry L. Hawthorne, '82, Second Artillery, was the first academy graduate to win the Medal of Honor, a distinction for which naval officers were not eligible until 1914. He was awarded the army medal for heroism in action against the Sioux at the Battle of Wounded Knee, the last major engagement of the Indian wars, on December 29, 1890.

Another who did not make the cut was Philo N. McGiffin, the wild man of the Class of 1882, whose legendary exploits live on in the collective memory of the brigade of midshipmen. In the words of his boyhood friend Richard Harding Davis: "To him discipline was extremely irksome. He could maintain it among others, but when it applied to himself it bored him." One of McGiffin's most noted misdeeds involved a decorative pyramid of cannon balls from the War of 1812 which stood on the landing of his floor in the New Quarters. To amuse himself one evening he rolled them down the stairs one at a time, with predictably ruinous effect on the steps, banisters, and walls encountered in their descent. For this he was confined on board the *Santee*, where he talked the old salt who kept the brig into giving him six powder charges. Upon his release, he used them to fire a midnight salute from the antique cannons flanking the Mexican Monument. McGiffin's daring was not demonstrated only in pranks, however. On another occasion he rescued two children from a burning house, an act for which he was commended by the secretary of the navy.

Prevented from following a naval career under his own flag, McGiffin offered his services to the Imperial Chinese Navy. Although the mandarins who interviewed him made it clear that they considered the twenty-four-

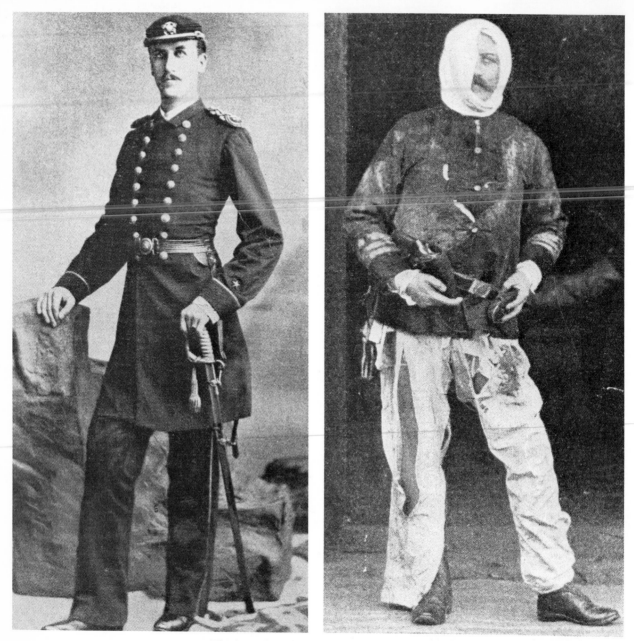

The legendary Philo McGiffin: at left, following his graduation from the Naval Academy in 1882; at right, after the Battle of the Yalu in 1894. Although academy graduates remained "naval cadets" during their two-year probationary sea duty, they were allowed to wear ensigns' uniforms. From Richard Harding Davis, *Real Soldiers of Fortune*.

year-old applicant a presumptuous boy, he did so well in the professional examinations they gave him that he was appointed professor of seamanship and gunnery at the Chinese Naval Academy at Tientsin. In a few years he was a commander. Classmates in the U.S. Asiatic Squadron, none of whom had reached the rank of lieutenant, visited his palatial quarters and wondered who had really had the luck. But McGiffin lived for the day when he would be readmitted to the U.S. Navy. In 1894, he resigned his commission and had arranged passage home when war broke out between China and Japan. It was not McGiffin's fight but he believed that honor obliged him to see it through.

The morning of September 17, 1894, found McGiffin serving as adviser to the captain of the battleship *Chen Yuen*, one of two new capital ships in a Chinese squadron lying off the mouth of the Yalu River. The approach of a Japanese squadron precipitated the first major sea fight of the battleship era. With twelve vessels each, the opposing forces were numerically equal, but the better-armed and better-handled Japanese squadron soon gained the upper hand. McGiffin assumed command of the *Chen Yuen* when her captain fled the bridge early in the engagement, in the course of which the ship took more than 150 hits. When the battered *Chen Yuen* reached port, she had only three shells left for her big guns. McGiffin was badly wounded. Threatened with blindness and in constant pain, he shot himself in a New York hospital in 1897.

The most immediate effect of the act of 1882, however, was to aggravate the disciplinary situation at the academy. The battalion was accustomed to Balch's indulgence when Captain Ramsay became superintendent. Ramsay's reforms antagonized the upper classmen, who viewed the change in the system of quartering and the introduction of a conduct grade as assaults on their time-honored class privileges. Now they were informed that they could not even count on being accepted into the navy. Under the circumstances, it is not surprising that the cadets began to feel and act aggrieved.

The academic year of 1882-83 was as troubled as any the academy has ever experienced. It all began in January 1883, when Cadet Petty Officer Charles E. Woodruff posted the answers to a mathematics examination he had just completed inside the door of a hall closet for the benefit of slower classmates. Ramsay rewarded his philanthropy by depriving him of his rank. The battalion was informed of the action during the customary "publication," or reading aloud, of orders at dinner formation one evening. After the meal, as Woodruff's division marched out of the mess hall, it gave him a cheer led by Cadet Lieutenant George W. Street. Ramsay was outraged. Street's explanation that such cheers were customary was not accepted and at dinner the next day the cadets learned that he, too, had lost his stripes. They responded with hisses and groans.

Captain Ramsay was not the man to tolerate insubordination. The entire first class was transferred to the *Santee* and the other classes were completely restricted. Thereupon, all the cadet officers, excepting only the lieutenant commander and one lieutenant, tendered their resignations from the academy. The commandant tried to persuade them to reconsider, but they were obdurate. Little good it did them. Ramsay refused to accept their resignations, reduced them to the ranks, ordered them placed in confinement on board the *Santee*, and appointed new cadet officers from the third class.

The reaction of the battalion was not far removed from mutiny. In formation the cadets expressed their opinion of orders by groans, hisses, derisory laughter, and impertinent cheers. They began calling the academy "Ramsay's Kindergarten," and complained to their parents, their congressmen, and Secretary of the Navy William E. Chandler that he seemed determined to "crush every particle of spirit which a cadet might reasonably be expected to possess." Their protests were in vain. Secretary Chandler supported the superintendent. Eventually, all except three of the cadet officers confined on the *Santee* apologized for their action, and

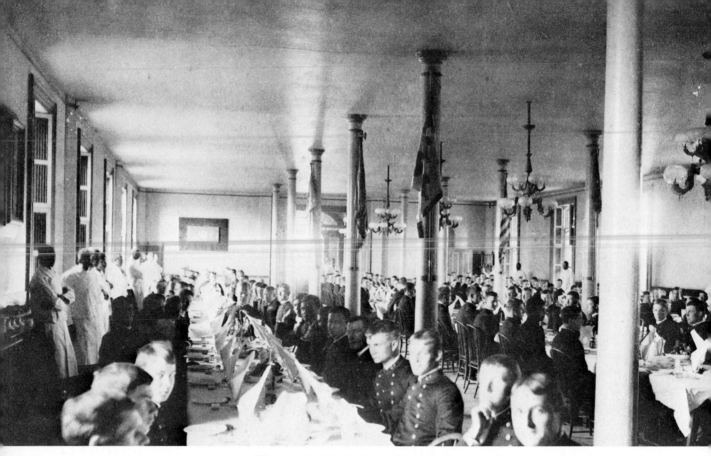

The mess hall in the New Quarters, where the disturbances that convulsed the academy in 1883 broke out. Courtesy: U.S. Naval History Division.

were reinstated in the battalion but not restored to their ranks. The three who refused to apologize were dismissed.

The trouble was not over, however. Its climax came at graduation. On the morning of June 9, 1883, the cadets, faculty, staff, distinguished guests, and parents assembled in the chapel for the presentation of diplomas. The speaker was Representative R. T. Mills of Texas, who discoursed on the necessity for cheerful obedience of orders. Following the congressman's address, Captain Ramsay arose to begin the presentation of diplomas. According to the account of a newsman present, he

leaned against the desk and looked straight forward into the audience. His lips were seen to work, but few of the spectators heard what he said. The name of Dana S. Greene, Jr., the honor man of the Class, was then called. As Cadet Greene stepped forward to receive his diploma, a number of cadets broke into cheers, the usual course on commencement day when a favorite steps to the front to receive the testimony of his graduation. In an instant the scene changed as Captain Ramsay said: "You show your insubordination and attempt to disgrace yourselves and the Naval Academy before the eyes of the country. Battalion, rise! Those who applauded, march to the front!" and there, to the astonishment of the spectators, twenty cadets left the ranks and formed around the platform before the indignant Superintendent. Turning to Lieutenant Greene, who had followed the cadets, Captain Ramsay said: "Take them to the *Santee* until further orders." Several of the convicted cadets' parents were present, and saw their sons march off to prison and nobody seemed to know what for. . . .

The "mutineers" of the Class of 1883—midshipmen officers who tendered their resignations in protest of Captain Ramsay's policies—display their defiance in this photograph. The insignia and accoutrements of their surrendered ranks are piled in the foreground. From left to right: W.J. Wilson, R.W. Barkley, T.H. Gignilliat, J.H. Barnard, T.S. O'Leary (seated), T.V. Toney, T.A. Witherspoon, and Harry George. O'Leary and George retired as captains; Barnard resigned permanently in August 1883; Toney died on the Asiatic Station in 1884; the others were discharged in 1885 under the provisions of the Personnel Act of 1882. U.S. Naval Institute Collection.

The diplomas were then handed to the remaining graduates in funereal silence, the situation being exceedingly painful and gloomy. This over, all the cadets were marched out to the new quarters, where they were dismissed. Then it was discovered . . . that the first words Captain Ramsay had spoken were that there would be no applauding, and the cadets, like nearly all the audience, had not heard them. Officers and cadets crowded around the Superintendent and represented the situation, and the Captain ordered all those who had not heard the order to be released. In an hour the cadets were once more at liberty. Before the order had reached the *Santee*, all the cadets had signed a pledge, on their honor, that they had not heard the order of the Superintendent.

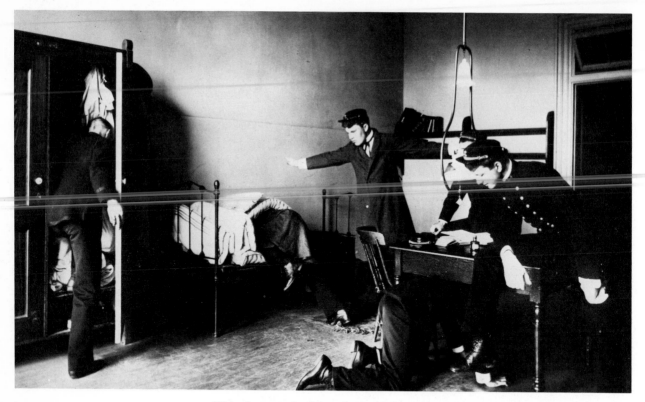

This photograph, although staged, is a realistic representation of the milder forms of hazing in the 1880s and '90s. Courtesy: U.S. Naval Academy Archives.

Captain Ramsay's mysterious order was soon explained. Just before the ceremony, he heard that the cadets planned to humiliate one of the cadet officers who had refused to resign with the others by loudly applauding his classmates when their diplomas were presented but leaving him to receive his in silence. It was to avert this ignominy that Ramsay forbade the cadets to applaud. Unfortunately, hardly anyone in the chapel, whose acoustics were poor, heard him.

This incident brought the June Week festivities to an inglorious end. The Class of 1883 canceled its graduation dance and repaired to Washington to hold a banquet at the Riggs House hotel. The comments passed on Captain Ramsay in the course of the evening, to quote a contemporary report, were "as may be imagined . . . anything else but good."

Those unhappy events served as a sort of corporate catharsis. There was a flare-up of hazing during the ensuing summer cruise, but the courts-martial that followed revealed that no real brutality was involved. Order had been restored by the time classes convened for the new academic year and the discipline of the battalion showed such improvement that at graduation Captain Ramsay could commend the Class of 1884.

The year 1883 also marked the beginning of the American naval renaissance. The turning-point came with congressional authorization for the construction of the navy's "White Squadron," the protected cruisers *Atlanta*, *Boston*, and *Chicago* and the dispatch boat *Dolphin*. Almost every navy budget for more than a decade thereafter included funds for new construction. America's first steel battleships, the *Maine* and the

Swordmaster Corbesier drills a group of plebes, some of them still in civilian clothes, in the manual of arms. Courtesy: U.S. Naval Academy Special Collections, Nimitz Library.

Texas, were authorized in 1886. Two years earlier, Commodore Luce had opened the Naval War College, at which Captain Mahan gave the lectures that provided the basis for his brilliant exposition *The Influence of Sea Power upon History*. Appearing in 1890, this vastly influential work was instrumental in convincing Americans of the need for a strong navy. The future of American sea power, which had seemed so dismal, grew brighter with every passing year.

The status of the academy's recent graduates also improved. Ever since the passage of the Personnel Act of 1882, graduates who entered the navy line had been protesting, quite justifiably, that it discriminated against them. While classmates who became Marines or engineers were granted commissions immediately upon passing the six-year, graduating examination, cadets who passed the same examination were merely appointed midshipmen, at a much lower salary, pending an opening in the rank of ensign. Captain Ramsay endorsed their complaint, and in 1884 Congress removed the inequity, stipulating that henceforth they would be commissioned at the same time as the others. Nevertheless, the surviving provisions of the act continued to impose an artificial limitation on the expanding navy's supply of junior officers until their belated repeal in 1889.

Captain Ramsay's relief by Commander W. T. Sampson in September 1886 was one of the rare instances of a reforming superintendent being succeeded by another. Sampson's reforms were not as dramatic as Ramsay's, but they did not need to be. The groundwork had been laid.

Commander William T. Sampson, the academy's thirteenth superintendent. Courtesy: U.S. Naval Academy Archives.

Honor man of the Class of 1861, Sampson had already served three tours—more than one-third of his career—at the academy, most recently as head of the Department of Physics and Chemistry, 1874-1879. No other superintendent has ever embarked upon his duties with such a wealth of academic experience to aid him in their discharge. An austere personality, he struck most people as cold and remote, but inspired the utmost devotion among the handful who came to know him well.

Upon his appointment, Sampson promised that he would prosecute any hazing offences with the full vigor of the law. The third class did not take him seriously until he court-martialed and dismissed nine of its members. The acts of which they were convicted were so trivial that President Grover Cleveland reduced the sentence to brief confinement in the *Santee*, but Sampson had made his point.

One of the first officers to appreciate the relevance of applied science to the naval profession, as a department head Sampson had introduced

Marine sentries guard Gate Three, at the foot of Maryland Avenue, in 1889.
Courtesy: U.S. Naval Academy Special Collections, Nimitz Library.

studies in electricity and metallurgy. As superintendent he emphasized
the technical aspects of the curriculum, especially practical work in the
academy's machine shops, and initiated the custom of inviting distinguished scientists to Annapolis to lecture to the cadets. Towards the
end of his tour, in March 1889, he finally persuaded Congress to adopt a
plan he had long advocated of reestablishing specialized studies for engineers. No distinction was made during the cadets' first three years at the
academy, but as first classmen they were divided into two sections, line
and engineer, for which different curricula were prescribed. This system
remained in effect until 1899, when the amalgamation of line officers and
engineers made it superfluous.

The most enduring of Sampson's innovations proved to be the "aptitude for the service" grade, which is still assigned today. Computed independently of classroom work, it was designed to measure a cadet's
potential as a naval officer, and was based on his performance of military
duties and conduct on cruise. Sampson also refined Ramsay's conduct
grade, separating it from academics and making the extent of the liberties
available to each cadet dependent upon his conduct grade for the preceding month.

Sampson's superintendency witnessed the revival of Naval Academy
athletics, although the initiative came from the cadets and concerned
alumni rather than from his administration. Since Admiral Porter's days
at the academy, the athletic programs he encouraged had been allowed
gradually to deteriorate. Physical education remained in the curriculum,
but sports were neglected. The cadets' interest was reawakened by the
evolution of American football away from the old, rugby rules into a
wholly new game. In 1882 Cadet Vaulx Carter, '84, provided the impetus
for the formation of a navy team, which played a Thanksgiving Day

"Instruction in electricity" was included in the academy's curriculum as early as 1889, when this photograph was made. Electrical lighting began to be used in ships in the 1880s. Courtesy: U.S. Naval Academy Special Collections, Nimitz Library.

match with Johns Hopkins University for the next three years. Navy won them all. In 1885 the single-game season was expanded to three games, and in 1886 to six. By then, football was becoming a vital part of academy life. The passion it aroused was reflected in a newspaper report of the aftermath of a game in which Navy was trounced by St. John's College, 22-6, in December 1888:

> As the game neared its close the rival spirit between the two clubs showed itself among the outsiders. The college had at one point about 30 fellow student backers, ranging in age from 12 to 20, who were showing their gratification at the . . . drubbing of the Cadets . . . by loud and incessant college cries, with several taunting exclamations personal to the Cadets.
>
> About 100 Cadets formed themselves in solid phalanx and rushed at the college boys, driving them 15 or 20 yards. The college boys made a stand, and one threw off his coat. Then the Cadets rushed them again and a number of blows were passed, and some of the smaller boys were picked up by the stalwart Cadets and thrown head over heels into the struggling mass of their comrades.
>
> Commander Sampson (the superintendent of the academy), Commander [Purnell F.] Harrington (commandant of Cadets) and Watchman Sloane

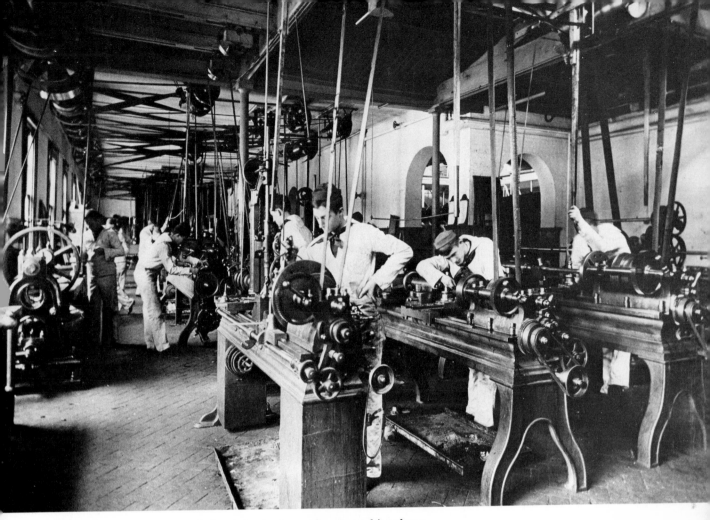

Midshipmen also received practical training in the academy's machine shops.
Courtesy: U.S. Naval Academy Special Collections, Nimitz Library.

made haste with calls and personal effort to stop the melee, which was soon ended. No one was seriously hurt, tho several of the college boys had black eyes.

The foundation of the Naval Academy Graduates' Association had taken place in 1886. In the course of their June Week reunions at the academy, its members, particularly those who remembered Porter's athletic regimen, remarked that many of the cadets did not appear to be in good physical condition. Colonel (by courtesy) Robert Means Thompson decided that something should be done. An inveterate doer, Thompson had resigned from the navy in 1871 and amassed a fortune as president of the Orford Copper Company. In a speech delivered at the 1890 reunion he asserted that an officer's academic attainments would be worthless if he proved physically incapable of bearing the strain of conflict. The following year he aided the officers attached to the academy in the formation of the Naval Academy Auxiliary Athletic Association, a private, non-profit organization devoted to the support of academy athletics. It has performed that mission with great success ever since.

The Navy "N" athletic letter was introduced in 1890, the same year in which the first Army-Navy game took place. This contest was instigated by West Point Cadet Dennis Michie, '92, who asked some midship-

Cadets model the academy's duty and athletic uniforms of 1890. From left to right: first row, baseball, tennis, football; second row, white working dress, foul weather, fencing, blue service dress–drill order, study (bathrobe and pajamas), and gymnastics; third row, blue service dress, full dress, cold weather. Courtesy: U.S. Naval Academy Special Collections, Nimitz Library.

men friends to send the Military Academy a challenge. His school had never fielded a team, but he felt justly confident that a challenge from Annapolis would produce one. The Navy team traveled to West Point for the game. It was played on November 29 on a frozen field cobbled with ice clods churned up during Army's practice sessions. Navy won, 24-0, which, in view of the West Pointers' inexperience, was only to be expected. Great indignation was felt on the Army side when a Navy player who had dropped back to punt ran for a touchdown. Brigadier General John A. Palmer, USMA '92, recalled that: "We expected the officials would recall the play. It was clearly a false official statement for an officer and a gentleman to announce that he was going to kick the ball and then do something else with it. To our surprise and disgust the officials let the play stand."

The Navy goat made his debut at this game. On the train to West Point the team decided it should have a mascot, comparable to the Yale bulldog, for which purpose a goat was filched from the area of the non-commissioned officers' quarters at the Military Academy. He only made a one-day stand, however, and in succeeding years various mascots were adopted. The credit for establishing Bill the Goat, as he came to be known, as Navy's mascot seems to belong to Commander Colby M. Chester, '64, commandant of cadets 1891-1894 and first president of the Naval Academy Athletic Association. Colby kept a celebrated goat as

The football team of 1890. Note the absence of helmets and padding. Courtesy: U.S. Naval Academy Special Collections, Nimitz Library.

ship's mascot while in command of the sloop *Galena* prior to coming to the academy, and would have been in a good position to promote the adoption of a goat there.

In 1891 the Army team came to Annapolis and Michie had the satisfaction of leading it to an upset victory, defeating Navy 32-16. Returning to West Point in 1892, the year navy blue and gold were adopted as the academy colors, Navy beat Army 12-4 and in 1893 it squeaked to victory in its home game, 6-4. During the latter season, Navy's star tackle, Cadet Joseph M. Reeves, '94, wore the first protective headgear seen on an American football field. Tired of stopping kicks with his skull, he had an Annapolis cobbler fashion him a crude leather helmet.

The Army-Navy game of 1894 was due to be played at West Point, but there was no Army-Navy game that year, or for some years thereafter. At the conclusion of the 1893 season, Colonel Oswald Ernst, superintendent at West Point, decided that, while in general football provided a wholesome outlet for the cadets' high spirits, the intense excitement generated by the Army-Navy game was disruptive of discipline. He wrote the secretary of war recommending its suppression. His reference to intense excitement was underscored by the fact that a brigadier general and a rear admiral had come close to fighting a duel over the last interservice game. The matter went all the way to a cabinet meeting, at which it was decided to have the secretaries of war and the navy issue orders prohibiting the academy teams from leaving their respective campuses. They could play football, but not with one another. In the following years,

The battalion parades in white drill order, 1892. Tecumseh surveys the scene from his pedestal beside the lyceum at right. Courtesy: U.S. Naval Academy Publications Office.

Navy did well against visiting teams of the caliber of Penn State, Princeton, Rutgers, and Lehigh, winding up the decade with six consecutive winning seasons.

Navy's athletic revival was not limited to football. There was an upsurge of interest in sports, in general. The baseball team entered intercollegiate competition. Winston Churchill, '94, later a best-selling novelist, was given leave to go to New Haven to observe the Yale crew. The Navy crew, of which he became captain, rowed its first race in 1893. Colonel Thompson arranged fencing matches with Harvard and Columbia, and presented the academy with the Thompson Trophy Cup, on which the name of the athlete of the year was to be engraved.

In June 1890 Sampson was succeeded by Captain Robert L. Phythian. A kindly man, Phythian took great pleasure in the social aspects of academy life, many of which had already assumed their modern forms. Among the most charming of the customs established by that date is the June Week Color Parade, at which a young lady chosen by the commander of the best-drilled company accepts the academy colors from the superintendent and presents them to what then becomes the color company. Another aspect of academy life that became a tradition had its start in 1894, the last year of Phythian's administration, with the appearance of the *Lucky Bag*, the academy's first real year book.

In his first annual report as superintendent, Captain Phythian paid a remarkably generous compliment to his predecessors by declaring that he could find no changes to make. The policy of his successor, Captain Philip H. Cooper, '64, was equally conservative. The academy ran on a force a distinguished twentieth-century superintendent christened "institutional impulsion"—the self-sustaining momentum of a successful routine.

Midshipmen embark in steam launches while others go aloft in the *Constellation*, behind the boat shed, left. At right is the *Santee*. Courtesy: U.S. Naval Academy Special Collections, Nimitz Library.

superintendents and Boards of Visitors had repeatedly invited congressional attention, was at best dilapidated and at worst dangerous. The walls of the New Quarters had cracked from top to bottom; seams had opened in the flooring, and fumes from the kitchen and laundry wafted through the cadets' rooms.

In 1895 a Board of Visitors whose members included the indefatigable Colonel Thompson submitted the strongest report to date. After roundly condemning the existing facilities, it asserted that the Naval Academy should be an institution second to none in the world and predicted that "a reconstruction of the buildings, grounds, and sanitation, upon the most approved modern architectural . . . lines, will not only be an incalculable benefit to the naval service, but . . . will meet the approval of the whole country."

As far as Colonel Thompson was concerned, that was just the beginning. Proceeding on his own initiative, he commissioned an eminent New York architect, Ernest Flagg, to develop an architectural and topographical master plan for a new academy. The result was the noble conception which forms the core of the Naval Academy of today. Concurrently with its development, Thompson prodded Secretary of the Navy Hilary A. Herbert to appoint a Board of Survey, headed by Commodore E. O. Matthews, to study the academy's needs. Its report, submitted in January 1896, endorsed the Flagg plan. All that remained was to obtain the congressional appropriation necessary to begin work, but no attempt to do so had been made by the time Secretary Herbert left office in March 1897.

The project had still not left the Navy Department when, on the evening of February 15, 1898, the battleship *Maine* was destroyed by an explosion in Havana Harbor.* Almost half her crew, 266 officers and men, were killed. Although the origin of the blast was uncertain, most

* Today her foremast stands in the academy yard; the ensign and jack that were lowered at sunset that day are in the museum.

Midshipmen go aloft for sail drill, around 1898. Courtesy: U.S. Naval Academy Archives.

whose midshipman days predated its foundation went ashore in the 1880s. Every ship's captain and every regular line officer who fought at Manila and Santiago was an alumnus. Watching the armored cruiser *Brooklyn*, Captain Francis A. Cook, '64, go into action at Santiago, the battleship *Oregon*'s Captain Charles E. Clark, proudly exclaimed, "My old roommate is in command of that ship!"

The cadets in Sampson's squadron acquitted themselves with distinction, if not always with discretion. At the height of the Battle of Santiago, Captain Robley D. "Fighting Bob" Evans, in command of the battleship *Iowa*, was appalled to find one young gentleman sitting atop the fore turret, calmly taking snapshots of the action. The battalion's only casualty was William A. Boardman, '00, who volunteered to accompany a party that was landed to restore order at San Juan, Puerto Rico, and was killed when a gun went off by accident.

The aftermath of the Battle of Santiago brought unexpected guests to Annapolis. The Spanish admiral, Don Pascual Cervera y Topete, and most of his surviving officers had been not so much captured as rescued when they beached their burning ships along the hostile Cuban coast. Transported to the Naval Academy for their confinement, Cervera and his senior officers were lodged in a house on Buchanan Row; his junior officers were assigned rooms in the Old Quarters. The academy's new superintendent, Rear Admiral Frederick V. McNair, arranged for them to be treated with every consideration. In exchange for their promise not to attempt to escape, they were given the liberty of the academy yard and the city of Annapolis. Their dignified deportment won the sympathy of all, and after their initial depression had passed they made the best of things, enjoying the hospitality of Annapolitan society, attending mass at St. Mary's Church and, in the case of the younger officers, exchanging language lessons with the local belles. Admiral Cervera, a tall old man with a sailor's rolling gait, incongruously outfitted with a blue civilian suit and umbrella, became a familiar figure on the city streets. Usually he was accompanied by Captain Eulate of the cruiser *Viscaya*. The most despondent of the prisoners, Eulate was wont to exclaim, "Oh! my beautiful ship." When a lady asked him to autograph a fan on which she was collecting the signatures of the Spanish officers, he did so with the comment, "A souvenir of misfortune." Years later an Annapolitan who knew them all wondered "whether officers of other nations would have conducted themselves with such good spirit and genuine sportsmanship under similar conditions." They were repatriated early in September.

CHAPTER SEVEN

Anchor's Aweigh

The year 1898 marked a turning-point in the history of the United States, its navy, and its Naval Academy. The defeat of Spain signaled the young republic's entry into world affairs. For the first time, its power had been exerted beyond the bounds of the North American continent. The destruction of Spanish rule in Cuba, Puerto Rico, the Philippines, and Guam presented it with an instant empire, soon enlarged by the acquisition of the Hawaiian Islands, Wake Island, and part of Samoa. The security of these far-flung territories demanded a first-rate fleet. So did the American people. Its smashing victories at Manila and Santiago made the navy the nation's delight. Books and articles on naval heroes, naval history, and naval affairs appeared in profusion. There was a Dewey-for-president boom. Suddenly, America's long-forgotten fleet became the object of unprecedented popular enthusiasm.

Thus it seems singularly appropriate that 1898 was the year in which the Naval Academy acquired a coat of arms. It was the creation of Park Benjamin, who joined Colonel Thompson in the organization of the Naval Academy Alumni Association of New York in 1897. Like Thompson, he resigned from the navy to make a fortune in business but never forgot his debt to the academy. The construction of a building for the University Club of New York, the exterior of which was to be decorated by the arms of its members' colleges, reminded Benjamin that the Naval Academy had none to display. He supplied the want. In his words: "The . . . arms of the Naval Academy has for its crest a hand grasping a trident, below which is a shield bearing an ancient galley coming into action, bows on, and below that an open book, indicative of education, and finally the motto, 'Ex Scientia Tridens' (From knowledge, the sea power)." Its adoption by the Navy Department was promoted by one of Benjamin's classmates, Jacob W. Miller, a founder of the New York Naval Militia.

America's commitment to sea power was clinched when a former assistant secretary of the navy, Theodore Roosevelt, friend and disciple of Mahan and himself the author of a naval history of the War of 1812, succeeded to the presidency following the assassination of William McKinley in September 1901. In his own celebrated summary, Roosevelt's policy was to walk softly and carry a big stick. In the international arena, his big stick was to be the U.S. Navy.

The result was a Golden Age of American sea power. The modest tempo of the naval renaissance of the nineties underwent a dramatic

Graduates are carried out of the New Quarters by new first classmen in the "class rush," a custom that died out soon after the completion of Bancroft Hall. Courtesy: U.S. Naval History Division.

acceleration as Congress tacitly accepted the goal of building a navy second only to that of Great Britain, traditional ruler of the waves. At least one battleship was authorized annually between 1898 and 1918, except for a single year when the shipyards were full.

At Annapolis the Golden Age began innocuously enough with a determination by the 1898 Board of Visitors that the Recitation Hall had become structurally unsafe. Secretary of the Navy John D. Long's decisive response was to ask Congress for $1,000,000 to begin the reconstruction of the entire academy in accordance with the Flagg project. The temper of the times assured that the money would be forthcoming. Work commenced on March 28, 1899, and was kept going by annual appropriations throughout the opening decade of the new century. Opposition of a sort arose over the second appropriation, when there was talk of stopping work on Flagg's plan and holding an architectural competition, but it was overcome.

Flagg's grand design called for the expansion of the yard by sizeable landfills along both its river and harbor shores and the creation of a ship basin on the former. It showed the buildings, in monumental, French Renaissance style, grouped in functional units, with a new dormitory in the southeastern section of the yard. Planned for 480 midshipmen, upon the suggestion of Colonel Thompson the dormitory was designed in such a manner that additional wings could be added as needed. Inside its main entrance was to be a magnificent, marble-floored rotunda, from which a broad flight of marble steps would lead directly to a great, cathedral-ceilinged room that would be consecrated to the memory of the navy's heroes and used for assemblies and social activities. Besides these public areas and the midshipmen's rooms, the dormitory was to contain the battalion mess hall and kitchen and offices for the disciplinary officers.

Bancroft Hall has been the home of the brigade of midshipmen since 1906.
Courtesy: U.S. Naval Academy Special Collections, Nimitz Library.

Flanking the dormitory and connected to it by long colonnades, the plan showed two large rectangular buildings. The one nearest the Severn, which Flagg designated the Boat-House (today's Macdonough Hall), was to accommodate the Department of Seamanship. Its twin, the Armory (Dahlgren Hall), was meant for the Department of Gunnery.

Directly opposite this complex, across the yard, stood the much smaller academic group, three adjoining buildings placed at right angles so as to form a courtyard opening towards the dormitory. They would house all of the remaining academic departments, except Steam Engineering and Naval Construction, which were to occupy a separate building (Isherwood Hall) immediately to their rear. The library and auditorium were in the center section (Mahan Hall) of the academic group.

A new chapel would be built on Blake Row, facing the Severn, approximately midway between the dormitory and the academic group. Designed in the form of a Greek cross, 120 feet square, it would seat 1,600 worshippers. The superintendent's house was shown on one side of it, the Administration Building on the other. The design also featured an officers' club on Goldsborough Row; spacious, duplex houses for department heads along Porter Row; and additional officers' quarters on Upshur and Rodgers rows.

Flagg's plan was modified in several respects during the course of construction. The little lighthouses he had drawn on the end of the breakwaters enclosing Dewey Basin and the amphitheatre overlooking it were eliminated, as was the colonnaded arch enclosing the courtyard of the academic group. On the whole, however, the finished academy was remarkably faithful to his original conception.

Dahlgren and Macdonough halls, with which construction started, were officially opened on March 7, 1903. Work was begun on the dormitory (later named Bancroft Hall) in 1901. The material used for these three buildings was granite. Thereafter, economic considerations caused the

Mahan Hall, the center of the academic group, was the home of the academy's library from 1907 to 1973. Courtesy: U.S. Naval Academy Archives.

substitution of grey brick. Because of the similarity of color, the change is almost imperceptible. The northeast wing of Bancroft Hall was ready for occupancy in 1904, the year in which Admiral Dewey laid the cornerstone of the chapel. The officers' club was finished in 1905. The remaining wings of Bancroft Hall and the superintendent's house were completed in 1906. The academic group and the Administration Building were ready in 1907. The first service was held in the new chapel on May 28, 1908. The magnificent bronze doors were unveiled on June 2, 1909. Designed by nineteen-year-old Miss Evelyn B. Longman, winner of a design competition sponsored by Colonel Thompson, they were presented to the academy by him in memory of the Class of 1868.

Fort Severn, initially scheduled for preservation as an historic monument, was demolished in 1909. With its disappearance, the only surviving remnants of the old academy were the two brick guardhouses at Gate Three. The new academy was completed in 1913 by the laying of underground power lines and the construction of a concrete bridge across College Creek. It covered 111 acres, 45 of which had been reclaimed, and had cost $8,465,000—$8,019,000 for buildings and $446,000 for seawalls and wharfs.

The chapel upon its completion in 1908. The terra-cotta covering of the dome
was replaced by copper sheathing in 1929 and the nave was extended in 1940.
Courtesy: U.S. Naval History Division.

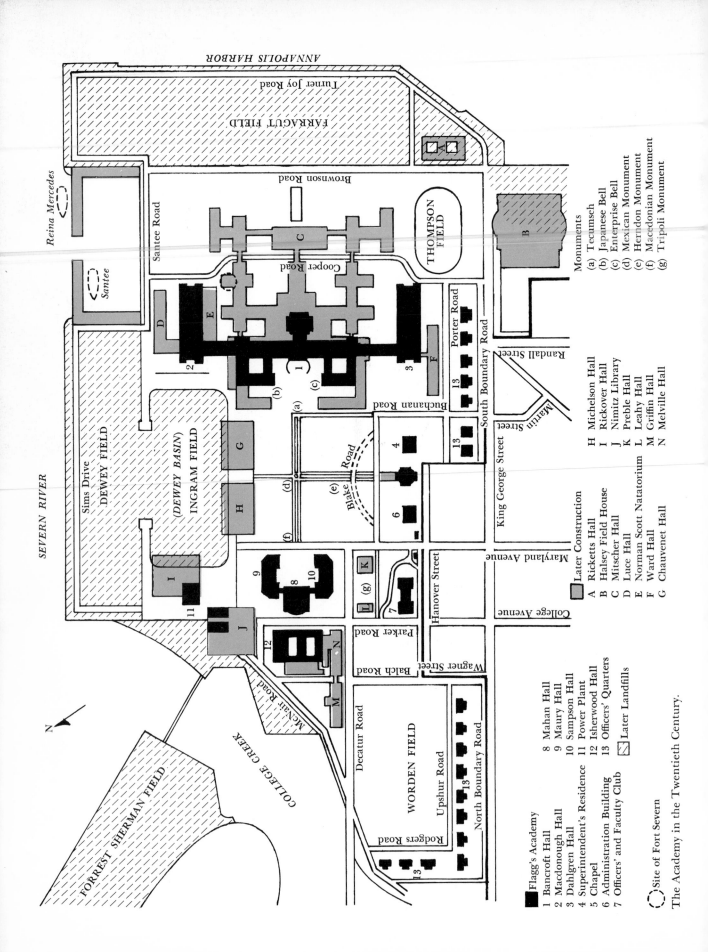

SEVERN RIVER

ANNAPOLIS HARBOR

Turner Joy Road

FARRAGUT FIELD

Reina Mercedes

Santee

Santee Road

Brownson Road

THOMPSON FIELD

Cooper Road

Sims Drive   DEWEY FIELD

(DEWEY BASIN)   INGRAM FIELD

Porter Road

Buchanan Road

South Boundary Road

Randall Street

Martin Street

Blake Road

King George Street

Maryland Avenue

College Avenue

Hanover Street

Wagner Street

Parker Road

Balch Road

McNair Road

Decatur Road

WORDEN FIELD

Upshur Road

Rodgers Road

North Boundary Road

FORREST SHERMAN FIELD

COLLEGE CREEK

N

Flagg's Academy
1 Bancroft Hall
2 Macdonough Hall
3 Dahlgren Hall
4 Superintendent's Residence
5 Chapel
6 Administration Building
7 Officers' and Faculty Club

8 Mahan Hall
9 Maury Hall
10 Sampson Hall
11 Power Plant
12 Isherwood Hall
13 Officers' Quarters

Later Construction
A Ricketts Hall
B Halsey Field House
C Mitscher Hall
D Luce Hall
E Norman Scott Natatorium
F Ward Hall
G Chauvenet Hall

H Michelson Hall
I Rickover Hall
J Nimitz Library
K Preble Hall
L Leahy Hall
M Griffin Hall
N Melville Hall

Later Landfills

Site of Fort Severn

Monuments
(a) Tecumseh
(b) Japanese Bell
(c) Enterprise Bell
(d) Mexican Monument
(e) Herndon Monument
(f) Macedonian Monument
(g) Tripoli Monument

The Academy in the Twentieth Century.

The superintendent's house was ready for occupancy in 1906. Its first resident was the last Civil War veteran to serve as superintendent, Rear Admiral James H. Sands. Courtesy: U.S. Naval Academy Special Collections, Nimitz Library.

The midshipmen who attended the academy during Theodore Roosevelt's presidencies became familiar with his bustling, frock-coated figure. While vice-president, he presented the diplomas to the Class of 1901. A year later he returned as president to deliver the famous "shots-that-hit" address in which he put himself behind the young reformers who were trying to improve the navy's antiquated gunnery. Learning that one member of the graduating class, Naval Cadet Emory S. Land, was in sick bay, Roosevelt stopped there after the ceremony and completed the presentations by handing the amazed Land his sheepskin. Naturally, the regiment marched in his inaugural parade.

By a happy chance, the construction of the new academy coincided with the discovery of the remains of John Paul Jones, which were found after a six-year search by General Horace Porter, American ambassador to France, in a cemetery in Paris in April 1905. Clearly, there could be no more fitting place to inter America's first naval hero than in its sparkling new Naval Academy. Theodore Roosevelt dispatched a cruiser squadron to bring Jones back to his adopted homeland. The French government entered into the spirit of the occasion and, following elaborate ceremonies in Paris, a special train transported the hero's coffin to Cherbourg for transfer by a French torpedo boat to the USS *Brooklyn*. Taken ashore at Annapolis on July 22, the body was placed in a temporary mausoleum which had been erected in the yard opposite the new chapel. On April

147

A frequent visitor to the academy during his terms of office, President Theodore Roosevelt presented diplomas to the Class of 1902. Courtesy: U.S. Naval History Division.

President Theodore Roosevelt was the principal speaker at the John Paul Jones Commemoration Ceremony in Dahlgren Hall on April 24, 1906. Jones's casket is directly below the speakers' platform. Courtesy: Library of Congress.

24, 1906, it was moved to Dahlgren Hall for a grand commemoration ceremony at which Roosevelt delivered the principal address.

The ceremony was followed by a prolonged anticlimax. Although Roosevelt had convinced Congress that Jones's final resting-place should be in the crypt of the Naval Academy chapel, the legislators put off appropriating the funds necessary to construct a crypt, and for the next six years the coffin was stored beneath the main staircase in Bancroft Hall. To Commander Robert E. Coontz, commandant of midshipmen 1910-1911, "it seemed a sacrilege to keep the corpse of the great naval hero in so undignified a place for so long a time even though there were many visitors who journeyed to Annapolis to do him honor." Irreverent midshipmen parodied a popular song of the day, "Everybody Works but Father," with the words:

> Everybody works but John Paul Jones!
>   He lies around all day,
> Body pickled in alcohol
>   On a permanent jag, they say.
> Middies stand around him
>   Doing honor to his bones;
> Everybody works in "Crabtown"
>   But John Paul Jones!

Finally, Representative George A. Loud, of Michigan, sponsored the necessary legislation. The result was worth the waiting. A circular crypt, designed in a style reminiscent of the tomb of Napoleon, was built beneath the chapel chancel. In its center stands a magnificent, twenty-one-ton sarcophagus of lustrous green Pyrénées marble, the work of the French sculptor Sylvain Salières. Jones was laid to rest in it on January 26, 1913.

These were exciting times at the academy. Greatly to everyone's delight, on July 1, 1902, Congress passed an act abolishing the term "naval cadet" and reinstated the time-honored title "midshipman." The following year the student body was expanded from four companies to eight and transformed into a brigade. The burgeoning fleet's need for junior officers was so great that the Classes of 1903 through 1906 were graduated in the middle of their first-class year. The Class of 1907 was divided into three sections, the first of which left the academy in September 1906, the second in February 1907, and the third in June. The strength of the following classes, which had entered the academy after the expansion of 1903, allowed them to be graduated on schedule. The final breakthrough came with the act of May 12, 1912, by which Congress eliminated the requirement for midshipmen to perform two years' probationary sea duty and provided for them to receive their commissions as ensigns with their diplomas. A month later, at the end of the graduation ceremonies of the Class of 1912, its members spontaneously hurled their hats into the air. Their jubilant gesture was repeated by succeeding classes and an eruption of white hats has been the climax of every graduation since that day.

The graduating classes of these decades included the men who would lead the navy to victory in World War Two. Foremost among them were Ernest J. King, '01, chief of naval operations 1942-45 and one of the shapers of American global strategy; Chester W. Nimitz, '05, commander in chief of the Pacific Fleet, the mightiest armada in history; dynamic, irrepressible William F. "Bull" Halsey, '04, and clear-thinking, deliberate Raymond A. Spruance, '07, who spearheaded the Central Pacific drive

Steam launches and cutters get under way from the academy's boat basin for fleet drill on the Severn, 1903. Courtesy: U.S. Naval History Division.

against Japan; and aviation pioneer Marc A. Mitscher, '10, commander of their fast carriers.

The backgrounds of these men, though scarcely a representative sampling, provide a cross section of the origins of midshipmen of the era. King and Nimitz came from comparatively humble circumstances. King's father was a foreman in a railroad shop in Cleveland, Ohio. Nimitz was born after his father had died; his stepfather managed a small hotel in Kerrville, Texas. King's interest in the Naval Academy was aroused by an article in *Youth's Companion*. Nimitz decided to apply for admission to West Point after talking to two young army officers who stopped at the Kerrville hotel. Informed by his congressman that no appointments were available at the Military Academy, he accepted the offer of one to the Naval Academy, of which until that moment he had never even heard. Halsey was a navy junior who spent three boyhood years at the academy while his father was an instructor there. His application for appointment was automatic. Spruance's early years were dominated by his mother, the

Left, Naval Cadet Ernest J. King. Courtesy: U.S. Naval History Division.
Right, Midshipman William F. Halsey. Courtesy: U.S. Naval Academy Archives.

strong-willed and intellectual daughter of a wealthy old Baltimore family that lost its money when he was in his teens. His application for the Naval Academy was dictated by financial necessity. Mitscher was the son of a self-made Oklahoman who decided it would be nice to have a boy at Annapolis and exerted his political influence to place one there.

The admirals' academy careers are a study in contrasts. King made the best record. He was one of the lucky plebes who reached the Caribbean during the Spanish-American War, although he missed the Battle of Santiago. A star man in academic standing and a member of the junior varsity football team, the Hustlers, throughout his four years at the academy, in his first-class year he was chosen to command the battalion and graduated number four in a class of sixty-seven. His last year was dangerous, however. Put on report three times for smoking, he narrowly escaped a spell in the *Santee* and invited much more serious trouble by frenching out to visit a girl in Annapolis. On one occasion a friend, learning of an unscheduled inspection at 10:00 p.m., loyally frenched out himself to bring King back on time. A few years later King was assigned to the Executive Department at the academy. At dinner with the midshipmen in Bancroft Hall one evening he was asked if he had ever frenched out. He admitted that he had.

The next question was, "Did you ever get caught?"

"No," King replied, "but I almost did."

"How did you manage not to?" the midshipman persisted.

151

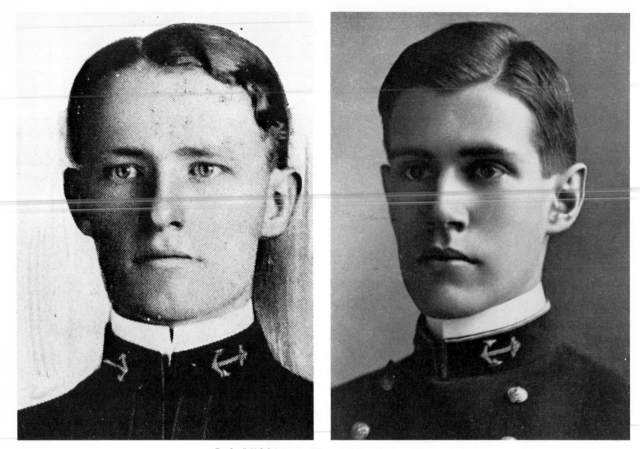

Left, Midshipman Chester W. Nimitz. Courtesy: U.S. Naval History Division. Right, Midshipman Raymond A. Spruance. Courtesy: Naval Historical Collection, Naval War College.

"I am afraid I cannot tell you now," King parried, "but when you graduate, come out to my house and I will give you a drink and tell you how to french out and not be caught."

Halsey, who belonged to the last class to enter the academy less than 100 strong, was the most athletic. A winner of the Thompson Trophy Cup, he was elected president of the Midshipmen's Athletic Association and was the starting fullback on the Navy teams of 1902 and 1903. In later life he liked to say that he was the poorest fullback on the poorest teams Navy ever produced (their two-year record was 8-14). He also took an active part in class activities, serving on the class supper, crest, Christmas card, graduation ball, and cotillion committees. He was less active in the classroom and finished forty-third of sixty-seven, wearing the stripes of Second Battalion adjutant. At graduation, the academy's chief master-at-arms congratulated him with the words, "I wish you all the luck in the world, Mr. Halsey, but you'll never be as good a naval officer as your father!"

Nimitz came to the academy in 1901, the year one of its texts provoked the notorious Sampson-Schley controversy. The book was the third volume of Edgar S. Maclay's *History of the United States Navy*, which covered the Spanish-American War. Maclay charged that Commodore Schley, who with Dewey and Sampson had emerged as one of the war's

Midshipman Marc A. Mitscher. Courtesy: U.S. Naval Academy Archives.

naval heroes, had bungled the search for Cervera and lost his nerve at the Battle of Santiago. The outraged Schley demanded that the work be withdrawn from the academy, which it was. Unfortunately, Schley did not stop there. He also demanded a court of inquiry to investigate his conduct throughout the entire war. This had the effect of polarizing naval opinion into two hostile camps, one of which agreed with Maclay's interpretation and held that Sampson deserved all the credit for Santiago, while the other supported Schley. The court did not help matters by turning in a majority report condemning Schley and a minority report exonerating him. The publicity attracted by this unseemly squabble proved an embarrassment to the navy as a whole, and the episode seems to have left a lasting impression on the minds of the midshipmen of Nimitz's generation. The extreme tact most of them later observed in discussing the command decisions they made as admirals in World War Two proceeded in part from a determination to avoid any more Sampson-Schley controversies.

Like King, Nimitz did well at the academy. A midshipman company commander, he graduated seventh in a class of 114 and pulled stroke on the varsity crew. And like King, he came close to disaster in his first-class year. At its beginning, his class was moved into the completed wing of Bancroft Hall. Nimitz was assigned a room on the third floor, from which he and his friends discovered a way to reach the roof of one of the wings still under construction. There they held moonlight beer parties, dropping their empties to explode with a gratifying crash on the blocks of granite piled below. One day it fell to Nimitz to pick up the beer from the back room of an obliging Maryland Avenue tailor. Also present at the tailor's was a distinguished-looking stranger in civilian clothes. At the next meeting of his navigation class, Nimitz was aghast to find the distinguished stranger at its head, this time in uniform. He was Lieutenant Commander Levi C. Bertolette, '87, who had just joined the academy staff. Certain that he was recognized, Nimitz awaited the summons that might herald his dismissal from the academy. It never came. Although it may have been simply that Bertolette did not place him, Nimitz was convinced that he had decided to give him another chance. Years later, he commented, "This escapade taught me a lesson on how to behave for the remainder of my stay at the academy." Of Nimitz the 1905 *Lucky Bag* noted: "Possesses that calm and steady-going Dutch way that gets to the bottom of things."

Reserved, cerebral Raymond A. Spruance passed through the academy without leaving a wake. His years there were not happy ones. He detested hazing (and refused to haze), loathed drill, and disliked the by-the-numbers system of instruction. It did not cause him any difficulty, however, and he graduated twenty-fifth of 209. His conduct record was equally good. *Lucky Bag* described him as a "shy young thing with a rather sober, earnest face and the innocent disposition of an ingenue. . . . Would never hurt anything or anybody except in the line of duty. . . . A faithful supporter of the lee rail on all summer cruises." His views of the academy were somewhat ambivalent. He left it with a vow never to return, but he acknowledged that it was a "fine place" to train naval officers and to eliminate the unfit.

Marc "Pete" Mitscher had the worst time of it. Never a scholar, he experienced academic difficulties from the day he entered the academy in September 1904. He also had disciplinary problems. In March 1906, three-quarters of the way through his third-class year, he resigned, having accumulated thirty more than the allowable 250 demerits. In addition, he had become involved in the greatest hazing scandal ever to rock the academy.

The trouble began when Mitscher's classmate, Minor Meriwether, Jr., '08, challenged James R. Branch, '07, to a fight. It took place after dinner one evening, the usual time, and was conducted according to the midshipmen's unwritten punctilio, with seconds, a timekeeper, and a referee. Meeting in Room 303 of Bancroft Hall, Meriwether and Branch went twenty-three rounds with three-ounce gloves. After the last blow had been struck, they shook hands and declared themselves satisfied. Branch thanked his seconds, showered, and went to bed. A friend gave him a rubdown and put hot towels on his left eye, which had swollen shut. The next morning he did not respond to efforts to awaken him. He was in a coma. Specialists were summoned from the Johns Hopkins University Medical School; Theodore Roosevelt dispatched the White House physician. It was hopeless. The following day, November 7, 1905, Branch died.

The incident made front-page news across the nation. Charged with manslaughter and two violations of naval regulations, Meriwether was tried by a court-martial presided over by Rear Admiral Francis M. Ramsay, the former superintendent. He was acquitted of manslaughter, but found guilty of "conduct prejudicial to good order," publicly reprimanded by Secretary of the Navy Charles J. Bonaparte, and sentenced to

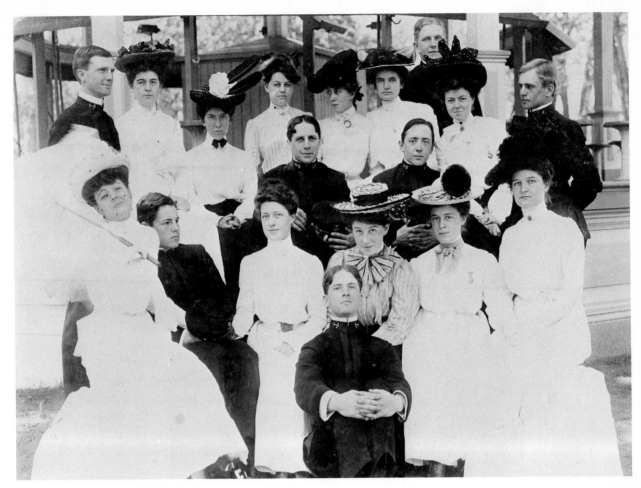

Belles and beaux of the Class of 1905 assemble at the bandstand. Note the meek-looking young man at lower left holding hands with two girls. Courtesy: U.S. Navy.

a year's restriction to the yard. The witnesses' unanimous testimony that it had been a fair fight evidently carried great weight with the court. Considering the seriousness of the case, Meriwether came out remarkably well.

Hardly had this tragedy faded from the headlines than a succession of exhausted plebes began to appear at the academy infirmary in need of medical attention from what was obviously excessive hazing. The ensuing investigation revealed that among the offenders was none other than Minor Meriwether. These disclosures provoked a public sensation. In the Senate, James B. "Champ" Clark, of Missouri, declared that if he appointed any more of his constituents to the academy he would equip them with Bowie knives and hatchets to defend themselves. It made no difference that some degree of hazing was carried out at most colleges; most colleges were not government institutions. The reputation of the academy demanded that firm action be taken, and taken it was. A marathon court-martial dismissed Meriwether and eleven other upper classmen. Theodore Roosevelt, apostle of the strenuous life, intervened with pardons for Meriwether and a first classman, but Meriwether decided to call it quits and resigned. A number of other midshipmen, apparently including Pete Mitscher, submitted their resignations in the shadow of the investigation.

Father Mitscher rose to the occasion. Ordering Pete to remain at Annapolis, he got his friendly congressman to procure a reappointment. It was duly arranged, and in June 1906 Pete Mitscher reentered the Naval Academy as a member of the Class of 1910. This meant that, besides dropping two years behind his contemporaries, he had the mortification of repeating plebe year. That hurt. One of his new classmates recalled that, far from being a class leader, Mitscher "was more like a private in the rear rank. He made aside remarks. He was negative and antisocial. He swore." On several occasions his total of demerits came perilously near the 250 mark. He did not qualify as a midshipman officer and, at graduation, his class standing was 113 of 131. Despite his lacklustre record, the editors of *Lucky Bag* showed remarkable prescience when they summed him up as "a true friend and a man on whom one can depend." How greatly he could be depended upon became evident thirty-four years later, on the evening of the Battle of the Philippine Sea, when he braved the danger of enemy submarines and illuminated the decks of his carriers to guide his weary pilots home.

The academy's last Japanese midshipman, Viscount Kinjiro Matsukata, was admitted in 1906, in which year the deterioration of Japanese-American relations led Congress to enact a law prohibiting the acceptance of students "from any foreign country." Altogether, a total of sixteen Japanese had attended the academy. Seven graduated; seven resigned or were recalled by their government; and two, one of whom was Matsukata, died at the academy. All were members of the nobility or samurai caste, and the majority of the fourteen who returned home enjoyed distinguished careers in the Imperial Japanese Navy.

Of the nongraduates, Sandanari Youchi, '91, who was badly deficient in English but impressed everyone with his technical aptitude, became a rear admiral and superintendent of the Japanese Engineer School. The popular Motohiko Takasaki, '95, designer of his class ring, was recalled to serve in the Sino-Japanese War of 1894-95 and was killed in action in the Russo-Japanese War a decade later. Lieutenant Commander Kagehazu Nire, '91, fell in the same conflict.

Of the graduates, two reached the rank of vice admiral, three became rear admirals, one retired as a captain, and one as a lieutenant commander. The two most fondly remembered by their classmates were Sotokichi Uriu, '81, and Hiroaki Tamura, '00, both later rear admirals. Uriu, who became an ardent Christian during a year at a preparatory school in Connecticut, was elected president of the Naval Academy YMCA. He also became an expert boxer. Assigned as an instructor at the Eta Jima Naval Academy upon his return to Japan, he literally silenced another officer's criticism of his religion by a knock-out punch on the chin. During the Russo-Japanese War, he commanded a cruiser force that destroyed two Russian cruisers off Inchon and subsequently played a leading part in the Japanese victory at Tsushima, one of the greatest naval battles ever fought. He returned to the United States to participate in the unveiling of the chapel doors during June Week 1909, and again when he was vice-president of the Japanese Commission at the Panama-Pacific Exposition of 1915.

Tamura ("Tam" or "Mike" to his classmates) became almost as popular as and even more Americanized than Uriu. He fell in love with the

Sunday afternoon in the yard, in 1905. Courtesy: Library of Congress.

daughter of a prominent Annapolis family and dreamed of becoming an American citizen and an officer in the U.S. Navy. The social conventions of the turn of the century doomed these ideas to remain a dream. Following his Annapolis years, he served in the Russo-Japanese War and World War I, and in 1917 was chosen to bring the remains of American Ambassador George W. Guthrie home from Japan. At the time of his death in January 1945, Tamura was the last of the Japanese midshipmen.

The adverse publicity of hazing scandals notwithstanding, the popular image of the new academy was highly favorable. The midshipman had always been a romantic figure in his own eyes, but now the majority of his countrymen came to share his vision. Between 1898 and 1918, Annapolis acquired its mystique.

The place the academy gained in the American imagination was reflected by a sudden spate of boys' books and stories. Naval subjects had long been a staple of juvenile literature and the first fictional accounts of midshipman life came out in the 1880s; but it was not until after the Spanish-American War that they began to appear in numbers. Captain Edward L. Beach, '88, drew upon his experience of three tours as an instructor and as disciplinary officer to trace Midshipman Robert Drake through the academy at the rate of a volume per year (1907-1910). Captain Richmond P. Hobson, '89, compressed the adventures of *Buck Jones at Annapolis* into a single volume (1907). A prolific professional writer, H. Irving Hancock, adopted Beach's book-a-year format to follow roommates Dave Darin and Dan Dalzell from plebe summer to graduation (1910-1911). As recruiting literature these publications, complemented by countless magazine articles, could hardly have been surpassed. Any boy who put one down without at least a fleeting desire to attend the academy must have been phlegmatic, indeed.

Aside from their often wildly improbable plots, the books presented realistic pictures of a midshipman's life. Their treatments of Annapolis and the academy were accurate, and a number of Captain Beach's characters are real people, easily identifiable in their fictional guise. In *Dave Darin's Second Year at Annapolis*, Hancock gives a good idea of why, regulations notwithstanding, hazing and fighting remained part of the academy scene. Priggish Lieutenant Willow ("one of those officers who are known as duty-mad") starts to report Dave for fighting to the officer-in-charge at Bancroft Hall, sympathetic, understanding Lieutenant Commander Stearns. "But, see here," Stearns interrupts, "if you make an official report, you'll force me to take action, even though it's something I'd secretly slap a midshipman on the shoulder for doing." When Willow informs him unofficially that Dave has thrashed a bully, Stearns decides that the matter should go no further. "My dear fellow, neither you nor I know anything about this fight—officially. The Navy, after all, is a fighting machine. Do you think the Navy can afford to lose a fighting man like that youngster?"

Plebes quickly discovered, in real life no less than in fiction, that they had entered a separate society, with its own laws and language. Their vocabularies expanded to encompass savoirs, red mikes, yard engines, pap sheets, Crabs, greasers, rhinos, drags (outstanding students, woman-haters, the daughters of families living on the academy grounds, bad conduct reports, Annapolitan belles, sycophants, chronic complainers, and young ladies on dates with midshipmen), and innumerable other equally esoteric terms. Among other things, they learned to keep their eyes "in the

Professor Paul J. Dashiell—"Skinny Paul"—played an important part in the development of academy athletics. Here he stands second from left, with his colleagues of the Department of Physics and Chemistry. The department's chairman, Professor Nathaniel M. Terry, seated on the steps, was a world-renowned physicist. The officers are, from left to right, Lieutenant (j.g.) John A. Hoogewerff, '81, Lieutenant Thomas B. Howard, '73, and Lieutenant (j.g.) Joseph W. Oram, '86. All three reached the rank of rear admiral. Courtesy: U.S. Naval Academy Archives.

wrestling, and gymnastics spanned ten years. Joining the academy faculty in 1892, he became one of the mainstays of the school's embryonic athletic program. He was also active on the national scene, officiating at major intercollegiate games and in 1896 taking the initiative in organizing the Football Rules Committee. His three seasons as Navy's head coach were all winning ones: 7-2-1, 10-1-1, and 9-2-1. Despite Dashiell's splendid record, in 1907 the academy decided to adopt the system of graduate coaching and replaced him with Commander Joseph M. Reeves.

Bandmaster Charles Zimmerman composed the music of Navy's famous fight song, "Anchor's Aweigh." Courtesy: U.S. Naval Academy Archives.

Whatever disappointment Dashiell might have felt was dispelled by the affection of the midshipmen, who honored him with the first navy cheer ever dedicated to an individual:

> Rah, rah, rah!
> Proud we feel,
> Our Paul, Skinny Paul,
> Paul Dashiell!

Dashiell remained at the academy as professor of chemistry long after his coaching days were over. Upon his retirement in July 1932, it was estimated that he had taught 13,000 midshipmen.

"Anchor's Aweigh," the academy's fight song, was sung at an Army-Navy game for the first time in 1907. For years it had been the custom for Bandmaster Charles A. Zimmerman to compose a march in honor of each graduating class, which expressed its appreciation by contributing another medal to his highly decorated chest. Most of his efforts were soon forgotten. That dedicated to the Class of 1907 was an exception. Its stirring strains inspired Midshipman Alfred Hart Miles, '07, to write the verses that begin, "Stand Navy down the field/ Sails set to the Sky." The result was "Anchor's Aweigh," one of the world's favorite marches.

At the time the song made its appearance, the future of football itself was in doubt. Since the turn of the century intercollegiate contests had grown increasingly violent. Eighteen players died of injuries in 1905 and the casualty rate remained high throughout the following years. None other than Theodore Roosevelt joined a chorus of national concern over instances of brutality and foul play. In October 1909 Navy quarterback Earl D. Wilson, '11, was carried out of the Villanova game with a broken neck. Only two week afterwards, while Wilson's life hung in the balance, Cadet Eugene Byrne was killed in the Army-Harvard game. He was the fifteenth college player to die in a season that was little more than half over. (Wilson succumbed months later.) Army canceled its remaining games, and anti-football agitation became intense. Fortunately, the rules committee that Paul Dashiell had helped to establish took matters in hand. Such dangerous practices as interlocking interference were abolished. This and various other changes in the rules of play produced a faster, cleaner, safer game.

Academy sports multiplied with almost every passing year. In 1900 Navy fielded four varsity teams: football, baseball, fencing, and crew. Track and small-bore rifle were added in 1904. Basketball became a varsity sport in 1907; tennis in 1909; wrestling in 1910; and swimming in 1911. Lacrosse and soccer were incorporated into the intramural athletic program around the same time, and sailing in the academy's little fleet of knockabouts and catboats was encouraged. Calisthenics ("the Swedish system") was introduced in 1912. By the academic year 1915-16, 452 of 918 midshipmen, almost exactly half the regiment, were training for an intercollegiate sport.

Extracurricular activities also increased. Aside from class committees, at the beginning of the new century there were exactly two approved midshipmen organizations: the choir, established when the school was at Newport, and the Naval Academy chapter of the YMCA, authorized in 1878. A great step forward was taken in 1907, when two traditional areas of midshipman activity were officially sanctioned by the foundation of the Masqueraders, the academy drama club, and the Musical Clubs, an umbrella association that included the Glee Club, an orchestra, a dance band known as the Naval Academy Ten, and a mandolin club. The first edition of *Reef Points*, the brigade's handbook and the plebes' bible, appeared two years earlier. *The Log*, a weekly newspaper that evolved into a monthly humor magazine, commenced publication late in 1913. By then *Lucky Bag* had grown from a modest collection of graduation photographs to a lavish production with art work by such famous illustrators as Howard Chandler Christy and James Montgomery Flagg.

In 1910 the academy took the surprising step of buying a 180-acre farm and establishing its own dairy across the Severn at Greenbury Point. This action followed the discovery by Pay Inspector Samuel Bryan, the academy's commissary officer, that the milk products being obtained from local dairies were of inferior quality. Three years later, the Greenbury Point facility proving inadequate, a 771-acre farm was purchased at Gambrills, ten miles northwest of Annapolis, and the dairy was moved there.

Howard Chandler Christy was one of many famous illustrators who did work for *Lucky Bag*. This watercolor, published in 1900, suggests that there was more than football to "The Army-Navy Game." Courtesy: *Lucky Bag*, 1900.

Its products proved to be more wholesome and less expensive than those available commercially. The midshipmen enjoy them to this day.

The advance of naval technology led to a number of anomalies in the academy's training program. Up-to-the-minute classroom courses in marine engineering alternated with traditional instruction in marlin-spike seamanship. The forty-year-old *Monongahela* made the last single-ship summer cruise in 1900. Later that year she was replaced by the new practice ship authorized in 1897, the steel-hulled square-rigger *Chesapeake*. The midshipmen had become too numerous to be accommodated in a single vessel, however, and in succeeding summers she was only one of a variety of ships constituting the Naval Academy Practice Squadron. Renamed the *Severn* in 1904, she made her final cruise in 1907 but was retained as a drill ship until 1910. The last midshipmen to cruise under sail did so in the sloop *Hartford*, Admiral Farragut's Civil War flagship, in 1909. Thereafter all the academy cruises were made by a squadron of three more or less modern battleships. Exceptions occurred in 1912 and 1913 when, as an experiment, the midshipmen were distributed among the battleships of the Atlantic Fleet, but the results were disappointing and squadron training was revived. The *Missouri, Wiscon-*

The battleship *Texas*, a veteran of the Battle of Santiago, was the flagship of the Naval Academy Practice Squadron during the summer cruises of 1904 and 1905. Courtesy: National Archives.

sin, and *Ohio* made the cr.... .... in the course of it became the first battleships to pass through the Panama Can...

While the midshipmen were still going aloft on the *Severn*, the navy's last sailing ship, they were also going down in the *Holland*, the navy's first submarine. Fifty-four feet in length and shaped rather like a bream, the *Holland* was based at the academy from 1900 until 1905.

Aviation came to Annapolis in the autumn of 1911, when the navy's first aerodrome was established at Greenbury Point. The decision to locate it there was probably determined by the presence of the Engineering Experiment Station (today the Naval Ship Research and Development Center) on the north shore of the Severn, opposite the academy. Naval aviation then consisted of three pilots, all of whom had learned to fly earlier that year, and three exceedingly primitive, pusher-type biplanes. The first of the pilots to arrive was Lieutenant John Rodgers, '03, who bore the designation Naval Aviator No. 2. The first airplane, the Wright-built B-1, was delivered in crates on September 6 and assembled that afternoon. The next day Rodgers took off from Farragut Field, the parade ground behind Bancroft Hall, executed a series of spirals, circles, and turns for the benefit of the spellbound midshipmen,

The USS *Bagley* (TB-24), one of the navy's first torpedo boats, secured at the academy's boat landing, around 1916. The cutter and barge in the foreground were used to train the midshipmen in laying mines. Courtesy: U.S. Naval History Division.

naval forces, they would constitute the mightiest fleet the world had ever seen.

The expansion of the academy program was ably administered by its twenty-fourth superintendent, Captain Edward W. Eberle, '85, a future chief of naval operations. One of the last American naval officers to wear a full beard and pince-nez, he commanded the fore turret of the battleship *Oregon*, "bulldog of the fleet," at the Battle of Santiago and later pioneered the development of destroyer tactics.

The academy opened the academic year 1916-17 with 1,240 midshipmen in attendance, 312 more than the year before. Classes were accelerated to turn out ensigns for the navy's new ships, and the Class of 1917 was graduated on March 29. Less than ten days later, the United States declared war on Germany.

The personnel situation was reminiscent of that at the beginning of the Civil War. If every one of the 4,822 officers the academy had graduated since 1845 had been available for active duty, the wartime fleet would still have had only a fraction of the number it needed. Most of its junior officers would have to come from the reserve force established by the Naval Act of 1916 and the navy's noncommissioned ranks.

In May 1917 Captain Eberle was directed to organize a ten-week crash course for a class of reserve line officers that would report to the academy in July. Around the same time the Class of 1918, scheduled to graduate in September 1917, was horrified to learn that the navy planned to grant temporary regular commissions to 1,000 outstanding warrant officers. Aghast at the prospect of losing 1,000 numbers on the seniority list, its members raised such an outcry that their graduation date was advanced to June 28. The reserve officers had come and gone by the opening of the academic year on September 24, but the program was adjudged so successful that a sixteen-week course was introduced to run throughout the war. The reserve officers were quartered in temporary barracks erected on the tennis courts between Bancroft and Sampson halls, wore khaki uniforms (in contrast to the midshipmen's blues and whites), and had their own company and battalion organization. Several years older than the midshipmen, most of them were business and professional men, and many were graduates of Ivy League schools. Some 2,098 entered the program, 93 per cent of whom successfully completed it. A much smaller number of reserve paymasters, electrical engineers, naval constructors, and aviation intelligence officers took shorter courses at the academy.

At first, there was some friction between the two student bodies. The midshipmen regarded the reservists as "ninety-day wonders" who were usurping their hard-won places on the seniority list, and, as one perceptive midshipman put it, the reserve officers considered them "callous young snobs." These antipathies were never personalized, however, and once the midshipmen realized that the reservists were wartime comrades, not lifelong competitors, relations improved. A member of the Class of 1919 recalled that: "We made some very good friends among them. They were a super blue ribbon bunch and did awfully well in the Fleet."

Meanwhile, the enlargement of the regular academy program continued at a rapid rate. Two new wings for Bancroft Hall were put under construction on July 30, 1917, and completed almost exactly a year later, increasing its capacity to 2,200 midshipmen. A second engineering building, Griffin Hall, was built around the same time. The plebe class of 1917, 744 strong, was nearly as large as the entire regiment had been only eighteen months before; the class that entered in 1918 was even larger, 898 men. By then Congress had provided for an almost 40 per cent increase in the size of the regiment, raising the number of appointments allowed each member of Congress from three to five. The last wartime graduation took place on June 6, 1918, when the 199 members of the Class of 1919 received their diplomas and orders to the European war zone.

The war to end war ended on November 11, 1918. At that date the U.S. Navy had more than 2,000 vessels in commission. They had not been called upon to fight the kind of battles marine painters celebrate on stirring canvases, but they had made a major contribution to the Allied victory. Five of America's newest dreadnoughts were sent to reinforce the British battle line in case the kaiser's fleet should come out for death or glory. Hundreds of wooden subchasers hunted U-boats from the Mediterranean to the North Sea. Perhaps most important of all, the ships of the Cruiser and Transport Force escorted more than 2,000,000 American soldiers to France without losing a single man through enemy action. Less than 8 per cent of the 45,000 officers who contributed to this great war record were academy graduates; but they formed the expert cadre which trained, directed the efforts and, in a very real sense, set the standard for all the others. Park Benjamin had summed it up twenty years earlier: Ex Scientia, Tridens.

CHAPTER EIGHT

Transition and Tradition

The task of bringing the academy back to normal was assigned to Captain Archibald H. Scales, '87, who came from command of one of the American dreadnoughts that had been attached to the British Grand Fleet. At the age of fifty the youngest superintendent since Buchanan, he found it no easy task. In February 1919, when he assumed his new duties, the strength of the regiment stood at 2,250, an increase of 300 per cent over what it had been only three years before. Inevitably, such rapid growth, coupled with the acceleration of the wartime curriculum, had disrupted the regular tenor of academy life. Hazing had taken an unpleasant new twist by the introduction of the custom of paddling plebes with broomsticks. Upper classmen often stood on table tops and literally swung from the ceiling to deliver the blows, which were no laughing matter to plebes ordered to "assume the position" on the receiving end.

These problems were aggravated by the reaction that always follows a major conflict. Rejecting the opportunity to assume world leadership, America was already returning to its traditional isolationism. The capital-ship construction program of 1916, shelved during the war to permit the mass production of destroyers and patrol craft to counter the U-boat threat, was revived; but when President Wilson asked Congress to enlarge it, his request was denied. Later that year his crusade for a new world order was repudiated by the Senate's veto of American entry into the League of Nations. Most of his countrymen felt that they had paid their dues to great causes; their new commitment was to business as usual.

A number of midshipmen who had entered the academy filled with patriotic fervor, including Worth B. Daniels, '22, a son of Secretary of the Navy Daniels, reconsidered their options, and resigned. Their classmates generally suspected their motives for entering in the first place, and Midshipman Daniel V. Gallery, '21, accused young Daniels of being a draft-dodger. Daniels challenged him to a fight, which, to avoid exposing Gallery to a hazing charge, was postponed until Daniels's resignation had been accepted. Only hours after Daniels became a civilian, the two met in Gallery's room, and Gallery knocked Daniels out. When Daniels came to, Gallery withdrew his remark and they shook hands. Somehow the story reached the newspapers and front-page stories reported that the secretary's son had been assaulted by a tough. Fortunately for Gallery, a sympathetic commandant of midshipmen, Captain William H. Standley, ruled that the incident could not be considered a hazing offense, and no action was taken against him.

The Gallery-Daniels fight was followed by the great segregation crisis of 1920. A letter home, in which a plebe described being paddled, sparked still another congressional investigation of hazing and, in October 1920, Superintendent Scales asked the first classmen to sign a pledge that there would be no hazing that year. Upon their refusal to do so, he retaliated by segregating the fourth class. Plebes were quartered on the upper four floors of two wings of Bancroft Hall; the stairs from the lower floors were guarded, and the doors to the other wings were padlocked. In the mess hall they ate in an area that was separated from the other classes by a barricade of tables and chairs. Neither the plebes nor the upper classmen appreciated these arrangements. The latter, feeling that they were being treated like children, resolved to act the part and cultivated an ostentatious enthusiasm for nursery games. "I remember," wrote Rear Admiral Winston P. Folk, '23, "seeing a D.O. [Duty Officer]— the one known as 'Big Hearted Bob'—come upon a group of marble shooting, top spinning midshipmen on the first deck of the third wing. Although he was on duty, all besworded, making a routine inspection, he made no attempt to break it up. He just passed by, shaking his head as if to say, 'Good Lord! What have we come to?'"

The climax was reached with the reading of the Thanksgiving Day liberty order in the mess hall one evening. It was announced that, instead of the routine liberty and dining-out privileges for all classes on Wednesday afternoon and liberty on Thanksgiving Day, the upper classes would have liberty Wednesday afternoon and the plebes on Thanksgiving. The indignant upper classmen raised such a ruckus that the duty officers marched them out of the mess hall twice. Returning for the third time, they sat in absolute silence at their tables. The plebes loyally followed suit. Back in their rooms, the upper classmen continued their protest by hurling the crockery wash basins, pitchers, and slop jars with which the old wings were still equipped out of the windows to shatter in the courtyard below. Scales, recently promoted to rear admiral, was definitely not impressed by these antics, and a few days later the first class capitulated. Its members promised to prevent any acts of hazing which, as they had originally insisted, proved beyond them, and the plebes were integrated into the regiment.

Despite these disorders, the academy gradually returned to normal. The Class of 1920 and the upper half of the Class of 1921 ('21-A), already well advanced in the three-year, wartime program, graduated in June 1919 and June 1920, respectively, but the four-year curriculum was reinstituted for the lower half of the Class of 1921 ('21-B) and succeeding classes. The first construction since the war was initiated by the ground-breaking for a new building for the Department of Seamanship and Navigation (Luce Hall) in April 1919. A high-power radio station and new quarters for the Marine detachment had been built on Greenbury Point during the conflict. The Postgraduate School, closed for the duration of the war, reopened in June 1919 under the direction of Captain Ernest J. King.

A number of Allied leaders visited the academy in the postwar years, the first wave of them appearing in 1920. Among them were Albert I, King of the Belgians, and Edward, Prince of Wales. After reviewing the regiment, the prince spoke to the midshipmen in Smoke Hall and was given a rousing "Four 'N'" Navy cheer. Later visitors included the Allied generalissimo, Marshal Ferdinand Foch, who addressed the midship-

Study hours in Bancroft Hall, around 1920. The midshipman is probably
Leon G. Tyler, '22. Courtesy: U.S. Naval History Division.

men in French, without the benefit of a translator, and the former
commander of the British Grand Fleet, Admiral Lord Beatty, then first
sea lord of the admiralty.

The naval lessons of the world war were among the matters covered in
a comprehensive *History of Sea Power* published in 1920 by two members
of the Department of English and History, Professors W. O. Stevens and
Allan Westcott. The first textbook to trace the workings of sea power from
ancient times to the modern world, it signaled a departure in American
undergraduate education. It also laid the foundation of the academy's
reputation as a center for naval history, a reputation that was to be
enriched in the years to come by the publications of faculty members
such as Charles Lee Lewis, Richard S. West, Jr., E. B. Potter, and others.

The Prince of Wales—later and briefly King Edward VIII—was one of the many distinguished Allied personalities who visited the academy in the immediate postwar years. From left to right: Assistant Secretary of the Navy Franklin D. Roosevelt; Secretary of the Navy Josephus Daniels; the prince; and, far right, Admiral Scales. Courtesy: U.S. Naval Academy Archives.

In July 1921, Admiral Scales was relieved by Rear Admiral Henry B. Wilson, '81. Commander of U.S. naval forces in France during the war, Wilson had just completed a tour as Commander in Chief, Atlantic Fleet, a four-star billet from which he reverted to rear admiral upon coming ashore. An imposing figure, exquisitely tailored and immaculately groomed, he created an indelible impression. Decades later a member of the Class of 1923 recalled: "His oversize cap, worn rakishly over his white hair as he strode briskly through the yard, swinging his cane with aplomb, was a sight to behold. Especially when he would whack that cane on the hood of an automobile for blowing its horn in the yard." Among the midshipmen, who feared and revered him, he was known as Uncle Henry.

Wilson came to the academy at a trying time. At the Washington Naval Conference in November 1921, the United States sacrificed its

Dapper Rear Admiral Henry B. Wilson was one of the academy's most dynamic superintendents. Courtesy: U.S. Naval Academy Archives.

growing lead in naval construction for the purpose of stabilizing the capital-ship strength of the American, British, and Japanese fleets at a tonnage ratio of 5:5:3. Sixty-one battleships and battle cruisers, built and building, almost half of them American, were scrapped and no others were to be laid down for a decade. Wits quipped that Secretary of State Charles E. Hughes, who masterminded the negotiations, had sunk more ships than any admiral who ever lived. The shrunken fleet was left with so great a surplus of line officers that for several years midshipmen were encouraged to resign their commissions on graduation.

Under such circumstances, Admiral Wilson had his work cut out for him. It was to see that, in a period of naval stagnation, the academy continued to progress. His very decided views on how to go about this were reflected in the first official statement of the academy's mission, issued early in his tenure: "To mould the material received into educated gentlemen, thoroughly indoctrinated with honor, uprightness, and

The Carvel Hall hotel, within easy walking distance of the academy, was a favorite rendezvous for midshipmen and officers from the time of its opening, around the turn of the century, through the 1950s. This photograph is a still from the motion picture "The Midshipman," starring Latin lover Ramon Novarro, filmed in Annapolis in 1920. The hotel, originally the home of Maryland Governor William Paca, a signer of the Declaration of Independence, was acquired by a historic trust and restored to its colonial appearance in the 1970s. Courtesy: U.S. Naval Academy Archives.

truth, with practical rather than academic minds, with thorough loyalty to country, [and] with a ground-work of educational fundamentals upon which experience afloat may build the finished Naval Officer. . . . Fullest efficiency under this mission can only be attained if, through humane yet firm and just discipline, the graduates carry into the Service respect and admiration for this academy." This statement provided an apt preamble to perhaps the most significant superintendency since David Porter's.

Wilson believed, as did Porter, that the academy's crucial task was the development of character. "Physical condition, scholastic attainment,

Another scene from "The Midshipman" was filmed inside the rotunda of Bancroft Hall. The flight of steps, center, leads to Memorial Hall. Courtesy: U.S. Naval Academy Archives.

gentlemanly qualities, all have important places," he declared; "but all are superstructures upon an adamant foundation which is character, with truth for the cornerstone." Consistent with this philosophy, he introduced the academy's first course in leadership. To heighten the midshipmen's appreciation of the navy's traditions and achievements, he arranged for the historical treasures previously scattered in various buildings to be collected in Mahan Hall; published a guidebook to the yard; and welcomed a plan to bring the *America* back to the academy, where she remained until 1942, when she was accidentally destroyed while undergoing repairs at a boat yard in Annapolis. Another reminder of days of glory, the Macedonian Monument, a marble replica of the figurehead of the British frigate *Macedonian* captured by Stephen Decatur in the War of 1812, was erected in 1924.

Midshipmen "roll their own" in Smoke Hall in 1922. One of Admiral Wilson's most popular reforms was the extension of smoking privileges to all four classes. Courtesy: U.S. Naval Academy Archives.

Wilson held that coercion was a poor substitute for inspiration. "While the fear of disciplinary action may make a midshipman prudent and industrious," he explained, "it is the hope of reward which leads him to do his best. He will be the more efficient the happier he is in his work." In accordance with this sentiment and to the dismay of many old graduates, he launched a campaign to make the academy "more human, more livable." Midshipmen had not been granted Christmas leave since 1848. Wilson revived it and inaugurated an Easter leave, as well. Liberty privileges for the first class were extended to allow them to go as far afield as Washington and Baltimore. All classes were allowed to smoke, play cards, and subscribe to newspapers. Every midshipman was invited to the superintendent's house at least once a year. Permission was given to organize a Radio Club and the Trident Society, a literary association that began to publish *Trident*, the midshipmen's serious magazine, and yearly calendars. Letters of commendation were awarded annually to

Nothing that had to do with the academy, from its entrance requirements to the appearance of its grounds, escaped Uncle Henry's attention. As a member of his staff put it, "he enjoyed keeping people on their toes." He introduced aptitude testing and took a particular interest in it. Himself a turnback, he had sympathy for bilgers who really tried. Learning that the midshipmen's examination scores were often substantially lower than their daily averages, he commissioned the preparation of a pamphlet entitled "Tactics for Examinations" and abolished the dreaded semiannual and annual comprehensives. He arranged for distinguished public figures to speak to the first class on current affairs, thus inaugurating the Friday night lectures familiar to succeeding generations of first classmen. The civilian faculty, greatly expanded during the war, was thinned out to give the midshipmen more exposure to officer instructors. At the end of 1922, the teaching staff consisted of 121 officers and 97 civilians.

Wilson was also conscious of the importance of public relations. Mass-produced automobiles had made America a nation of tourists. He ensured that those who visited the Naval Academy received a friendly welcome. Dissatisfied with the services of commercial guides, he detailed academy watchmen to take small parties through the yard and provided officer escorts for large groups. To keep the navy informed of the academy's progress, he published and distributed his *Annual Report of the Superintendent, United States Naval Academy* in the form of an illustrated booklet printed by the Naval Academy Press. By actively soliciting parental support "in the administration of the Academy and assistance in the proper guidance of their sons," Wilson sought to change the impression of many parents that they lost sons who entered the academy.

The athletic program, especially the Army-Navy rivalry, enjoyed Wilson's enthusiastic support. When the secretary of the navy launched an investigation of alleged misbehavior by the midshipmen in Philadelphia following the 1922 Army-Navy game, he brought the proceedings to a dead end by declaring that he accepted full responsibility for the conduct of the regiment and had faith in his young men. In 1923, he was proud to report that academy teams had participated in fifteen intercollegiate sports and won the boxing and gymnastic championships. Keenly aware of the publicity value of Navy football, he eagerly accepted an invitation for the academy to play Washington University in the Rose Bowl at Pasadena, California, on New Year's Day 1924. The game ended in a tie, 14-14. A natatorium, later named in honor of Rear Admiral Norman B. Scott, '11, a hero of World War Two, was completed that spring.

The importance Wilson attached to athletics was also signified by the creation of a Department of Physical Training in 1923. Its original members included two of the best-loved men ever associated with academy athletics: Hamilton W. "Spike" Webb and Augustus K. "Doc" Snyder. A veteran of more than one hundred professional fights, Spike was a trainer with the American Expeditionary Force in France in World War One and came to the academy as boxing coach in 1919. Between 1920 and 1941, when boxing was a varsity sport, his teams were among the nation's best; in one eleven-year period they did not lose a single match. Eventually, the level of competition, spurred on by Spike's successes, reached semiprofessional standards, and the resultant risk of serious injury to the participants caused the academy to limit boxing to intra-

"Spike" Webb was one of the most popular coaches in the history of the academy. This photograph dates from the 1930s. Courtesy: Naval Academy Athletic Association.

mural contests. Spike also worked with underprivileged boys in Baltimore. Among his protégés was Walker Smith, better known as Sugar Ray Robinson. When Spike retired in 1954, 200 officers attended his farewell banquet and Admiral Halsey wired: "The Naval Academy will not be the same without you."

Doc Snyder began his military career in the U.S. cavalry in 1903. Following a hitch in the Marines during the occupation of Cuba, he joined the navy and was assigned to the academy as a trainer in 1911. Called away to sea duty in World War One, he returned in 1919 and was engaged as a civilian employee of the Naval Academy Athletic Association after retiring from the navy in 1922. As resident MD (midshipmen's doctor) in Misery Hall, he greeted generations of bruised and battered athletes with a kindly "Well, son, what can I do for you today?" Before his second retirement in 1947 he was made an honorary member of four

First-class ducking was discontinued after a midshipman accidentally drowned.
Courtesy: U.S. Naval Academy Alumni Association.

classes and became the only man besides Paul Dashiell to whom the midshipmen ever dedicated a cheer:

> Iodine, iodine,
> Epsom salts and pills!
> We've got a doctor
> But we don't pay his bills.
> Doc Snyder!

One of the academy's more riotous customs was abolished and one of
its most romantic instituted following a fatal accident that occurred in
May 1924. Traditionally, second classmen put on their class rings for
the first time immediately upon completing their last navigation examination and, as they left the classroom building, were seized by the first
classmen, dragged to Dewey Basin, and tossed into the Severn. In the
excitement of the ducking in 1924 no one noticed that Midshipman
Leicester R. Smith did not come up. Apparently, he had hit his head
on the seawall. To prevent similar tragedies academy authorities introduced the Ring Dance. The highlight of the evening comes when the
second classman and his One and Only approach a gigantic replica of his
class ring. The lady dips his ring in three basins containing water from
the Atlantic, the Pacific and the Caribbean and slips it on his finger as
the couple passes through the huge ring. The ceremony is sealed
with a kiss.

183

Midshipman Arleigh A. Burke. Courtesy: U.S. Naval History Division.

Among Wilson's graduates were two who were destined for greatness: Hyman G. Rickover, '22, the father of the nuclear navy; and Arleigh A. Burke, '23, who served an unprecedented three tours as chief of naval operations, 1955-1961. Neither could have afforded the expense of a private civilian college. Burke was a farm boy from Boulder, Colorado; Rickover, the son of a Polish tailor who brought his family to America when the future admiral was six years old. Asked for his favorite academy anecdote, Admiral Burke replied: "This is not my favorite anecdote, but it is the one I remember most vividly. I won my numerals in wrestling my second class year. Quite naturally I was eager to get them sewed on my sweater just as soon as I could. The seamstress had her shop in the gymnasium right next to the swimming pool dressing room. The only entrance to her shop was from that dressing room. Those were the days when the only swimming pool was the small one in the gym. I took my sweater down with pride and great impatience to get it back as soon as possible. The seamstress assured me I could have it back by ten o'clock the next day but I could not, repeat not, get it before that time. The next day

Midshipmen practice gun drill on the 1925 summer cruise. Courtesy: U.S. Naval Academy Archives.

The onset of the Great Depression was registered by the stock-market crash of October 1929. The year was a good one for the academy, however. Midshipmen won six of the country's twelve Rhodes scholarships. The yellow terra cotta "cup custard" chapel dome, which had begun cracking as early as 1913, was replaced by a new one sheathed in copper; and a permanent boat house, Hubbard Hall, was built on the north shore of College Creek for the Navy crew. It was the first academy building to be named in honor of a living man: Rear Admiral John Hubbard, '70, the stroke on Admiral Porter's crew.

In 1930, the academy was accredited by the Association of American Universities, which entitled it to confer the degree of bachelor of science; nine years later, Congress authorized the degree to be awarded retroactively to all living graduates.

Since the turn of the century, Tecumseh had led a literally moving existence. Carried from his position beside the lyceum into Macdonough Hall during the demolition of the old academy, he was transferred to Dahlgren Hall in 1909, and finally set up outside Bancroft Hall in 1917. There, he resumed his function as "the god of 2.5," to whom formations

A conservative disciplinarian, Rear Admiral Thomas C. Hart proved to be a progressive educator. In this studio portrait he wears the full dress uniform of 1922, which fell into disuse during World War Two and was abolished in 1947. Courtesy: U.S. Naval Academy Archives.

of midshipmen on their way to examinations flipped pennies as offerings for passing grades. In the late twenties it was discovered that, after more than five decades' exposure to wind and weather, the deity was in a state of advanced decay. The Class of 1890 thereupon subscribed the cost of casting a bronze replica, in which fragments of the first Tecumseh were embedded to preserve his medicine. At the beginning of June Week 1930, the bronze bust of Tecumseh was placed on a pedestal facing Bancroft Hall. (The original figurehead, treated with chemical preservatives, is displayed in the Halsey Field House.)

Colonel R. M. Thompson, the academy's greatest private benefactor, died at Ticonderoga, New York, in September 1930. The following year the bleachers at Farragut Field—made from the steel of a battleship scrapped by the Washington Naval Treaty—were named Thompson Stadium in his honor.

The impact of the depression was severely felt at the academy during the administration of Rear Admiral Thomas C. Hart, '97, who succeeded Admiral Robison in 1931. By the end of the following year, industrial production had fallen to roughly half its 1929 level and one out of every four American workers was unemployed. The government responded

according to orthodox economic theory, with an austerity progr`'
eral salaries were cut by 15 per cent. A drastic reduction in th   ;y
budget necessitated the discharge of a number of civilian   ors.
Finally, in the fall of 1932, it was announced that only the to`   of the
Class of 1933 and subsequent classes would be commissioned until the
number of navy line officers, then around 5,700, had been reduced to the
authorized total of 5,449. It was the 1880s all over again, with selection
on the basis of class standing. In the event, 431 midshipmen were graduated in 1933; 13 resigned voluntarily; 41 were found physically dis-
qualified; and 127 were honorably discharged, leaving an even 250 to be
commissioned, 216 of whom entered the navy line. Happily, this de-
moralizing process was not repeated. The Roosevelt administration,
entering office in March 1933, embarked on a program of economic
stimulus. Before many months had passed, it was obvious that, although
hard times still lay ahead, the country was on the road to recovery. In
May 1934 Congress authorized the president to commission that year's
entire graduating class and to offer commissions to the discharged members of the Class of 1933.

Admiral Hart was known, and with good reason, as one of the navy's
strictest disciplinarians. A pleasant, even playful, man in a circle of
friends, in official matters he was as unbending as his high, starched
collars. The Hart touch came through clearly in his first annual report,
when he wrote: "During the past year the conduct and discipline of the
Regiment have been maintained at a satisfactory level at the expense of a
few individuals who could not live up to the standards expected of
them."

Conservative as he was in many respects, Hart had an open mind.
Considerably to the surprise of his contemporaries, during his second
year as superintendent he carried out the most liberal curriculum reform since the foundation of the academy. In 1931 the Board of Visitors
was headed by James Rowland Angell, president of Yale University. As a
member of the 1923 Board of Visitors, he had complained of the limited
time the curriculum allotted to the humanities. Now he expressed the
same criticism in stronger terms, deploring the absence "of any economics,
of any substantial course in government, of any biology, geography, ethics
or social science, or of any of the literature of foreign languages, or of any
of the fine arts which play so large a part in the cultural life of all
peoples." At the same time, he acknowledged that professional subjects
had to take priority in the allocation of classroom time, and confessed
that he had no solution "to the perplexing educational problem thus
disclosed."

Tommy Hart did. A review undertaken on his orders showed that, if
some of the practical instruction in professional courses were eliminated,
it would be possible both to emphasize fundamentals in the sciences and
spend more time on cultural subjects. A Department of Economics and
Government was created to offer second classmen courses in U.S. and
European governments and first classmen courses in economics. The
Department of English and History introduced a course in comparative
literature for second classmen. The result was to increase the proportion
of time devoted to the humanities from 21.6 to 31.6 per cent. These
changes were completed by the beginning of the academic year 1933-34.

Reaction was not long in coming. In June 1934, Admiral Hart was relieved by Rear Admiral David F. Sellers, '94, past Commander in Chief,

189

A double room in Bancroft Hall is ready for inspection, 1939. The radio on the table shows that its occupants are upper classmen; plebes were not allowed to have radios. Courtesy: U.S. Naval Academy Archives.

Midshipmen prepare to shove off from the boat sheds on the Severn for cutter drill in 1939. Courtesy: U.S. Naval Academy Archives.

The graduation ceremony for the Class of 1939, 581 men strong, was held at
Thompson Field on June 1, 1939. Courtesy: U.S. Naval Academy Archives.

U.S. Fleet. While he recognized that "the naval officer's education should
supply that degree of general culture which is the basis of a better understanding of human contact and relationship," Sellers believed that the
expanded cultural coverage of the new curriculum had been achieved at
an unacceptable sacrifice of professional education. "[The Naval Acad-
emy] has one justification for existence," he wrote, "to educate and train
officers to fight the fleet. No matter what may be the result from a standpoint of erudition and culture, if the Academy fails in the one single
particular for which it was created, it has failed to justify its existence.
. . . Any element introduced into the Naval Academy curriculum which
takes its place at the expense of professional training and development
. . . should be excised forthwith." In answer to concerns of the sort expressed by Dr. Angell, Admiral Sellers declared, "I can say without hesitation that in my opinion success or failure in battle with the fleet is in
no way dependent upon a knowledge of biology, geology, ethics, social
science, the literature of foreign languages or the fine arts."

Beginning with the academic year 1935-36, Sellers gradually restored
the hours that had been taken from professional subjects by reducing
those allotted to the humanities. In 1937, the new Department of Economics and Government was merged with English and History to form a
Department of English, History, and Government. The process continued
following Sellers's relief by Rear Admiral Wilson Brown, '02, in February
1938. By the start of the academic year 1938-39 the humanities' share of
the curriculum had been pared to 17.6 per cent. In partial compensation
for the elimination of comparative literature, newly commissioned ensigns
were required to read a title chosen from a list of great books and write a

191

The academy in 1939. In the Santee Basin, right foreground, are the *Reina Mercedes,* left, and the *Cumberland,* which housed many of the enlisted men attached to the academy. The *America* is alongside the pier at Dewey Basin, directly above the *Reina.* Courtesy: U.S. Naval Academy Archives.

1,000-word report on it within eighteen months of graduation. This program was terminated in 1940. Even after the cutback, however, the academy allocated more time to cultural studies than did civilian engineering schools.

The only architectural addition made to the yard during the depression occurred in May 1932, when, on the twenty-fifth anniversary of its graduation, the Class of 1907 presented the academy with the handsome, Indiana limestone piers and wrought-iron grillwork at Gate Three. With the return of prosperity, Admiral Brown was able to obtain the appropriations necessary to undertake the most extensive building program since the completion of the new academy in 1913. Two more wings were added to Bancroft Hall, raising its capacity to 3,100 midshipmen, for whom the mess hall was completely renovated. The chapel was enlarged and, by extending the nave towards the Severn, its form was changed from a Greek to a Latin cross. A new engineering building, Melville Hall, was erected adjacent to Isherwood. The dispensary was moved from the

CHAPTER NINE

Men of Annapolis

The summer cruise of 1938 took the midshipmen to northern Europe. After a liberty call in England, the practice squadron crossed the North Sea to Germany. Five years had passed since the birth of the Third Reich. Austria had been snuffed out that spring; in the meanwhile, Hitler had begun to demand the dismemberment of Czechoslovakia, which was counting on support from Britain and France. For the second time in a generation, Europe trembled on the brink of war. "We went to Germany," wrote the historian of the Class of 1940,

> expecting we hardly knew what. We found, to our surprise, a warm and cordial welcome and a real attempt on the part of everyone we met to insure that we had a good time. Berlin, Cologne, Coblenz, Heidelberg, Hildesheim, Hamburg—all were grand places for seeing sights and for staying too. Whatever we thought of the government, we left Germany with a sincere respect and liking for the German people.

This was the midshipmen's last visit to the New Germany. Britain and France backed down over Czechoslovakia, but when, a little over a year later, Hitler invaded Poland, they finally took a stand. World War Two began on September 1, 1939.

Although most Americans hoped that their country would be able to isolate itself from this new war, as they had hoped it could from the last, the shock of Germany's blitzkrieg victory in France in May and June of 1940 spurred them to prepare for the worst. Defense spending bottomed out in the mid-thirties. The first substantial new naval construction since the Washington Conference was authorized following the expiration of the treaty limitations in 1936. Until the fall of France, however, the pace of American rearmament was slow. It accelerated overnight. Congress approved the first peacetime draft in American history and voted funds to build a two-ocean navy. Simultaneously, President Roosevelt announced that the United States would extend "all aid to Britain short of war."

The Naval Academy went on a wartime schedule in the summer of 1940. The graduation date of the Class of 1941 was advanced to February 1941 and that of Class 1942 to December 1941. A three-year curriculum was designed for the Class of 1943 and its successors. Shifting some of the classroom instruction to the summer months made it possible to provide 88 per cent of the course work contained in the four-year curriculum. Civilian educators and engineers newly commissioned in the Naval Reserve were assigned to the academic departments, releasing regular officers for sea duty. Foreign cruises were canceled and midshipmen became "salty sailors of the Chesapeake," crisscrossing the bay in yard patrol boats and elderly battleships. The number of appointees allowed each member of Congress, reduced to four after World War One, was moved back to five. Plans were also made to revive the reserve officer training program which had proved so successful in the war years. By February 1, 1941, when Admiral Russell Willson, '06, relieved Admiral Brown to become the academy's thirty-second superintendent, war preparations were complete. The first class of college-graduate reserve midshipmen, 696 strong, reported on February 14; 583 were graduated and commissioned ensigns on May 15. Eighty-five per cent of them volunteered and were accepted for immediate active duty.

For some, duty soon became extremely active. In August, President Roosevelt responded to an urgent British request for assistance in escorting convoys. By the end of September the U.S. Navy was fighting an undeclared war with German submarines in the North Atlantic. But it was in the Pacific, where in midsummer the president moved to halt Japanese aggression by imposing an oil embargo, that the flash point was reached.

December 7, 1941, began like any other Sunday at the academy. The regiment attended chapel. Visitors toured the yard. In the afternoon there was a hop in Smoke Hall. It was still under way when word came of the Japanese attack on Pearl Harbor. Armed watchmen escorted the girls out the gates; others collected the sightseers; and small craft put out to scout the waterfront. "That night," recorded a member of the Class of 1943,

> the academy went wild with excitement. Immediately armed security guards were posted to patrol Bancroft's basements and terrace deck. . . . Mates began keeping a running information column on their black boards. Monday found the academy without a single visitor. Only escorted guests, civilian employees bearing identification cards, midshipmen and officers were allowed within the gates. Shortly afterwards, blackout shades were installed in all offices, and opaque shades were put in the windows of the lower three decks. An air raid bulletin was published that designated fire watchers and patrols. It assigned the first and second decks as air raid shelters. Descriptions of all types of incendiary bombs with instructions as to extinguishing them were posted and read to the regiment.

Three days later Germany and Italy honored the terms of their pact with Japan by declaring war on the United States.

Other than increased security measures, the outbreak of war brought little change to the operation of the academy. In most respects, hostilities had been anticipated by a year and a half. On January 31, 1942, Admiral Willson was called to Washington to become chief of staff to the new chief of naval operations, Admiral Ernest J. King. His replacement was Rear Admiral John R. Beardall, '08, a former naval aide to President Roosevelt. Under Beardall's able leadership, the academy ran smoothly throughout the war. Emphasis on the immediately employable ensign was stronger than ever. Professional courses were kept up-to-the-minute and provided with the latest equipment. In addition to instruction in survival techniques and the utilization of a host of innovative training devices, such as antisubmarine warfare attack simulators, heavy emphasis was given to the naval applications of the revolutionary breakthroughs in high-frequency electronics. The fact that many of these courses were

Secretary of the Navy James V. Forrestal presents diplomas to the Class of 1946
in Dahlgren Hall on June 6, 1945. Courtesy: U.S. Naval Academy Archives.

taught by officers fresh from combat duty added to their immediacy. The
athletic program was restructured to assure 100 per cent participation
and a twenty-two-acre playing field was dredged up off Cemetery Point.
Serious consideration was given to expanding the academy grounds by
annexing the campus of St. John's College, but that idea was abandoned.
Altogether, between February 1941 and June 1945, the academy contributed more than 7,500 officers to the fleet: 4,304 regular midshipmen
and 3,319 reservists.

Outside class, life at the academy was not very different than it had
been before the war. Traditional social functions and athletic events
continued to be held, and midshipmen remained irrepressible as ever.
The war waited for them, but it did not weigh on them. They cheered
their football teams to an unbroken series of winning seasons. They found
accommodations for their "drags" in the furnished attics and spare rooms
of quiet old Annapolitan homes ("drag houses") within walking distance
of the academy and raced the clock back to Bancroft Hall. They left the
telltale brick outside the door of the unfortunate adjudged to have
"dragged" the plainest girl. They celebrated Hundredth Night (before
graduation), when all rates were reversed and plebes could have their
way with upper classmen, restrained only by the realization that everything would return to normal in the morning. As firsties, they donated a

dollar apiece to the fund awarded their class anchor man. They listened with keen interest to lieutenant commanders talk tactics, but found VIP lectures on grand strategy a sure cure for insomnia. As a member of the plebe class of 1944 summed it up: "Of course, we read about the war in the newspapers and we expected that we'd be getting into it, but it didn't really worry us. We were eighteen or nineteen years old, and in the final analysis the war wasn't something that concerned us at that moment. We wanted to have a good time while we could."

The sea war to which these young men went was the greatest ever fought. Before the conflict ended, the U.S. Navy had become the most powerful naval force in history. Its contribution to victory was immense. In the Atlantic it worked together with the Royal Navy to defeat Admiral Dönitz's wolf packs. In North Africa, Sicily, Italy, and France, it provided amphibious lift and gunfire support for the largest landings in the annals of warfare. But it was in the Pacific, above all, that the navy demonstrated the meaning of sea power, defeating the might of the Japanese Empire in campaigns conducted across a watery expanse in which the continent of Europe might be misplaced. Nothing could have been more fitting than that the Japanese Instrument of Surrender was signed on the deck of the battleship *Missouri* in Tokyo Bay.

By then the navy had grown to approximately twenty times its prewar size. Barely 5 per cent of its officers were academy graduates. Its victory was a tribute to the tens of thousands of reserve and wartime officers who made up the 95 per cent, without whom the navy could not have waged, much less won, the war at sea. It was also a tribute to the academy's alumni. They comprised the professional nucleus around which the navy's prodigious expansion took place, and they supplied a sense of continuity, commitment, and cohesion that was instrumental in its success.

Not counting midshipmen still at the academy in 1945, members of fifty-four classes (1892, 1894-1946) took part in the war. Six per cent of them were killed in action. The last ten classes to graduate prior to Pearl Harbor, which furnished a high percentage of the destroyer, submarine, and air squadron commanders, averaged twice that figure. The losses of the Classes of 1934, 1935, and 1936 were 12, 14, and 16 per cent, respectively. The pages of the Alumni Association's *Register of Alumni* tell the story: "died 01 Mar '42 loss USS Edsall vicinity of Java enemy action. . . . died 05 June '42 USS Enterprise plane shot down in battle of Midway. . . . lost in USS Wahoo 11 Oct. '43 Japanese area enemy action. . . . missing in action 24 Dec. '43 USS Leary Lant Ocean. . . . died 05 March '45 Iwo Jima Volcano Islands enemy action." Among the dead were two former regimental commanders, Henry M. Mullinnix, '16, and Willis E. Maxson III, '43.

Twenty-seven alumni won the Medal of Honor, all of them in the Pacific, fourteen of them posthumously. The recipients' ranks ranged from rear admiral to lieutenant (junior grade), their classes from 1906 to 1945, their ages from fifty-seven to twenty-three. Typical of their valor were the deeds performed by Lieutenant Richard M. McCool, Jr., '45. Scarcely a year after his graduation, McCool found himself in command of *LCS(L)-122* during the invasion of Okinawa. On June 10, 1945, he assisted in rescuing the survivors of a sinking destroyer that had been rammed by a kamikaze. The following day, McCool's own ship was attacked by two kamikazes. One was shot down, but the other, to quote the

Regulations were relaxed for the riotous celebration of V-J Day, August 14, 1945. Courtesy: U.S. Naval Academy Archives.

citation for McCool's Medal of Honor, "crashed his station in the conning tower and engulfed the immediate area in a mass of flames. Although suffering from shrapnel wounds and painful burns, he rallied his concussion-shocked crew and initiated vigorous firefighting measures and then proceeded to the rescue of several trapped in a blazing compartment, subsequently carrying one man to safety despite the excruciating pain of additional severe burns. Unmindful of all personal danger, he continued his efforts without respite until aid arrived from other ships and he was evacuated. By his stanch leadership, capable direction and indomitable determination throughout the crisis, Lieutenant McCool saved the lives of many who might otherwise have perished and contributed materially to the saving of his ship."

199

A future commander in chief, James Earl Carter, Jr., was among the first classmen written up in *Lucky Bag*, 1947: "During plebe year Jimmy spent a large part of his time learning songs for the first classmen, but the only time he raised his voice after that was to shout, 'Brace up!' or 'Square that cap!' Studies never bothered Jimmy. In fact, the only times he opened his books were when his classmates desired help on problems. This lack of study did not, however, prevent him from standing in the upper part of his class. Jimmy's many friends will remember him for his cheerful disposition and his ability to see the humorous side of any situation." Courtesy: U.S. Naval Academy Archives.

When the cease-fire in the Pacific was announced on August 14, 1945, the academy's disciplinary regulations were relaxed for a riotous V-J Day. In the words of the Class of 1947 historian:

> Six days we waited for the uncertain news to settle down and to hear the official news from the President. Finally, it came, a two-day holiday was declared, and pandemonium broke loose. Tecumseh Court was the site for the first hours of the celebration. The Japanese bell clanged ceaselessly and our god of 2.5 even seemed to smile. Near the end of the noisy rejoicing, time was taken by all, either at the service in the Chapel or in the rooms of Bancroft Hall, to offer a solemn and earnest Thanksgiving.

Not every midshipman was able to share in the fun. Some had the misfortune to be on cruise. Among the latter was a first classman destined to become the only academy alumnus ever to become commander in chief, Jimmy Carter, '47. "We were especially envious of those who were celebrating the victory in Times Square," he recalled.

Upon learning of his assignment to the academy, Holloway immersed himself in two books whose principles became the cornerstones of his superintendency: *On Education*, by Sir Richard Livingstone, president of Corpus Christi College, Oxford; and the Harvard University report on *General Education in a Free Society*. Both emphasized the importance of concentrating on fundamentals in undergraduate education, a concept with which Holloway was in complete accord. Although he favored a fixed curriculum, he recognized that it offered a tempting framework on which to peg "an ever-increasing load of somewhat unrelated yet currently employed techniques of short-range implication." He rejected that temptation, declaring:

> Adherence to fundamentals appears to me particularly appropriate, as the very complexity of the modern Navy in a material and scientific sense demands that we strongly resist the centrifugal forces of detailed specialization at the undergraduate level. This complexity demands that there be established as a foundation basic knowledge and principles in the fundamental sciences, in the . . . humanities and in the basic professional areas. Without this foundation the young officer is totally unequipped to deal with the varied and ever-changing problems he will encounter in a service career of three decades.

In consonance with this philosophy, Holloway promoted a balanced, basic curriculum of mutually supporting courses. Literary work, which had been limited to the first two years, was extended over the full four. Altogether, thirty-nine semester hours, representing 23.4 per cent of the classroom and laboratory time (in contrast to 18.9 per cent at MIT), were devoted to the humanities, languages, and psychology. In response to persons who advocated the addition of advanced professional courses to the curriculum, he was apt to quote Sir Richard Livingstone's dictum: "It is not profitable to study theory without some practical experience of the facts to which it relates." It seems a singularly appropriate coincidence that 1947, Holloway's first year as superintendent, was the year in which the academy was first accredited by the Middle States Association of Colleges and Secondary Schools.

Simultaneously, steps were taken to boost the morale of students and faculty. Adopting a tactic employed by Admiral Henry B. Wilson, under whom he had taught, in October 1947 Holloway published an "Open Letter to the First Class," in which he appealed for its support in the maintenance of high military standards in the brigade. He counterpointed this measure, as had Wilson, by revoking a number of outmoded regulations. First classmen were allowed to own cars. When midshipmen reached the legal age, they were allowed to drink, providing they obeyed an archaic Maryland law prohibiting them from doing so within a seven-mile radius of the State House. The chapel, which had conducted only a Protestant Episcopal service on Sundays, began to hold Catholic services, and an antiphonal choir was established. The practice of marching to class was suspended, but the results were not deemed satisfactory and it was promptly reinstated.

Holloway took a particular interest in the revival of navy sailing, which had suffered an unavoidable eclipse during the war years. With the enthusiastic support of John Nicholas Brown, assistant secretary of the navy for air, and DeCoursey Fales, commodore of the New York Yacht Club, the Naval Academy Yacht Squadron was replaced by the more efficiently organized Naval Academy Sailing Squadron. Among the principal problems the squadron faced was a shortage of maintenance personnel. The academy was authorized only 1,000 enlisted men, including mess stewards—hardly enough to perform routine housekeeping, much less to look after its sailing fleet. Decades earlier, when the academy began acquiring land on the north side of the Severn, the superintendent of the Naval Academy had automatically become commander of the Severn River Naval Command. Acting in the latter capacity, Holloway detached the installation across the river from the academy and constituted a separate support facility, Naval Station, Annapolis, with its own complement of personnel. Maintenance of the academy's boats was among its assigned missions. Holloway's contribution to academy sailing was recognized at the end of his tour, when an overnight, big-boat competition was instituted for the Holloway Cup, a trophy presented to the brigade of midshipmen by a group of private donors headed by DeCoursey Fales.

During the last year of his superintendency, Holloway was again called upon to defend the academy against a plan whose implementation would have destroyed its traditional, time-tested character. Immediately after World War Two there arose a powerful movement, spearheaded by the army, to unify the armed forces under a single command. The navy opposed it, fearful that such a system would be dominated by soldiers and airmen unfamiliar with the navy's missions and unsympathetic to its needs. Most issues of the ensuing unification struggle were settled by the National Security Act of 1947, a compromise in which the fundamental interests of the navy were respected.

The act did not, however, address the possibility of unifying military education, which was privately favored by President Harry S. Truman. This question was taken up in March 1949, when Secretary Forrestal, the first head of the newly established Department of Defense, constituted the Service Academy Board to review the whole subject of basic military education. Better known as the Stearns-Eisenhower Board, it was composed of Dr. Robert L. Stearns, president of the University of Colorado, chairman; General of the Army Dwight D. Eisenhower, president of Columbia University, vice-chairman; four distinguished civilian educators, including a former member of the Holloway Board, James P. Baxter, president of Williams College; Major General Bryant E. Moore, U.S. Army, superintendent of West Point; Major General David M. Schlatter, U.S. Air Force, former deputy commandant of the Air University; and Admiral Holloway.

At the beginning of the board's deliberations, Eisenhower and its civilian members supported the concept of a combined academy for officer candidates, who would later be given specialized training at West Point, Annapolis, or an air force academy—the system Alexander Hamilton had advocated almost 150 years earlier. The three active-duty military members of the board formed a minority, with Holloway as its spokesman, that called for the retention of the established program at the two academies and the immediate foundation of a four-year air force academy. Years later, Holloway recalled:

"Our first meeting was held in the Pentagon, just as Mr. Forrestal was being relieved by Mr. Louis Johnson. The two of them came in and addressed the board and when they left, Ike in his enthusiasm said, 'Yes, we're going to have a common education now and then we'll have an army specialist and an air force specialist and a navy specialist.' I said, 'General, there is no such thing as a navy specialist. The navy is a profound and deeply rooted, traditional profession on its own.' Ike was a man of some temper and he turned red up to his ears; but he could also exercise great self-control, so he just 'hmphed' a little at this rather than pinning my ears back, because I was an exceedingly junior rear admiral and Ike was the hero of the nation."

Despite this grim start, in subsequent sessions Holloway succeeded in gradually swinging the board around to the academies' standpoint. His friend Baxter, the other civilians, and, finally, Eisenhower were converted. The board's preliminary report, submitted in April 1949, recommended that the existing system of military education be retained.

That recommendation was not welcome to Secretary Johnson, who had become the leading proponent of educational unification. In the following months, while the Stearns-Eisenhower Board prepared an elaborate final report, he directed the three service secretaries and the Joint Chiefs of Staff to examine the question, pointedly indicating his own preference. He met a united front of professional opposition. The Joint Chiefs' study was completed in August. Its conclusions anticipated the Stearns-Eisenhower Board's December report, of which the punch line, written by Admiral Holloway, endorsed the academies' "integrity and service identity." Secretary Johnson gave up. For the second time, Holloway had played a vital part in defeating a plan whose provisions ignored the record of a century of success.

Among the members of the Class of 1949 was Wesley A. Brown, the first black American to graduate from the Naval Academy. In the seventy years since Reconstruction, only two other blacks had entered the academy, James Lee Johnson in 1936 and George J. Trivers in 1937, and neither stayed more than a semester. For Brown, attending the academy was the realization of a boyhood dream more durable than its rivals of becoming a policeman, lawyer, or cowboy. An after-school job as a junior clerk in the Navy Department had confirmed his resolve, and in the spring of 1945, he secured an appointment from Congressman Adam Clayton Powell.

Brown described his academy experiences in an article published by *The Saturday Evening Post* shortly after his graduation. Like midshipmen from time immemorial, he found plebe summer hectic. "We had more to do than there were hours in the day," he recalled. "We ran to formation, learned customs and regulations, memorized 'can's and can't's' until our eyes popped. We shot on the rifle range, sailed, rowed, tied knots, practiced semaphore and blinker, and soaked up salt from the seamanship chiefs. We drilled, drilled, drilled until the bottoms of our feet had half-inch calluses." The frustration of stenciling clothing and gear also left a lasting memory: "That sticky black ink and clumsy little stenciling brush made me feel as if I were standing on a giant piece of flypaper with everyone in the world throwing inky sponges at me."

Brown ran into more serious problems at the commencement of the academic year in September, when "a small group of upperclassmen really worked me over," putting him on report at the slightest provocation. The deluge of demerits led him to suspect that this group might be trying to force him out of the academy. Fearful of being dismissed for bad conduct, he began brooding, which only made matters worse. Both his battalion officer and the upper classman assigned as his mentor invited him to come to them if he encountered undue difficulties, but he was reluctant to ask for help. By Christmas his conduct grade was one of the lowest in his class. He was not doing well in his studies, either, "clutching" (academy slang for freezing up) even on easy questions in his anxiety to pass.

Traditionally, midshipmen call the period between the end of Christmas leave and the coming of spring "the dark ages." The worst of Brown's troubles ended with them. His perseverance paid. "After about six months of Plebe Year," he related, "I got oriented, and the novelty of having a black midshipman around was forgotten by the others. Life became more pleasant." He learned to relax at recitations; his conduct grade gradually improved; and he went on to graduate in the top half of his class.

Looking back over his midshipman career, Brown concluded that the academy had given him all he ever wanted: the opportunity to make good on his own. "I was no angel and broke my share of regulations," he wrote. "When I got in hot water I kept reminding myself, *Brown, you're in trouble because you're a dumb cluck and have made a mistake. You're getting the same treatment as your classmates, and that's how it should be.* . . . All through my years at the Naval Academy my instructors treated me impartially. I never received special attention, either positive or negative. It was a lesson in democracy which many institutions could imitate."

In April 1950 Holloway was relieved by Vice Admiral Harry W. Hill, '11, who had distinguished himself as a commander of amphibious assault forces in the war in the Pacific. An active, sports-minded man, known since his midshipman days as "Handsome Harry," at the age of sixty Hill never simply walked up stairs; he sprinted up, two at a time. During football season it was a rare afternoon he could not be found in the bleachers behind Bancroft Hall, watching the team practice. He brought with him to the academy the ship's bell from the World War Two carrier *Enterprise*. Mounted in Tecumseh Court opposite the Japanese Bell, it is rung to celebrate victories over Army in sports other than football.

Early in his tour, Hill introduced the custom of designating Medal of Honor rooms in Bancroft Hall. In 1950 and 1951 bronze memorial plaques were affixed to the doors of the rooms that had been occupied by the academy's seventeen posthumous Medal of Honor winners and dedicated with appropriate ceremonies on the approximate anniversaries of their deeds. Another of Hill's innovations was an "open house" for the parents of fourth classmen at the close of plebe summer 1951. A great success, it was repeated in following years, gradually evolving into Parents' Weekend, one of the major events on the academy's calendar today.

The first sizeable postwar construction was a 17,500-square-foot addition to the midshipmen's mess hall. Completed in 1952, it raised the hall's seating capacity to 4,000. Additional administrative space was gained in 1951, when the Naval Postgraduate School moved to more commodious quarters at Monterey, California. The school's prewar facilities at the academy, ample for a navy with 5,000 line officers, were wholly inadequate to the postwar needs of a navy with 50,000 line officers. Its old classrooms in Halligan Hall became the offices of the academy's pay and personnel sections.

Unlike the two world wars, the Korean conflict did not necessitate a curtailment of the academy's curriculum; the navy's regular intake of ensigns was sufficient to permit graduations to continue on schedule. The

The brigade of midshipmen more than filled the mess hall in 1950. The
facility was enlarged two years later. Courtesy: U.S. Naval Academy Archives.

struggle did, however, give the lie to the unification-era argument that,
with the advent of the strategic bomber, navies belonged to yesterday.
The most brilliant action of the war, General Douglas MacArthur's assault on Inchon in September 1950, was made possible by the navy's
amphibious expertise. Four months later, the navy carried out an equally
dexterous amphibious operation in reverse, extricating 100,000 troops
and almost as many refugees from the jaws of a Chinese Communist
pincer that was closing on the port of Hungnam. Throughout the war,
carrier air strikes and naval bombardment rendered invaluable assistance
to the fighting men ashore. Three academy graduates won the Medal of
Honor in the course of the conflict. One medal went to a navy pilot; the
others, both awarded posthumously, to Marine lieutenants.

Admiral Hill retired in August 1952. His replacement was Vice Admiral C. Turner Joy, '16. Commander, Naval Forces, Far East, at the outbreak of the Korean War, Joy served with distinction in that post during the crucial, opening year of the conflict and was then appointed senior U.S. delegate to the truce talks at Panmunjom. A quiet, soft-spoken man, he was extremely popular with both midshipmen and faculty. Firmly opposed to the detachment of staff members in the course of the academic year, he relented upon learning that one of his department heads had been offered command of a new cruiser, providing he could be released early. "I would never keep anyone from getting a fine command like that," he declared.

Admiral Joy believed that in an undergraduate program "specialization must yield to breadth of coverage and mastery of fundamentals." During a meeting of the Academic Board, the senior professor of the Department of Electrical and Mechanical Engineering presented a proposal for a new engineering course, which was to be fitted into the curriculum by dropping a course taught by the Department of English, History, and Government. The latter's chairman, Captain John F. Davidson, '29, who had studied under the professor, spoke out against it. "In the twenty-four years I've been in the navy," he asserted, "I don't think I've ever had to so much as change a tube in a piece of equipment, much less know what you tried to teach me about what goes on inside them." Joy supported him. "I've never felt so inadequate as I did when I began to negotiate with the Communists," he commented, "because I'd never learned to communicate as effectively as they could." English, History, and Government kept its course.

The curriculum was by no means static, however. Throughout the postwar decade, the accelerating advance of naval-related technology was recognized by the introduction and continual updating of such fields of study as nuclear physics, jet propulsion, and electronics, unknown at the prewar academy. The midshipmen continued to call the subjects into which these new sciences were integrated by the names familiar to past generations: naval engineering was still "steam," electrical engineering still "juice," physics and chemistry still "skinny"; but only the names were unchanged.

Greatly to his surprise, Rear Admiral Walter F. Boone, '21, who had neither served nor requested duty at the academy since his graduation, was appointed superintendent upon Joy's retirement in August 1954. Inheriting the usual postwar slump in the aftermath of the Korean conflict, he worked through the first classmen in an attempt to brush up the military bearing and appearance of the brigade. A serious decline in the number of applicants for appointment, another typical postwar phenomenon, he countered with a multi-faceted publicity program, including the precursor of today's Operation Information, in which selected upper-class volunteers are detailed to speak at schools and youth groups in their home towns. The turning point seemed to be the Sugar Bowl Game at New Orleans on New Year's Day 1955, when a national television audience estimated at 65,000,000 watched Navy defeat the favored University of Mississippi, 21-0. In the following months, virtually every index of navy recruitment and retention, including applications to the academy, showed a significant change for the better. "The after-effects of that game . . . convinced many of us," wrote Boone, "that good Navy athletic teams are good for the Naval Academy and good for the Navy."

The upset victory over Mississippi in the midshipmen's first bowl game in thirty years also signaled the resurgence of Navy football from its postwar nadir. A number of the academy's wartime stars resigned upon the conclusion of peace, with disastrous effects on its gridiron fortunes. In 1945 Navy lost only one game; in 1946 it won only one. Two years later, in 1948, the most dismal season in Navy's history ended with a record of 0-8-1. Things began to change in February 1950, when Edward J. "Eddie" Erdelatz, former line coach of the San Francisco Forty-Niners, was appointed head coach at the academy. It took him two years to lead Navy back into the winners' column, but thereafter its recovery was remarkable. Beginning in 1952, the midshipmen scored seven consecutive winning seasons, achieving a record of 45-14-7, and were consistently rated among the twenty best collegiate teams in the country.

A potential disciplinary problem loomed when the assistant secretary of the navy for personnel, Albert Pratt, began to question the academy's honor concept, delaying a decision on several cases in which the administration recommended dismissing midshipmen for honor offenses. Admiral Boone recalled that, "when I attempted to explain to him the appropriateness of our recommended actions under the honor system, I found that he felt our standards of conduct were too high—that we should make a distinction between little lies and big lies, between petty theft and grand larceny, between small scale cheating and flagrant cheating—and tailor our punishments accordingly, as he indicated the practice to be in some major civilian universities.

"The Commandant, Captain [Robert T.] Keith, to his great credit, suggested a means to overcome this opposition to our honor standards. He proposed that we send a delegation of midshipmen leaders . . . to meet privately with the Assistant Secretary to give him their views. A meeting was arranged. The group of midshipmen I took to Washington consisted of the Brigade Commander, the Chairman of the Midshipmen Honor committee, the President of the three upper classes (the plebe class did not have a president), and a midshipman who had made a special study of the honor system. I carefully avoided any instructions as to what they might tell the Assistant Secretary; on the contrary, I impressed upon them that they should freely express their individual personal views. I introduced the group to the Assistant Secretary in his office and withdrew. When the group emerged about an hour later the Assistant Secretary told me that, to his astonishment, the midshipmen were unanimous in considering that the standards of conduct at the Naval Academy were not too high, if anything not tough enough. They had said that they did not want to serve with any officer who had been guilty of theft, lying or cheating in any degree at the Naval Academy. We had no further trouble in obtaining support . . . for our recommended disciplinary actions."

Upon becoming superintendent, Boone was impressed by the absence, rather than the incidence, of change at the academy in the thirty-four years since his graduation. One change that he found for the worse was that ballroom dancing was no longer being taught. Observing at hops that "with few exceptions the midshipmen were conspicuously inept on the dance floor," he revived mandatory, Sunday-afternoon dancing classes (known to the midshipmen as "tea fights") in Memorial Hall. "But this time," he wrote, "contrary to the practice in my day, we provided girls and plebes did not have to dance with one another. The young ladies

Midshipmen throng the library tables in Mahan Hall. By the beginning of the 1950s the library was serving a student body four times the size of that for which it was designed. Courtesy: U.S. Naval Academy Special Collections, Nimitz Library.

were carefully chosen by a group of matrons in Annapolis. . . . The dancing class immediately became so popular that many plebes who had demonstrated passing ability elected to attend voluntarily, even though a small fee to defray expenses was charged."

Meanwhile, the academy's enrollment had again outgrown its facilities. A master plan for the expansion of its plant was drawn up by a board headed by Rear Admiral J. J. Manning in 1948, but lack of funds had prevented it from being carried out. By the mid-fifties the average strength of the brigade of midshipmen was approaching 4,000, and Bancroft Hall had space for only 3,100. Now almost every room held an extra occupant. Elsewhere in the yard, the situation was even worse. Neither the academic group nor the field house had been enlarged since their completion for a student population of less than 1,000 nearly fifty years before.

The first big breakthrough came in 1954, when Congress approved an appropriation for the construction of a new 158,000-square-foot field house (later named in honor of Admiral Halsey) in the southwestern corner of the yard. Work began in 1955. That same year, a new master development plan, superseding the Manning Board program, was submitted to the Navy Department. Strongly endorsed by the Board of Visitors, it called for the addition of two wings to Bancroft Hall; the expansion of the yard by both landfills and purchases; and the construction of a new auditorium and a major academic building. Another project approved by the board was a football stadium, to be built on the outskirts of Annapolis on ground owned by the Naval Academy Athletic Association. The association had tried unsuccessfully to find the funds to start work several years earlier. Admiral Boone attempted to revive the project but, after sounding out authorities in the Navy Department and civilian friends of the navy, he concluded that the needed support would not be forthcoming.

In March 1956, Boone was promoted to four-star rank, skipping the vice-admiral level, and appointed commander in chief of U.S. naval forces in the Eastern Atlantic and Mediterranean. His successor as superintendent was Rear Admiral William R. Smedberg III, '26, during whose tour the academy's long-delayed expansion finally got under way. Although the development plan was not accepted in its entirety, an appropriation for filling the boat basins and extending Farragut Field was approved for fiscal year 1957. In the event, Santee Basin was retained and extra ground acquired by extending Dewey Field into the Severn. This landfill spelled the end of the *Reina Mercedes*, which was sold for scrap after forty-five years at the academy. The building of the seventh and eighth wings of Bancroft Hall began in 1959. By then, still a third master plan had been prepared.

Admiral Smedberg contributed to the building program by accepting the challenge of raising the money for a football stadium. A total of $3,100,000 was needed, of which the Naval Academy Athletic Association held $1,000,000. The ensuing drive, conducted in concert with the Athletic and Alumni associations, was directed by Captain Eugene B. Fluckey, '35, head of the Department of Electrical and Mechanical Engineering, who won the Medal of Honor for his exploits as skipper of the submarine *Barb* in 1945. His efforts were so successful that work was able to begin in the summer of 1958. Not one cent came from public funds.

During the 1957-58 television season, millions of Americans vicariously visited the academy through the medium of the prime-time series, "Men of Annapolis." An electronic update of the fiction that flourished early in the century, its background footage had actually been filmed in the yard. The pattern of the life it recorded was unchanged in essence since the days when Teddy Roosevelt was handing out diplomas. The midshipmen still marched to class in sections. They marched through the curriculum the same way, regardless of whether they came straight from high school or had completed two years of college. Their only elective was in the choice of a foreign language. Otherwise the lockstep was unbroken. All this, and much more, was soon to change.

expressed in his restatement of the academy's mission, approved by Secretary of the Navy Franke in March 1960:

> To develop midshipmen, morally, mentally, and physically, and to imbue them with the highest ideals of duty, honor, and loyalty in order to provide graduates who are dedicated to a career of naval service and have potential for future development in mind and character to assume the highest responsibilities of command, citizenship and government.

The new curriculum had been decided upon by the time Admiral Melson left the academy in June 1960. It went into effect in September under his successor, Rear Admiral John F. Davidson. A man of great charm, former head of the Department of English, History, and Government, Davidson commanded the submarine *Blackfin* in World War Two. "But," he remarked, "I wasn't one of those people who said they were never scared." On learning of his appointment to the academy, he asked a friend at the Bureau of Personnel how he had come to be chosen. He was told that the members of the selection board had listed the ten officers being considered for the job in order of preference; next, they had made out a similar list of the candidates' wives—"And you and Ann were the only people married to one another." Their judgment was sound and the Davidsons established a warm rapport with the brigade, which christened them "Big Daddy" and "Big Momma" and presented them with white working uniforms so stenciled. Amazed that parades were never rained out and the weather was always in synchronization with seasonal uniform changes, the midshipmen decided "Johnny talks with God," a notion Chaplain James W. Kelly put to verse:

> Now it all started two years ago this summer, you might say—
> When the Class of '64 was forming up to march on the field one day.
> The weather was threatening and the sky was heavy with rain—
> Everyone felt that the parade would be cancelled, but Johnny wasn't in any strain.
> As usual, the car was awaiting at the carriage entrance for him and his Ann—
> He had talked with God and knew that only a coward ever ran. . . .
>
> When they arrived at the canopy section and saw the people with foul-weather gear,
> They wondered why more people didn't talk to God and have less fear.
> And on the field the plebes marched at their best,
> Wondering why the rain had not come so they could have a rest.
> What they didn't know as they went through the parade and stood on the sod—
> Was that Johnny talked with God.
> Every parade came off just as scheduled, until one day—
> Johnny was away from the Academy and there was no one to pray.

Introduction of the new academic program was not the only change over which Davidson presided. Greatly to the dismay of many old graduates, he eliminated the practice of having the midshipmen march to class. With the abolition of the lockstep curriculum, it became altogether impractical. A subcritical nuclear reactor and a computer center were installed in 1960. In April 1961 the first Naval Academy Foreign Affairs Conference (NAFAC) brought 125 students from 50 colleges and universities to join the midshipmen and distinguished guests in discussions of "United States Foreign Policy in Africa and the Near East." Continued

Every midshipman is required to participate in either intramural or varsity athletics. Courtesy: U.S. Naval Academy Public Affairs Office.

on an annual basis, NAFAC soon became one of the most prestigious undergraduate conferences in the country.

The seventh and eighth wings of Bancroft Hall were completed in 1961. The determination of a master plan for the other urgently needed new buildings was still stalled, however. An attempt to reach a decision was made in June 1961 with the appointment of a Special Advisory Commission to the chief of naval personnel, headed by Admiral Ben Moreell, U.S. Navy (Retired). The report the commission submitted in January 1962 offered a comprehensive solution to the academy's needs. It was predicated on the acquisition of the three city blocks between Hanover and King George streets, a recommendation that went back half a century. Twenty-seven acres altogether, this tract offered ample space for the new construction.

While the report was still under consideration in the Navy Department a copy of it was leaked to the Baltimore *Sun*. Its unauthorized publication, before academy officials had conferred with local leaders, created the unhappy impression that the community was to be confronted with a fait accompli. The ensuing outburst of indignation was led by Historic Annapolis, Incorporated, a powerful organization dedicated to safeguarding the city's architectural heritage. Academy spokesmen pointed out that the plan provided for the preservation of the historically significant houses in the area. An informal opinion poll showed that only 6 per cent of the respondents objected to the academy's expansion, but Historic Annapolis refused to be reconciled. The climax came at an emotion-charged town meeting held in the auditorium of Mahan Hall. Admiral Davidson took the podium in an attempt to placate the plan's opponents, and found that he had stepped into a hornets' nest. By the end of the evening it had become evident that local leaders were inflexibly opposed to the project.

The impasse was still unresolved when Davidson's successor, Rear Admiral Charles C. Kirkpatrick, '31, took over on August 18, 1962. A submarine ace in World War Two, Kirkpatrick sank ten Japanese ships in the course of three action-packed patrols before being appointed an aide to Admiral King. A charismatic leader, he made an immediate hit with the midshipmen, who dubbed him "Uncle Charlie."

The expansion plan had by then become a highly political issue. Letters of protest had reached President Kennedy, and Secretary of Defense Robert S. McNamara told Kirkpatrick that, while he supported the academy in the expansion of its existing plant, he would not do so in a struggle with the city of Annapolis. The only thing to do was forget the Moreell report and start anew. Accordingly, in June 1963 the architectural firm of John Carl Warnecke and Associates was retained to develop a master plan. Warnecke told academy authorities he did not see why they had made such a fight for the three blocks; there was plenty of room for the proposed buildings on the grounds they had.

The academic aspects of Kirkpatrick's superintendency were equally eventful. The appointment of an academic dean had been under discussion for some time. Successive superintendents, fearful that a civilian administrator would seek to subordinate the professional portion of the curriculum to purely academic concerns, had steadfastly resisted the idea.

The issue was decided shortly before Admiral Davidson's detachment, when Secretary of the Navy Fred Korth formally directed the superintendent to obtain a civilian educator of national prominence to serve as academic dean. In the same letter the secretary addressed another controversial subject: the academic credentials of the officer instructors. In 1961 the Board of Visitors declared it "educationally imperative" that officers have at least a master's degree; but only 15 per cent did. Korth offered a drastic solution. The officer faculty would be replaced by civilians, unless officers of equal qualifications could be obtained. Determined to preserve the academy's traditional faculty mix, the navy moved swiftly. Between 1963 and 1965 the number of officers with master's degrees was increased to 51 per cent, and the idea of installing a strictly civilian faculty was abandoned.

The search for an academic dean was entrusted to the incoming secretary of the Academic Board, Commander Robert W. McNitt. His choice, from a field of more than seventy candidates, was A. Bernard "Ben" Drought, dean of engineering at Marquette University. "He recognized that Annapolis was the Navy's school," McNitt wrote, "and that his job would be to produce the best possible academic program in response to the policy set by the Superintendent and the Academic Board, with his advice as a valued input. When I asked him how he felt about being a civilian among all the blue suits, he smiled and said that he was used to working with a uniformed service at Marquette, and had even succeeded in persuading the Jesuit fathers to cut out a number of courses in religion in order to strengthen the engineering and humanities offering. Clearly this was our man."

In August 1963 Drought was named academic dean pro tem. His recognition of the navy's needs soon dispelled the officers' apprehensions about the addition of a civilian educator to the academy's administration, and a year later he was confirmed in his post.

The first step towards a minors program, the logical extension of the overload/electives option, was taken in 1963. Although the midshipmen's response to elective offerings was highly gratifying, most of them wound up taking a smorgasbord of unrelated courses. Obviously, it would be preferable to channel their enthusiasm into areas of academic concentration relevant to a naval career. Accordingly, a committee was constituted to examine the possibility of introducing a minors program. Its proposal called for a curriculum consisting of 75 per cent required courses and 25 per cent elective courses (minors), the latter grouped in recognized disciplines. Admiral Kirkpatrick approved, and plans to implement such a program were set in motion. This represented a fundamental change in the academy's educational philosophy: renunciation of the notion that, although he might supplement it, every midshipman had to complete the same, prescribed, four-year curriculum.

Another committee recommended the replacement of the academy's numerical grading system, unchanged since 1850. It found that whereas students at leading civilian engineering schools were awarded 30 to 40 per cent As and Bs, midshipmen were receiving no more than 8 to 10 per cent of the numerical equivalents. Officers interested in postgraduate education were therefore at an undeserved disadvantage. This situation was remedied by the adoption of a letter-grade system similar to that used in civilian colleges. The change was more than administrative. Coupled with a reduction of the traditional emphasis on daily grades, it produced a better-balanced grade distribution and contributed to the growth of a more stimulating classroom atmosphere.

The inauguration of the Trident Scholars program of independent study was Admiral Kirkpatrick's personal inspiration. While visiting Yale, he was intrigued to learn of its Scholars of the House, outstanding seniors who were excused from classes to conduct approved research projects. He returned to Annapolis determined to establish a comparable program at the academy. Because only a very small number of midshipmen would be affected, he was able to do so with a minimum of bureaucratic complications, and the first six Trident Scholars, members of the Class of '64, were designated in the spring of 1963. Successful from the start, the program has produced a staggeringly sophisticated level of undergraduate research.

Kirkpatrick achieved a long-standing academy objective by putting an end to interservice transfers. An agreement made in 1949 allowed up to 25 per cent of the academy's graduating classes to volunteer for the Air Force. In the academy's view, whatever justification there had originally been for this arrangement disappeared with the opening of the Air Force

Halfback Joe Bellino was the first midshipman to win the coveted Heisman Trophy, awarded annually to the outstanding college football player in the the nation. Courtesy: Naval Academy Athletic Association.

Academy in 1955. The program continued in force, however, and each year scores of midshipmen opted for what they conceived to be a glamorous life in Air Force blue. This situation did nothing to promote the development of a sense of professional commitment within the brigade. Kirkpatrick had the matter brought to the personal attention of President Kennedy, who ordered the practice to cease. Thereafter, every midshipman knew that, barring some exceptional circumstance, his choice was between the navy and the Marine Corps. Those with a yearning for the wide, blue yonder could hope to satisfy it in the aviation components of those two services.

Roger Staubach was Navy's second Heisman Trophy winner. Courtesy: Naval Academy Athletic Association.

The late fifties and early sixties were among the most exciting periods in the annals of Navy football. In 1959 Eddie Erdelatz was succeeded as head coach by Wayne Hardin, a fiery, thirty-two-year-old redhead who joined the coaching staff in 1955. During Hardin's six years at the helm, the midshipmen had only one losing season, compiling a record of 38-20-2, and for the first time winning five consecutive Army-Navy games. In 1960 and again in 1963, when Navy was unofficially ranked the number two team in the nation, 9-1 seasons were rewarded by invitations to bowl games. The postseason fates were unkind, however, and Navy lost both:

the Orange Bowl in 1960 to the University of Missouri, 21-14; and the Cotton Bowl in 1963 to the University of Texas, the team that was rated number one, 28-6.

Hardin's squads included the two most famous players ever to take the field for Navy: halfback Joseph M. Bellino, '60, and quarterback Roger T. Staubach, '65. Small for football at 5 feet 9 inches and 185 pounds, Bellino excelled at broken-field running. In the course of his playing career, he set a total of thirteen academy football records, nine of which are still unsurpassed. In his first-class year he was a unanimous choice for the All America team; became the first Navy player to win the Heisman Trophy, presented by the Downtown Athletic Club of New York City to "the outstanding college football player in the nation"; and was the first midshipman in four decades to win both of the academy's top athletic awards—the Naval Academy Athletic Association Sword and the Thompson Trophy Cup—the same year. As a signal honor, at the request of the brigade of midshipmen his No. 27 jersey was retired at the close of the 1959 season. No other player had ever been paid such a tribute.

Five years later, Staubach's No. 12 jersey joined Bellino's in a display case in the Halsey Field House. The greatest Navy quarterback of all time, Staubach was a superlative scrambler whose inspired footwork suggested the sobriquet "Roger the Dodger." In 1963 he was acclaimed by both wire services as the collegiate player of the year. The first midshipman to be awarded the Thompson Trophy three times, like Bellino he was a unanimous choice for All America, a Heisman Trophy winner and, as a first classman, the recipient of the Naval Academy Athletic Association Sword.

But Bellino and Staubach were not only athletes. They were also fine young men. Father Joseph Ryan, the academy's Catholic chaplain, remembered his first meeting with Staubach: "Roger asked me . . . 'What time is daily Mass?' I said 5:30 AM and thought to myself, 'Poor guy! He doesn't know how tough this place is going to be.' But he was there every morning of plebe summer. He never missed many during his four years."

Following graduation, the two men served regular duty assignments: Bellino aboard a minesweeper in the South China Sea, Staubach ashore at a navy supply depot in Vietnam. At the end of their service commitments, they entered professional football. Bellino played three seasons with the Boston Patriots before leaving football to go into business. Staubach became the quarterback of the Dallas Cowboys, leading his team into the Super Bowls of 1971, 1975, 1977, and 1979, and winning two out of the four. Looking back, both Bellino and Staubach consider their decision to attend the academy a wise one. In a recent interview, Bellino said: "It was the perfect place for me to go to school with my abilities and with what I wanted to do in athletics. If I had it to do again, I would select the Naval Academy."

In January 1964 Admiral Kirkpatrick was transferred to the Bureau of Personnel. The Warnecke master development plan was then nearing completion. To maintain continuity of command at this critical juncture, as his successor Kirkpatrick secured the appointment of his commandant of midshipmen, newly promoted Rear Admiral Charles S. Minter, Jr., '37, who had shared in every phase of the planning process. The first commandant of midshipmen ever to move directly into the superintendency, Minter was an open-minded, articulate man. Tall and trim at forty-nine, he had a distinguished record in naval aviation. Now he was determined to see that nothing disrupted the plans for the construction of which, after so many false starts, the academy stood in such need.

The master plan was completed later that year. Its dominant feature was a science and mathematics complex on the riverfront between Bancroft Hall and the academic group. The two buildings (later christened Chauvenet and Michelson halls) contained a combined area of almost 300,000 square feet. Their architecture, though modern in spirit, was designed to harmonize with Flagg's French Renaissance style. The next largest element in the plan, an auditorium, was to be situated between the academic group and the Severn. Other features included a barracks for enlisted men (Ricketts Hall), and the rehabilitation of Mahan, Sampson, and Maury halls.

Painstakingly promoted by Minter, the plan won general acceptance and, in 1965, Congress authorized the construction of Michelson Hall. Although it was later revised in important respects, the academy's first major construction program since the turn of the century was finally under way.

Minter also obtained approval of the plan to introduce a minors program. The academy was authorized to allocate 15 per cent of the curriculum—10 per cent less than proposed—to the program. In practice, this meant that every midshipman would take forty core courses and at least six electives. Every one would have a minor, and students with the energy to earn four elective-course credits could qualify for a major. The program was put into effect in September 1964. It was understood that if it proved successful, the case for a 25 per cent elective offering could be revived.

Several other planned actions were carried out around the same time. The post of dean of admissions was created. The number of companies in the brigade was increased from twenty-four to thirty-six, reducing the strength of each company from 175 to 115 midshipmen. This served both to multiply opportunities for midshipmen to exert leadership and to enable company officers to become better acquainted with their men. Finally, a system was established under which upper-class squad leaders were responsible for the indoctrination and training of the plebes in their squads.

Like the "limited" war in Korea, the Vietnam conflict, in which the United States became involved on a large scale in 1965, did not necessitate the curtailment of the academy's curriculum. The navy performed all of the missions it had in the earlier, essentially conventional struggle, providing air, fire, amphibious, and logistical support for operations ashore. In addition, it became involved in the counterinsurgency effort, organizing riverine forces to control the waterways of South Vietnam and monitoring coastal junk traffic to prevent the infiltration of men and supplies from the north. At the academy there was a rush for Pacific Fleet assignments, as graduating midshipmen competed to go where the action was. One hundred and twenty-two graduates were killed in action, and Captain James B. Stockdale, '47, was awarded the Medal of Honor, the seventy-first bestowed on an alumnus, for heroism while a prisoner-of-war in North Vietnam.

In June 1965, by which time he had spent four and one-half years at the academy, Minter was relieved by Rear Admiral Draper L. Kauffman, '33, who had enjoyed the most exotic career of any superintendent

During the academic year, midshipmen receive seamanship training on board yard patrol boats in the Severn. Courtesy: U.S. Naval Academy Archives.

since Porter. Compelled to resign from the navy at graduation on account of poor eyesight, he went to sea with the United States Lines. At the beginning of World War Two, he joined the American Volunteer Ambulance Corps in France and was captured when the Germans overran the country. Released in August 1940, he obtained a commission as a sublieutenant in the Royal Naval Volunteer Reserve and became a bombdisposal expert, for which work he received a commendation from King George VI. Following America's entry into the war, he resigned to take a commission in the U.S. Naval Reserve, serving with distinction as the leader of an underwater demolition team in the Pacific campaigns. In 1946, thirteen years after his graduation from the academy, he became an officer in the regular navy.

At the time Kauffman became superintendent, there was no question that the "academic revolution," as he called it, was a success. Between 1959 and 1965 the number of courses offered by the academy increased from 40 to 200; by 1968 it had reached 366. During this period recitation grades almost disappeared. Now instructors really instructed. The passing of the recitation system was lamented by those who felt that the responsibility it placed on the individual midshipman was the best possible training for later life, but the new technique was clearly a success in the classroom. In 1965 midshipmen won eleven postgraduate scholarships; in 1966 they won thirty.

The only question was whether the academic revolution had succeeded too well. In meeting with midshipmen, senior officers were disconcerted to note that talk revolved around graduate study rather than duty assignments. Admiral Smedberg had a particularly perplexing experience. Visiting the academy on the last day of spring football practice, he was invited to dine in the midshipmen's mess hall. He expected that the principal topic of conversation would be the day's scrimmage, but the midshipmen never even mentioned it. They discussed their plans for graduate school. Towards the end of the meal, there was a commotion at one end of the hall and a number of midshipmen were hoisted up in their chairs and paraded down the center aisle by cheering classmates. Assuming that the football players were being honored, Smedberg asked his host who they were. The answer was a stunning, "Oh, those are the Trident Scholars, sir."

After a year at the academy Kauffman became convinced that the scales had tipped too far. The balance between education and training had been weighted in favor of the former. To restore it, he launched what he described to the Board of Visitors as a "professional revolution." In February 1967, he established a Professional Training and Education Board to review the training program, and consistent efforts to strengthen it were made throughout the remainder of his tour. The number of professional courses was increased and the midshipmen's performance in them was given heavy emphasis in the determination of class standing. With these measures, the scales began to swing back towards equilibrium.

The midshipmen's increased interest in academic pursuits did not denote any diminution of their sense of fun. In reference to the succession of curricular changes that took place during their four years at the academy, the midshipmen who entered in 1964 called themselves the Class of 1968X—"X" for experimental. When duty officers were away, the labyrinthine passageways of Bancroft Hall became the scene of high jinks similar to those taking place in college dormitories across the nation, as midshipmen doused one another's rooms in water fights and dueled with aerosol cans of shaving lather. But the most celebrated prank of the period occurred out of doors. The folklore of the hall holds that the two antique bronze cannon that face one another across the entrance to Tecumseh Court go off every time a virgin walks between them. Of course, they very seldom go off; but one day a small group of midshipmen decided that they should. The patinaed barrels were secretly loaded with powder charges and Ajax, the foaming cleanser, and wired so that they could be fired from a distance. Zero hour was set for the Saturday noon meal formation, a martial ceremony observed by the usual throng of visitors to the yard. At the moment of truth, a conspirator who had managed to be excused from formation pushed the button. The ancient

Corps, the chapel choir, six foreign-language clubs, a rifle club, several musical groups, and the Brigade Hop Committee. Evening meal formation was at 6:30. Compulsory study hours began at 8:00. Taps was sounded at 11:00 p.m.

A change was occurring in the character of plebe year, however. Since the fifties, the academy's administrations had striven with gradually increasing success to establish a distinction between "plebe indoctrination" and "hazing." Plebe indoctrination was defined as the process by which fourth classmen were initiated into the life of the brigade. Sanctioned by the authorities, it accustomed plebes to conform to a highly demanding code of conduct. Its object was to lay the foundation of military character: self-reliance, respect for authority, the ability to function under pressure, and esprit de corps. Among its specific features were those that required plebes to learn and respect upper-class prerogatives; to know the mess-hall menu, front-page news stories, the number of panes of glass in the skylight of Bancroft Hall (489), and what movies were playing in Annapolis; to "come around" to the rooms of upper classmen who would cause them to repent their misdeeds; and to be able to recite a catechism called "Table Salts," according to which, for example, the response to the question "Why didn't you say sir?" is:

> Sir, sir is a subservient word surviving from the surly days in Old Serbia, when certain serfs, too ignorant to remember their lords' names, yet too servile to blaspheme them, circumvented the situation by serogating the subservient word, sir, by which I now belatedly address a certain senior cirruped, who correctly surmised that I was syrupy enough to say sir after every word I said, sir.

The traditional upper-class rate of requiring a plebe to do calisthenics, the usual conclusion of a "come around" and at one time approved as plebe indoctrination, was limited to ten sets of any given exercise and finally abolished. Thereafter it was considered hazing, that is, the exploitation of upper-class authority to compel plebes to perform actions not sanctioned by the plebe indoctrination system. Though still practiced in the mid-sixties, hazing had begun to take forms that, at least in comparison with past norms, were relatively harmless. A plebe might get it in the end, but the instrument of his chastisement was a rolled magazine or *The Book of Navy Songs*, not a broom. The custom of making plebes into sandwiches—wedging them between mattresses—had almost disappeared. More common were "airplane races," in which they were called upon to dash down a passageway and make a "carrier landing" on a mattress at the end. Other favored sports included "locker races," in which contestants curled up inside their respective footlockers competed to see who could change his uniform the fastest, and a unique form of handball played by raincoat-clad plebes in a shower room with every spout running full blast. Philosophical fourth classmen accepted these diversions as comic relief from the daily routine.

Meanwhile, the academy was taking vigorous steps to correct two situations with which an evaluation team of the Middle States Association of Colleges and Secondary Schools expressed serious dissatisfaction following its accreditation visit to the academy in 1966. Although it had been generous in its praise of the academic progress of recent years, it was sharply critical of the library facilities and the limited role the civilian faculty played in administrative affairs. Rejecting the planned rehabilita-

Vice Admiral James F. Calvert wrote that the academy must preserve the balance between Athens and Sparta. Courtesy: U.S. Naval Academy Archives.

tion of Mahan Hall as inadequate, it called for the construction of a new library with accommodations for at least 650 readers. To provide the professors with a stronger voice in the governance of the academy, it recommended the organization of several standing faculty committees and the appointment of civilians to departmental chairmanships, traditionally restricted to navy captains.

The decision to build a new library, on which the academy's accreditation was made contingent, required a major revision of the master development plan. Entrusted to the Warnecke firm, the revision was ready within a year. Besides the library, it incorporated an imposing new engineering building to replace antiquated Melville and Isherwood halls. They were to be demolished upon the new building's completion, and the projected auditorium erected in their place. With the exception of the demolitions and the auditorium, these works were accomplished within a decade.

The administrative reforms were more quickly effected. An Academic Advisory Board, composed of distinguished educators, business leaders, and naval officers, was constituted in 1966. An Academic Council made up of the superintendent, the academic dean, the assistant dean, department heads, and senior professors, and a Faculty Forum were organized that same year. A Civilian Faculty Affairs Committee, with elected representatives from each department, was instituted soon thereafter. Departmental chairmanships were opened to professors and a pyramid of predominantly civilian committees for curriculum review was established. Taken together, these measures gave the faculty more influence in the administration of the academy than it had had since the Civil War. They ensured that, although the determination of policy still rested, quite properly, with the superintendent, the academicians would be represented in its formulation.

Both the academic and the professional revolutions were carried to completion by Rear Admiral James F. Calvert, '43, who assumed the duties of superintendent on July 20, 1968. At forty-seven the youngest flag officer ever appointed to that position, he received a third star in the course of his tour. A veteran of nine World War Two submarine patrols in the Pacific, in 1959 he commanded the nuclear submarine *Skate* on her historic cruise under the Arctic ice to the North Pole.

Calvert's concept of the academy was basically conservative. Especially in light of the turmoil which the antiwar and youth movements, at their peak at the start of his superintendency, were creating on the nation's campuses, he thought it vital for "the Navy [to] have firm roots in a stable and relatively conservative institution. . . . It is important that [the academy] remain a . . . tradition-oriented influence within the officer corps. There will be no shortage of other influences." The essence of the academy program, as he perceived it, was the inculcation of "a sense of self-confidence, responsibility, purpose, and overall identification with the Navy. . . . All the other things we do could be accomplished somewhere else more cheaply." In discussing the tension between education and training, he often used the metaphor of Athens and Sparta. "The balance between Athens and Sparta must be maintained," he wrote, "but . . . Annapolis became world famous as a training institution that produced effective leaders, not as an educational institution that produced renowned scholars. Both are highly important, both can exist together with benefit, but the Naval Academy will succeed or fail . . . to the degree that it produces professional officers who have the dedication and loyalty to remain with the naval service."

At the same time, Calvert realized that the academy could not afford blindly to resist change. During the transfer of command, Kauffman expressed three concerns. The first was that, despite steps to strengthen it, the professional training program remained weak; the second, that some of the required engineering courses had become so sophisticated that at least one-third of the midshipmen were having difficulty doing more than memorizing their way through exams; the third, that, overall, the midshipmen were performing much better in their minors than in the core curriculum. A fourth problem, common to all the service academies, was a marked decline in the number of applicants for admission and a rise in voluntary resignations. A consequence of the increasingly unpopular war in Vietnam, the trend began with a 10 per cent drop in applications for the Class of 1969 and continued in a steady downward curve.

By the spring of 1969, after more than six months of study, Calvert concluded that the curriculum would have to be completely overhauled. The question, as he phrased it, was "How could we both increase the professional shipboard-oriented programs . . . and, at the same time, pro-

On cruise: a petty officer instructs a group of midshipmen in gunnery. Courtesy: U.S. Naval Academy.

duce academic programs capable of keeping the Naval Academy attractive to the realistic and better-educated youth of today?" His answer was a major cutback in the core curriculum. This made possible the introduction of a majors program, for which the door had been left open in 1963, and a virtual doubling of the hours allocated to professional subjects. Underlying these actions was a subtle but fundamental change in the academy's philosophy. "We had to stop asking, 'What must every Naval Academy graduate be able to bring to the Fleet?' " Calvert wrote, "and start asking, 'What must every Naval Academy class bring to the Fleet?' " Henceforth, instead of attempting to qualify each midshipman for any assignment, the academy would qualify each class for every assignment.

The majors program went into effect in September 1969. Twenty-four majors were offered, ranging from hard sciences to the liberal arts. In addition to their majors requirements, all midshipmen had to complete the expanded professional program, several semesters of science and mathematics, and two semesters each of English and history. Ceilings were

The traditional climax of graduation ceremony: hats in the air. Courtesy:
U.S. Naval Academy Archives.

placed on the number of midshipmen taking different majors to ensure
that the distribution corresponded to the needs of the navy, and the
academic side of the house was reorganized into eighteen departments
grouped in five divisions (Engineering and Weapons, Mathematics and
Science, Naval Command and Management, U.S. and International
Studies, and English and History). In 1971, following the retirement of
Ben Drought, Bruce M. Davidson became the academy's second academic
dean. That same year, the majors' distribution was fixed at 40 per cent
for engineering, 30 per cent for mathematics and the sciences, 20 per
cent for the humanities, and 10 per cent for management.

An intensive recruiting effort was also undertaken. Its success became
startlingly evident in the spring of 1970, when 7,065 young men, almost
1,000 more than had set the existing record in 1962, obtained nomina-
tions for the Class of 1974. The reasons for this sudden reversal, in a year
during which enrollment in the navy's other officer-producing programs
continued to decline, defy analysis; but it seems safe to say that the intro-

233

Michelson Hall, shown here at the time of its completion in 1968, and Chauvenet Hall were the beginning of the academy's first major construction program in more than half a century. Courtesy: U.S. Naval Academy Publications Office.

duction of the majors program was not least among them. In 1971 the strength of the brigade exceeded 4,000 for the first time since 1965. The upward trend continued in the following years, with the number of candidates for each successive class breaking the record set by its predecessor.

Steady progress was made on the building of the new facilities. Chauvenet and Michelson halls were completed in the summer of 1968. The final revision of the master development plan was made around the same time, when the sites for the library and engineering buildings were determined. The rehabilitation of the academic group began in 1969. By then the plans for the new buildings were ready. Congress appropriated funds to begin construction in 1970 and 1971.

Admiral Calvert was detached from the academy in June 1972. The new superintendent was Vice Admiral William P. Mack, '37, who came from command of the Seventh Fleet, off Vietnam. The instructions he received from the chief of naval operations, Admiral Elmo R. Zumwalt, Jr., '43, were ones any officer could envy: "Do what you think is best, and if you do anything radical, tell me." A courteous man with an air of paternal authority, Mack inspired the esteem of both students and faculty. Recalling how remote the superintendents had seemed during his student years, he took care to make himself accessible to midshipmen.

Emphasis on professional training remained strong. To monitor the effectiveness of the program, in December 1972 a professional-readiness examination was introduced for first classmen as a prerequisite for graduation. Another innovation was the development of a four-and-a-half-year "stretch" program designed to give midshipmen in academic difficulties a chance to recover.

A star Navy quarterback of the 1950s, George Welsh was appointed head football coach in 1972. Courtesy: U.S. Naval Academy Publications Office.

In 1974 the constitution of the academy faculty was challenged by the report of the Department of Defense Committee on Excellence in Education. This committee, chaired by Undersecretary of Defense William Clemens, was charged to review the operation of the service academies. It recommended replacing the civilian component of the Annapolis faculty with long-service officer instructors, the system in effect at West Point. Mack firmly upheld the advantages of the traditional faculty mix, with its blend of academic excellence and professional expertise, and the matter was soon forgotten.

In the meantime, Navy football had fallen on lean years. The astronomical salaries being offered by professional football teams to college stars immediately upon their graduation made it difficult for the academy, whose graduates incur a four-year, active-duty obligation, to recruit promising high-school players. Between 1964, Wayne Hardin's last year

Bill XX, a recent link in a long line of Navy goats. Courtesy: Naval Academy Athletic Association.

at the academy, and 1970, the midshipmen had only one winning season (1967) and lost five out of seven Army-Navy games.

Better days began with the appointment of George T. Welsh, '56, as head coach in February 1973. The first academy graduate to hold that position in a quarter-century, Welsh was Navy's starting quarterback for three years in the mid-fifties. He engineered the upset victory over the University of Mississippi in the 1955 Sugar Bowl, and as a first classman he led the nation in both passing and total offensive gains. His relaxed, unassuming personality and disarmingly candid, low-key style presented a refreshing contrast to the calculated flamboyance of many figures in the sports world.

In 1975 Welsh led Navy to its first winning season (7-4) in more than a decade. In recognition of his performance, the New York Football Writers' Association chose him as the East's major college Coach of the Year. Even in losing seasons, however, it was evident to all observers that Navy was playing better football. Four straight victories over Army, 1973-1976, also bolstered Welsh's stature among Navy fans. As he summed up his coaching philosophy: "Football can be simple. If you give the players this life-and-death stuff, you can make them too tight. Winning doesn't override everything. Our approach is to do the best we can."

Rickover Hall, center, was named in honor of the father of the navy's nuclear-power program. Courtesy: U.S. Naval Academy Publications Office.

Gradually, the construction that had long been so much a part of the academy scene came to an end. The library, named in honor of Admiral Nimitz, was opened in September 1973; the engineering building, named in honor of Admiral Rickover, in April 1975. The Robert Crown Sailing Center, home of the Intercollegiate Sailing Hall of Fame, was ready for use in the spring of 1974, and Dahlgren Hall opened as a student union in 1975. The latter two projects were privately funded through the Alumni Association and the Naval Academy Memorial Fund.

Its physical face was not the only aspect of the academy that had undergone dramatic changes since the mid-sixties. A new look had also become apparent in the faculty. The first Marine officers, a mere handful, to be assigned to the staff arrived at the end of World War Two. By 1975 more than forty Marines were serving in positions ranging from instructors to company officers to director of the Division of English and History. Exchange officers from foreign navies also joined the staff. Dr. Samuel P. Massie, Jr., subsequently chairman of the Chemistry Depart-

The Robert Crown Center is the headquarters of academy sailing. Courtesy: U.S. Naval Academy Publications Office.

ment, became the academy's first black professor in 1966. The first woman instructor, Lieutenant Commander Georgia Clark, came aboard in 1972. Other women, civilian as well as military, were added to the teaching staff in following years, and in 1977 Lieutenant Susan H. Stephens gained the distinction of becoming the first woman to serve as a company officer.

Equally important changes took place in the brigade. Hazing was finally eliminated by the efforts of Admiral Calvert and Admiral Mack. Recognizing that the practice would persist, libraries of regulations notwithstanding, so long as it enjoyed the internal sanction of the brigade, they undermined that sanction by persuading the upper classmen that hazing was childish. The institutional stresses of plebe indoctrination were deliberately retained as part of every midshipman's learning experience. Calvert was less successful in defending compulsory chapel attendance, a policy that dated back to the foundation of the academy but was being challenged on constitutional grounds. Despite his eloquent argument for its retention, the courts suddenly found that the custom violated the principle of separation of church and state.

Beginning in 1970, the number of midshipmen who came from minority groups in the population increased rapidly. As of 1965, the brigade included only nine black midshipmen. A minority recruitment program was launched that same year, and between 1970 and 1974 the total minorities' enrollment climbed from 27 to 178. To prevent the racial troubles that were an unhappy feature of the military scene during that period from arising in Bancroft Hall, Admiral Mack instituted a comprehensive human-relations course for midshipmen, "The Junior Officer

Midshipmen on their way to class. Courtesy: U.S. Naval Academy Publications Office.

and the Human Person." There were no incidents, and the program was subsequently adopted by several other commands.

But the most highly publicized, not to say sensational, change took place under Mack's successor, Rear Admiral Kinnaird R. McKee, '51. A nuclear submariner who was promoted vice admiral while superintendent, McKee arrived at the academy in August 1975, in time to direct preparations for the reception of the first female midshipmen. Long regarded as ludicrous, the idea of admitting women to the service academies ceased to be a laughing matter with the rise of the women's liberation movement in the 1960s. The services were unanimously opposed. As late as February 1972, Secretary of the Navy John H. Chafee announced that the academy would not enroll women in the foreseeable future, though they would be welcome in the NROTC. The navy based its stand on Section 6015, Title 10, of the U.S. Code, which prohibited women from being assigned to combat duty or serving in naval vessels other than transports and hospital ships. The academy's argument was that, while there was no doubt that qualified women could complete the program, these provisions would prevent them from participating in at-sea training and from becoming the combat officers the academy existed to produce. These objections were ignored by an amendment to the 1976 Defense Appropriations Bill that authorized the admission of women to all three academies, "consistent with the needs of the services." Approved by congressional voice vote, it was signed into law by President Gerald R. Ford on October 8, 1975.

In the following months, the academy proceeded to get ready for the girls. The first 81, selected from 530 applicants, were sworn into the Class

The academy today. Courtesy: U.S. Naval Academy Publications Office.

The first female midshipmen were admitted to the academy in 1976. Courtesy: Norm Goldberg.

After Color Parade, jubilant first classmen celebrate at the traditional frolic in
the Reflecting Pool behind Mitscher Hall. Courtesy: *The Evening Capital,*
Annapolis.

The Class of 1982 pledges the oath of a midshipman in Tecumseh Court,
July 6, 1978. Courtesy: U.S. Naval Academy Public Affairs Office.

of 1980 in Tecumseh Court on July 9, 1976. The admission of females to
the academies caught the public fancy and the yard was the scene of a
media blitz, as newsmen and television crews converged to cover the
event. Although in general the male members of the brigade looked on
the appearance of female midshipmen with considerable distaste, their
attitude towards the individual female midshipman was one of sympathetic, if sometimes bemused, acceptance.

The administration had decided that apart from adjusting some aspects
of the physical training program on physiological grounds, the girls would
be required to meet the same standards as any other midshipman. They
showed that they expected nothing less, and their conduct soon dispelled many of the more extreme male notions concerning helpless,
hysterical females. At the end of the academic year it was found that the
female midshipmen had about the same attrition rate and slightly higher

grades than their male counterparts. In July 1977, eighty-three girls became members of the Class of 1981.

Never in its long history had the academy experienced a period of such rapid and extensive change as it did in the twenty years between 1958 and 1978. The fixed curriculum, in effect since its foundation, was replaced by elective majors. The number of courses offered increased from 40 to more than 500. An independent studies program was instituted. The civilian faculty regained a voice in the administration. Hazing was eliminated. Minorities achieved significant representation in the brigade, and women were admitted to its ranks.

Inevitably, there were old graduates to whom one or more of these developments was anathema. Some concluded that the academy was going to the devil. Yet, if its history has a message, it is that the academy has been going to the devil since the day it was founded. It was going to the devil when David Dixon Porter decided that it was permissible for midshipmen to have fun; when William T. Sampson emphasized the scientific side of the curriculum; and when Henry B. Wilson began to liberalize rates. But the devil is still waiting and must continue to wait so long as young Americans take the oath:

> I, ..., having been appointed a midshipman in the United States Navy, do solemnly swear (or affirm) that I will support and defend the Constitution of the United States against all enemies, foreign and domestic; that I will bear true faith and allegiance to the same; that I take this obligation freely, without any mental reservation or purpose of evasion; and that I will well and faithfully discharge the duties of the office on which I am about to enter: So help me God.

Appendix

Superintendents of the U.S. Naval Academy

Ranks are those held as of dates of appointment — Assumed command

	Assumed command
Commander Franklin Buchanan	Sept. 3, 1845
Commander George P. Upshur	Mar. 15, 1847
Commander Cornelius K. Stribling	July 1, 1850
Commander Louis M. Goldsborough	Nov. 1, 1853
Captain George S. Blake	Sept. 15, 1857
Rear Admiral David D. Porter	Sept. 9, 1865
Commodore John L. Worden	Dec. 1, 1869
Rear Admiral Christopher R.P. Rodgers	Sept. 22, 1874
Commodore Foxhall A. Parker	July 1, 1878
Rear Admiral George B. Balch	Aug. 2, 1879
Rear Admiral Christopher R.P. Rodgers	June 13, 1881
Captain Francis M. Ramsay	Nov. 14, 1881
Commander William T. Sampson	Sept. 9, 1886
Captain Robert L. Phythian	June 13, 1890
Captain Philip H. Cooper	Nov. 15, 1894
Rear Admiral Frederick V. McNair	July 15, 1898
Commander Richard Wainwright	Mar. 15, 1900
Captain Willard H. Brownson	Nov. 6, 1902
Rear Admiral James H. Sands	July 1, 1905
Captain Charles J. Badger	July 15, 1907
Captain John M. Bowyer	June 10, 1909
Captain John H. Gibbons	May 15, 1911
Captain William F. Fullam	Feb. 7, 1914
Captain Edward W. Eberle	Sept. 20, 1915
Captain Archibald H. Scales	Feb. 12, 1919
Rear Admiral Henry B. Wilson	July 5, 1921
Rear Admiral Louis M. Nulton	Feb. 23, 1925
Rear Admiral Samuel S. Robison	June 16, 1928
Rear Admiral Thomas C. Hart	May 1, 1931
Rear Admiral David F. Sellers	June 18, 1934
Rear Admiral Wilson Brown	Feb. 1, 1938
Rear Admiral Russell Willson	Feb. 1, 1941
Rear Admiral John R. Beardall	Jan. 31, 1942
Vice Admiral Aubrey W. Fitch	Aug. 16, 1945
Rear Admiral James L. Holloway, Jr.	Jan. 15, 1947

Vice Admiral Harry W. Hill	Apr. 28, 1950
Vice Admiral C. Turner Joy	Aug. 4, 1952
Rear Admiral Walter F. Boone	Aug. 12, 1954
Rear Admiral William R. Smedberg III	Mar. 16, 1956
Rear Admiral Charles L. Melson	June 27, 1958
Rear Admiral John F. Davidson	June 22, 1960
Rear Admiral Charles C. Kirkpatrick	Aug. 18, 1962
Rear Admiral Charles S. Minter, Jr.	Jan. 11, 1964
Rear Admiral Draper L. Kauffman	June 12, 1965
Captain Lawrence Heyworth, Jr. (temporary)	June 22, 1968
Rear Admiral James F. Calvert	July 20, 1968
Vice Admiral William P. Mack	June 16, 1972
Rear Admiral Kinnaird R. McKee	Aug. 1, 1975
Rear Admiral William P. Lawrence	Aug. 28, 1978

Notes

CHAPTER ONE

Page No.

3–4   *Somers* mutiny. This account is based on: Harrison Hayford, editor, *The Somers Mutiny Affair*; Frederic F. Van De Water, *The Captain Called It Mutiny*; and Samuel Eliot Morison, *"Old Bruin": Commodore Matthew Calbraith Perry*.

3   a crew of 121. Morison, *"Old Bruin,"* p. 148.

3   "of medium height. . . ." Hayford, p. 25.

4   "a determined attempt. . . ." Park Benjamin, *The United States Naval Academy*, p. 136.

4   "It seemed to be a mania. . . ." Hayford, p. 45.

4   "You can judge. . . ." *Ibid.*, p. 72.

4   "I am no pirate. . . ." *Ibid.*

4   "hearty ones they were." *Ibid.*

5   "catching them young." For a more detailed account of the evolution of the rank of midshipman and training in the Royal Navy, *see* Benjamin, pp. 3–14.

6   Jones's recommendations. Samuel Eliot Morison, *John Paul Jones: A Sailor's Biography*, pp. 334, 431.

6   Hamilton's "fundamental school." Stephen E. Ambrose, *Duty, Honor, Country: A History of West Point*, p. 13.

6   Williams's proposal. James Russell Soley, *Historical Sketch of the United States Naval Academy*, p. 14.

8   chaplains as schoolmasters. *Naval Regulations, 1802*, p. 18.

8   pay and status of schoolmasters. Soley, pp. 11, 26–27.

8   Maury explained. Henry Francis Sturdy, "The Establishment of the Naval School at Annapolis," p. 2.

9   Perry took care. Morison, *"Old Bruin,"* pp. 117–18.

9   lieutenants' examination. Benjamin, pp. 48, 104.

9   Maury chalked problems. *Ibid.*, p. 107.

9   sketch of Southard. Charles Oscar Paullin, *Paullin's History of Naval Administration 1775–1911*, pp. 160, 163.

9   *"Instruction is not less necessary. . . ."* Soley, p. 15.

9   special report of January 1825. *Ibid.*, p. 16.

9   ". . . daily increasing aggravation." *Ibid.*, p. 20.

9   Congressional actions of 1826–27. *Ibid.*, pp. 21–22.

10   "glamor of a naval education." Lt. F.M. Brown, U.S. Air Force, "A Half Century of Frustration: A Study of the Failure of Naval Academy Legislation between 1800 and 1845," p. 633.

10   "ducks in a garret." Benjamin, p. 143.

10   Midshipman Jarvis. *Ibid.*, p. 22.

11 schools established at New York and Norfolk. *Ibid.*, p. 108.

11 Branch's recommendations. *Ibid.*, pp. 108–09.

11 board of 1832. *Ibid.*, p. 112.

11 foundation of a school at Boston. *Ibid.*, pp. 109–10.

11 Maury deplored. Sturdy, "The Establishment of the Naval School," p. 5.

11 *Constitution* and *Vandalia* petitions. Soley, pp. 27–31.

11 Southard's bill. *Ibid.*, pp. 31, 239–40.

11 Paulding echoes its arguments. *Ibid.*, p. 31.

11 organization of the Naval Asylum School. Benjamin, p. 119.

11 "a different order of scientific knowledge. . . ." Soley, p. 30.

12 recommendation of December 1842. *Ibid.*, p. 34.

12 sketch of Chauvenet. "The First Academic Staff," p. 1393; Benjamin, p. 123.

12 Admiral Franklin recalled. Rear Admiral Samuel R. Franklin, *Memories of a Rear Admiral*, p. 89.

12 Chauvenet at the Naval Asylum. Benjamin, p. 124.

13 Chauvenet's project. *Ibid.*, pp. 125–26. Chevalier Thomas G. Ford, "History of the United States Naval Academy," Ch. 20. Unpublished manuscript, 1887.

13 "the first object. . . ." Chauvenet to Ford, October 20, 1860, Ford, Ch. 7, p. 58ff.

13 Chauvenet's project rejected. Benjamin, p. 126; Paullin, p. 206.

13 Chauvenet's achievements at the Asylum School. Benjamin, p. 126.

13 *Vincennes* petition; Commodore Stewart's report. Soley, pp. 36–37.

14–15 sketch of Bancroft. Russel B. Nye, *George Bancroft: Brahmin Rebel*.

14 "I cannot but wonder. . . ." *Ibid.*, p. 54.

15 Bancroft as secretary. Paullin, pp. 207, 208, 239.

15–16 Bancroft's plan to found the academy. Benjamin, pp. 149–51; Sturdy, "The Establishment of the Naval School," pp. 4–5; Ford, Ch. 20; Edward Chauncey Marshall, *History of the Naval Academy*, pp. 25–26, which notes that General Winfield Scott was consulted prior to the transfer. The suggestion sometimes made that Bancroft pulled a fast one on the army is unwarranted.

16 Bancroft to the examining board. Soley, p. 43.

16 the board's reply. *Ibid.*, p. 44.

16 review board constituted. Benjamin, p. 148.

16 Bancroft visits Annapolis. Soley, p. 44.

16 Bancroft to Buchanan. *Ibid.*, pp. 51–54.

17 Transfer of Fort Severn; professors. *Ibid.*, pp. 54–59; Benjamin, pp. 150–51.

17 *Maryland Republican* quotation. Soley, p. 67.

CHAPTER TWO

19 sketch of Buchanan. Charles Lee Lewis, *Admiral Franklin Buchanan: Fearless Man of Action*.

19 "There he stood. . . ." *Ibid.*, p. 69.

19 Buchanan's opening address. James Russell Soley, *Historical Sketch of the United States Naval Academy*, p. 65.

19 "Rules and Regulations." Lewis, p. 104.

19 Lieutenant Ward. "The First Academic Staff," pp. 1392–93; Soley, p. 62n.

20 Passed Midshipman Marcy. "The First Academic Staff," pp. 1402–03.

20–21 Professor Lockwood. *Ibid.*, pp. 1395–97.

21–22 Professor Girault. *Ibid.*, pp. 1397–99.

23 Surgeon Lockwood. *Ibid.*, pp. 1401–02.

23 Chaplain Jones. *Ibid.*, pp. 1399–1400.

23 Surgeon DuBarry on Annapolis. Sturdy, "The Establishment of the Naval School at Annapolis," p. 6.

23 *National Intelligencer* quotation. Soley, p. 66.

23 rents. Sturdy, "The Establishment of the Naval School," p. 6.

23 Maryland General Assembly. Soley, p. 21.

25 description of Fort Severn. *Ibid.*, pp. 115, 123–28.

25–26 conversion of the barracks. Henry Francis Sturdy, "The Founding of the Naval Academy by Bancroft and Buchanan," p. 1370.

26 Brandywine Cottage. Rear Admiral Samuel R. Franklin, *Memories of a Rear Admiral*, p. 91.

26 Apollo Row. Park Benjamin, *The United States Naval Academy*, p. 161.

26 Gas House. *Ibid.*, p. 162.

26 Rowdy Row. Franklin, p. 91.

26 the Abbey; frenching out. Benjamin, p. 162.

26–27 school program. Sturdy, "The Establishment of the Naval School," p. 16.

27 requirements for admission. *Ibid.*, p. 11.

27 things did not work so smoothly. *Ibid.*, p. 16.

27 administration of the school. *Ibid.*, pp. 10–12.

27–28 no military training or organization. Benjamin, pp. 185–86.

28–29 the midshipmen's day; curriculum. *Ibid.*, p. 169; Soley, pp. 67–70.

29 Girault and the Board of Examiners. Benjamin, p. 187.

29 Spirits Club. *Ibid.*, p. 164; Lewis, p. 108.

29 Ballsegurs. Lewis, p. 109.

29 Midshipman Nones dismissed. Sturdy, "The Founding of the Naval Academy," p. 1374.

29 "dissipation is the cause. . . ." *Ibid.*

30 Bancroft's letter. Lewis, p. 108.

30 dismissals effective. Sturdy, "The Founding of the Naval Academy," pp. 1374–75.

30 Buchanan and the academy library. Sturdy, "The Establishment of the Naval School," p. 9.

30 Buchanan to Lockwood. Sturdy, "The Founding of the Naval Academy," p. 1376.

30 "Natural Philosophy is a highly important branch. . . ." *Ibid.*, p. 1377.

30 Buchanan's marriage. Lewis, pp. 74–76.

30 naval ball. *Ibid.*, p. 109; Benjamin, p. 164.

30–31 "Lady of Lyons." Benjamin, p. 164.

31 Mexican War service. Louis H. Bolander, "The Naval Academy in Five Wars," pp. 35–36.

31 Bancroft to Buchanan. Lewis, p. 112.

31 Mexican Monument. Benjamin, pp. 172–73; [Lieutenant Commander Edward P. Lull], *Description and History of the U.S. Naval Academy from its Origin to the Present Time*, p. 63.

31 Bancroft submits the new budget. Soley, pp. 82–83.

31 Bancroft's visit, 1878. Chevalier Thomas G. Ford, "History of the United States Naval Academy," Ch. 22, p. 50.

32 second year of operation. Soley, p. 83.

32 library and lyceum organized. Ford, Ch. 37, p. 14; Captain Harry A. Baldridge, U.S. Navy (Ret.), "Naval Academy Museum: The First Hundred Years," p. 85.

33 Lockwood to his wife. Sturdy, "The Founding of the Naval Academy," p. 1382.

33 second naval ball. Soley, pp. 128–29.

33 Buchanan detached. Lewis, pp. 113–22.

33 *Nautical Magazine* quotation. Soley, pp. 123–24.

35 Upshur's career. James Russell Soley, *Historical Sketch of the United States Naval Academy*, p. 334.

35 Lockwood on Upshur. Sturdy, "The Founding of the Naval Academy," p. 1384.

35 Parker on Upshur. Captain William Harwar Parker, *Recollections of a Naval Officer, 1841–1865*, p. 119.

35 midshipmen ran amok. Park Benjamin, *The United States Naval Academy*, pp. 175–80.

35 Franklin confessed. Rear Admiral Samuel R. Franklin, *Memories of a Rear Admiral*, pp. 93–94.

36 "Word was passed. . . ." *Ibid.*, p. 88.

36 "Raining as it was. . . ." *Ibid.*

36 "I cannot govern you. . . ." Benjamin, p. 180.

36 "Alphabet Song." The full text appears *ibid.*, pp. 175–77.

36 dueling. Franklin, pp. 38–39.

36 rumored duels under Buchanan. Charles Lee Lewis, *Admiral Franklin Buchanan*, p. 109.

36–37 Queen-Stevenson duel. Upshur to Secretary of the Navy John Y. Mason, May 5, 1848, Record Group 45, Naval Academy Letters, National Archives.

36 "What distance?" Benjamin, p. 181.

37 Upshur's report. Upshur to Mason, May 12, 1848, Record Group 45, Naval Academy Letters, National Archives.

37 what really upset him. Upshur to Mason, May 5, 1848, *ibid.*

37 "slanderous reports. . . ." Gardner W. Allen, editor, *The Papers of Francis Gregory Dallas, United States Navy*, p. 108.

37 Dallas hit. *Ibid.*, pp. 30–32.

37 Introduction of military drill. Benjamin, p. 183.

37 brass six-pounders. [Lieutenant Commander Edward P. Lull], *Description and History of the U.S. Naval Academy*, p. 24.

37 midshipman resistance. Benjamin, pp. 182, 185.

37–38 Lockwood hung in effigy; the aftermath. *Ibid.*, p. 182.

38 "haw-haw-haw!" *Ibid.*, p. 185.

38 "wh-why d-don't you. . . ." *Ibid.*, p. 212.

38–39 regulations of 1850. *Ibid.*, pp. 188–90.

40 a military character. *Ibid.*, pp. 194–211.

40 clubs abolished. *Ibid.*, pp. 190–91.

40 Stribling's career. Edward Chauncey Marshall, *History of the Naval Academy*, p. 89.

40 midshipman mischief. Benjamin, pp. 198–99.

40–41 Stribling recalled. Stribling to Ford, 1860, Chevalier Thomas G. Ford, "History of the United States Naval Academy," Ch. 11.

42 practice cruise of 1851. [Lull], p. 15.

42 four-year course established. Soley, pp. 96–97.

42 warrants restricted to graduates. Benjamin, p. 193.

43 construction. *Ibid.*, p. 163; Soley, pp. 129–30; [Lull], p. 61.

45 land purchases of 1847 and 1853. Soley, pp. 117–19.

45 appointments. Ford, Ch. 13–14.

45 "as tall as a sequoia. . . ." Rear Admiral Caspar F. Goodrich, *Rope Yarns from the Old Navy*, p. 30.

45 Franklin recalled. Franklin, p. 143.

45 Goldberry. Ford, Ch. 13, p. 34.

45–46 progress under Goldsborough. Benjamin, p. 204.

45 teaching staff had grown. Ford, Ch. 14, p. 1.

45 first graduation exercise. Thomas O. Selfridge, *Memoirs of Thomas O. Selfridge, Jr., Rear Admiral, USN*, pp. 9–10.

45 Date of 1850 graduations. Soley, p. 101.

45–46 cruises of 1852 and 1853. Benjamin, p. 202.

46 "Proper provision. . . ." Franklin, p. 146.

47 *Plymouth* replaces *Preble*. Benjamin, p. 202.

47 new dormitories. Marshall, pp. 51, 52, 135.

47–48 Matthews's story. Benjamin, p. 201.

47 new construction. Soley, p. 130.

48 Bull Pup. Benjamin, p. 213; Robert Seager II and Doris D. Maguire, editors, *Letters and Papers of Alfred Thayer Mahan*, I, p. 63.

48 guns disassembled. Alfred Thayer Mahan, *From Sail to Steam*, pp. 64–65.

49 superintendent's fence disappeared. Benjamin, pp. 212–13.

49 "A general good-humored tolerance. . . ." Mahan, p. 56.

49 brusque brush-offs. Benjamin, p. 203.

49 versified address. Mahan, pp. 59–60.

50 "Mr. McThorne went. . . ." Goldsborough to Dobbin, November 14, 1853, Record Group 45, Naval Academy Letters, National Archives.

50 "hazing not practiced. . . ." Mahan, p. 54.

51 "I liked things to happen. . . ." Admiral of the Navy George Dewey, *Autobiography*, p. 5.

51 "Fistic arbitration. . . ." Dewey, p. 19.

51 Dewey's academic record. *Ibid.*, p. 14.

51 "one endless grind. . . ." *Ibid.*, p. 17.

51 his memory rankled. *Ibid.*, pp. 17–19.

51 "The things we knew. . . ." *Ibid.*, p. 21.

51 "I think now. . . ." Mahan, p. xiv.

52 Mahan's classmates. Seager and Maguire, I, p. 3.

52 romantic novels. *Ibid.*, p. 14.

52 "Life at sea. . . ." *Ibid.*, p. 4.

52 Nannie Craven. *Ibid.*, pp. 20–21; Captain W.D. Puleston, *Mahan*, p. 21.

52 classmates outraged. Seager and Maguire, I, pp. 11–13.

52 Mahan in Coventry. *Ibid.*, p. 82.

52 Mahan's recollections. Mahan, pp. 84–85.

53 "The Academy constituted. . . ." *Ibid.*, p. 84.

53 Board of Visitors' report. Marshall, p. 37.

CHAPTER FOUR

55 Blake's career. James Russell Soley, *Historical Sketch of the United States Naval Academy*, p. 108n; Park Benjamin, *The United States Naval Academy*, p. 218.

55 "I can lay my hand. . . ." Rear Admiral Charles E. Clark, *My Fifty Years in the Navy*, p. 14.

55 letters. Benjamin, p. 258.

55 Craven and summer cruise. *Ibid.*, pp. 219–20.

55 Craven's report. Edward Chauncey Marshall, *History of the Naval Academy*, pp. 42–43.

55 alcohol and tobacco. Lieutenant Charles M. Todorich, USN, "The Naval Academy in the Pre-Civil War Era: 1845–61," pp. 15, 18.

55 Lawrence Literary Society. Marshall, p. 85.

56 Foote beats Lockwood's maid. Todorich, p. 17.

56 Foote tarred and feathered. Edgar S. Maclay, editor, *The Life and Adventures of Jack Philip, Rear Admiral, USN*, p. 28.

56 vigilantes dismissed. Robert Seager II and Doris D. Maguire, *Letters and Papers of Alfred Thayer Mahan*, I, p. 72n.

56 faculty in 1859. Benjamin, pp. 473–75.

56 Parker on Chauvenet. Captain William Harwar Parker, *Recollections of a Naval Officer, 1841–1865*, p. 121.

56 Chauvenet's subsequent career. Soley, pp. 102–03n.

57 *Plymouth* and *Constitution. Ibid.,* pp. 102–03; Benjamin, p. 221.

57 "must, undoubtedly, exercise. . . ." Marshall, p. 39.

57 student body in October 1860. Benjamin, p. 226.

57 construction. Soley, p. 130; [Lieutenant Commander Edward P. Lull], *Description and History of the U.S. Naval Academy,* p. 61.

57 Japanese Bell. Soley, p. 222.

57 Herndon Monument. Chevalier Thomas G. Ford, "History of the United States Naval Academy," Ch. 15; Commander Leland P. Lovette, *School of the Sea: The Annapolis Tradition in American Life,* pp. 355–56.

57 Tripoli Monument. Dody W. Smith, "The Tripoli Monument."

57 Chesterfield of the Navy. Richard S. West, Jr., "The Superintendents of the Naval Academy," p. 61.

57 "embodiment of dignity. . . ." James Morris Morgan, *Recollections of a Rebel Reefer,* p. 23.

57 a sort of aristocracy. Benjamin, p. 219.

57–58 academic stars. Ford, Ch. 15, p. 5.

58 Clark recalled. Clark, p. 23.

59 "Go on, gentlemen." Benjamin, p. 228.

59 "There goes Foxhall. . . ." Clark, p. 18.

59 Davidson and Wood. *Ibid.*

59 Evans and his mother. Robley D. Evans, *A Sailor's Log: Recollections of Forty Years of Naval Life,* pp. 46–47.

59 practice battery dismounted. Clark, pp. 27–28.

59–60 "many of whom are little boys. . . ." Benjamin, p. 229.

60 Blake's plan. Soley, p. 104.

60 Parker spoke for them. Parker, p. 202.

60 Welles to Blake. Benjamin, p. 230.

60–61 rumored attack. *Ibid.*

61 Blake and Butler. Benjamin F. Butler, *Butler's Book: Autobiography and Personal Reminiscences of Major-General Benj. F. Butler,* p. 192.

61 *Constitution* grounded. Benjamin, p. 232.

61–62 Hicks's protest; the landing. Butler, pp. 195–99.

62 regiments in the yard; Lockwood's drill. Benjamin, pp. 232–33.

62 Blake writes Welles. Soley, p. 106.

62 midshipmen ordered to assemble; peace pipe. Benjamin, pp. 233–34.

63 "The wharf was crowded. . . ." Clark, pp. 34–35.

63 "Never mind!" *Ibid.,* p. 34.

63 arrival at Newport. Soley, p. 107.

63 vessels in commission. E.B. Potter and Fleet Admiral Chester W. Nimitz, editors, *Sea Power: A Naval History,* p. 250.

63 volunteers commissioned. Charles Oscar Paullin, *Paullin's History of Naval Administration, 1775–1911,* p. 299.

63 Classes of 1861–63 detached. Soley, p. 107; Marshall, p. 47.

63 Rodgers's protest. Benjamin, p. 237.

63 Fort Adams. Soley, p. 107; Marshall, p. 47.

63 Class of 1865. Marshall, p. 48.

63–64 Atlantic House. *Ibid.,* p. 47; Soley, p. 108; Benjamin, pp. 239–40.

64 *Constitution* at Goat Island. Benjamin, p. 240.

64 *Santee. Ibid.,* p. 241; Captain W.D. Puleston, USN, *Annapolis: Gangway to the Quarterdeck,* pp. 80–81.

64 "Nothing could have been more desolate. . . ." Benjamin, pp. 241–42.

65 Goodrich recalled. Rear Admiral Caspar F. Goodrich, *Rope Yarns from the Old Navy,* p. 9.

65 Annapolis a center of activity. P.H. Magruder, "The U.S. Naval Academy and Annapolis during the Civil War 1861–1865," pp. 69–72.

66 Burnside expedition. *Ibid.,* p. 69.

66 Welles asks War Department; Early's raid. *Ibid.,* p. 72; cf; Louis H. Bolander, "Civil War Annapolis."

66 academy at Newport. Benjamin, pp. 242–43, 255.

67 Midshipman Welles thrown overboard. Ford, Ch. 20, notes.

67 only 1,000 books unpacked. Marshall, p. 52.

67 Sigsbee recalled. West, "The Superintendents of the Naval Academy," p. 61.

67 Captain Goodenough's diary. Louis H. Bolander, "The Naval Academy in Five Wars," p. 40.

67 full-fledged midshipmen. Benjamin, pp. 250, 256–57.

67 "Our lads did not falter. . . ." *Ibid.,* p. 237.

68 1862 cruise. *Ibid.,* p. 247.

69 "the universal admiration. . . ." Caspar Goodrich, quoted in Rear Admiral Albert Gleaves, *Life and Letters of Rear Admiral Stephen B. Luce,* p. 89.

70 Luce recalled to the academy. *Ibid.,* pp. 76–77.

70 origins of Luce's *Seamanship. Ibid.,* p. 79; Benjamin, pp. 221–22.

70–71 1863 cruise. Benjamin, p. 295.

70–71 *America. Ibid.,* pp. 295–96.

71 Clark on Mahan. Clark, p. 46.

72 Luce disguises the *Macedonian.* Benjamin, pp. 247–48.

72 former classmates meet in Paris. Clark, pp. 67–68.

72 Duc de Penthièvre. Benjamin, p. 235.

72 "If d'Orléans felt. . . ." Clark, p. 45.

72 Luce's order. Gleaves, p. 85.

73–74. 1864 cruise. Benjamin, pp. 249–50.

74 alumni war records. Bolander, "The Naval Academy in Five Wars," p. 37; The United States Naval Academy Alumni Association, Inc., *Register of Alumni, 1976,* Classes of 1846–1865.

74 Lieutenant Waddell. James D. Horan, editor, *C.S.S. Shenandoah: The Memoirs of Lieutenant Commanding James I. Waddell.*

74 Carter and Nelson. Captain Frank V. Rigler, USN (Ret.), "Commandants of Midshipmen," p. 32; Rear Admiral Samuel R. Franklin, *Memories of a Rear Admiral,* p. 104.

75 "Now, how the devil. . . ." Admiral of the Navy George Dewey, *Autobiography,* p. 108.

75 Midshipman Porter. Benjamin, p. 251.

75 Cushing's exploits; his academic obituary. Ralph J. Roske and Charles Van Doren, *Lincoln's Commando: The Biography of Commander W.B. Cushing, U.S.N.,* pp. 87–88.

75 "a delicate-looking youth." Parker, p. 340.

75 alumni killed in action. *Register of Alumni,* Classes of 1846–1865.

75 "a strikingly handsome old man. . . ." Charles Lee Lewis, *Admiral Franklin Buchanan,* pp. 246–47.

75–76 Buchanan's Civil War service. *Ibid.,* pp. 219–45.

76 Ward killed. Marshall, p. 123.

76 Marcy mortally injured. *Ibid.,* pp. 114–15.

76 Lockwood's Civil War service. Benjamin, p. 235; Lieutenant Colonel Mark M. Boatner III, USA, *The Civil War Dictionary,* pp. 191–92, 486, 589.

76 "some form of education. . . ." G. Melville Herndon, "The Confederate States Naval Academy," p. 304.

76 establishment of the Confederate Naval Academy. *Ibid.,* pp. 304–05.

76 organization of C. S. Naval Academy. *Ibid.,* pp. 305, 310.

77 classes opened; faculty. *Ibid.,* pp. 306–07.

77 Mallory to Davis. *Ibid.,* p. 312.

77 two classes were graduated. *Ibid.,* p. 315.

78 "the most realistic war college. . . ." Morgan, pp. 204–05.

78   Palmer Saunders. *Ibid.*, p. 206.

79   academic excellence rewarded by combat duty. Herndon, pp. 309–10.

79   Brooke to Mallory. *Ibid.*, p. 309.

79   Morgan's recollections. Morgan, p. 205.

79   the South's leading families. J.T. Scharf, *History of the Confederate States Navy*, p. 781.

79–80   midshipmen escort the treasure train. *Ibid.*, pp. 314–15; Parker, pp. 362–65.

79   "Foot-sore and ragged. . . ." Parker, p. 352.

80   "Report!" *Ibid.*, p. 354.

80–81   postwar career of Buchanan: Lewis, pp. 253–61; of Parker: Scharf, p. 773n; of Waddell: Horan, p. 48; of Kell: Norman C. Delaney, *John McIntosh Kell of the Raider* Alabama.

81   Confederate officers in Egyptian service. William B. Hesseltine and Hazel C. Wolf, *The Blue and the Grey on the Nile*, passim; Morgan, pp. 280–81.

81   Lieutenant Fry. Jeanie Mort Walker, *Life of Captain Joseph Fry*, p. 191ff.

81   Fry's letter. *Ibid.*, p. 444.

CHAPTER FIVE

83   return to Annapolis. Park Benjamin, *The United States Naval Academy*, pp. 243–44, 258, 260.

84   sketch of Porter. Richard S. West, Jr., *The Second Admiral: A Life of David Dixon Porter, 1813–1891*, pp. 1–60.

84   Porter promoted vice admiral. *Ibid.*, p. 299.

84   Porter to Fox. *Ibid.*, p. 146.

84   imminence of war. *Ibid.*, p. 305.

84   "a welcome substitute. . . ." Benjamin, p. 263.

84   wartime legislation. *Ibid.*, p. 279.

84   a great national institution. West, p. 305.

84–85   Maryland Government House. James Russell Soley, *Historical Sketch of the United States Naval Academy*, p. 121; [Lieutenant Commander Edward P. Lull], *Description and History of the U.S. Naval Academy*, p. 62; P.H. Magruder, "The Colonial Government House of Maryland," pp. 1407–11.

85   College Lot. Soley, p. 121.

85   Strawberry Hill. *Ibid.*

85   Naval Academy Cemetery. Ruby R. Duval, "The Naval Academy Cemetery on 'Strawberry Hill,' " pp. 75–79.

85–87   new construction. Soley, pp. 110, 132; [Lull], p. 62.

87   "an ugly factory." Benjamin, p. 280.

87   New Quarters. Soley, p. 132; [Lull], pp. 62–63.

87   Old Quarters. Benjamin, p. 281.

87   Tecumseh. Chevalier Thomas G. Ford, "History of the United States Naval Academy," Ch. 22, p. 48.

87   faculty at war's end. Benjamin, p. 265.

88   Welles had foreseen. West, p. 305.

88   civilian faculty reduced. Benjamin, p. 265.

88   Schley at the academy. Rear Admiral Winfield Scott Schley, *Forty-five Years Under the Flag*, p. 63.

88   faculty members. Benjamin, p. 264; "The First Academic Staff," pp. 1397, 1399.

89   Porter's guiding idea. West, p. 306.

89   the superintendent had three votes. Ford, Ch. 20, pp. 5, 24.

89   instructors rotated. Ford, Ch. 20, p. 7.

89   the faculty was warned. [Lull], p. 25.

89   mathematics simplified. West, p. 306.

89   *Santee* transformed. *Ibid.*, p. 307.

89   *Tonawanda*. Ford, Ch. 20, p. 29.

89   ship models. West, p. 306.

89   sail drill. *Ibid.*

90   line officers and engineers. Benjamin, p. 259.

90   W_4O_2D. *Ibid.*, pp. 264, 271.

90   midshipmen alternated watches. *Ibid.*, pp. 272–73.

90   midshipman resistance; two-year engineering course. *Ibid.*, pp. 273–74; Soley, pp. 110–11.

90–91 *Albemarle* disaster. Benjamin, pp. 274–75.

91   1866 Board of Visitors. *Ibid.*, pp. 277–78.

91   discipline was restored. *Ibid.*, p. 275.

91   working off demerits. *Ibid.*

91–92 Porter's poetic justice. West, p. 308.

93   honor concept. Benjamin, p. 269.

93   "commit less wrong. . . ." *Ibid.*, p. 275.

93   "I loosen or tighten the reins. . . ." Ford, Ch. 20, p. 3.

93   athletics were encouraged. West, p. 310.

93   Corbesier. Ford, Ch. 20, p. 13.

93   "polished as an ambassador. . . ." Captain J.M. Ellicott, "The Passing of the Cadet Engineers," p. 1130.

93   Matthew Strohm. Walter Aamold, "Naval Academy Athletics—1845 to 1945," p. 106.

94   Porter went a round. Benjamin, pp. 266–67.

94   "I don't want anyone. . . ." West, p. 310.

94   Quaker City Boat Club. Ford, Ch. 20, p. 54.

94   military reorganization. [Lull], p. 26.

94   Marine detachment. Midshipman Barton D. Strong, "A History of the Marine Barracks, Annapolis, Maryland," p. 1.

94   midshipmen's uniform redesigned. Benjamin, p. 266.

95   dress parade. [Lull], p. 74.

95   Old Denver. West, p. 309.

95   "in a way that aroused. . . ." Benjamin, p. 268.

95   call at West Point. *Ibid.*, p. 279; Ford, Ch. 25, pp. 37–38.

95   Mrs. Porter. West, pp. 309, 311.

95   "a very refining influence. . . ." [Lull], p. 73.

95   *Dieu et les dames*. Rear Admiral Seaton Schroeder, USN (Ret.), *A Half-Century of Naval Service*, p. 4.

97   Goldsborough quipped. Ford, Ch. 20, p. 58.

97   graduation exercises of 1867 and 1869. Lieutenant C.T. Houpt, USNR, "Graduation Exercises at the Naval Academy, 1854–1914," pp. 132–33.

97   Benjamin recalled. Benjamin, p. 267.

97   Musical Club and minstrel troop. *Ibid.*; West, p. 309; Ford, Ch. 20, Parts I and II, notes and inserts.

97   Porter to Thompson. Midshipman E.A. Grantham, USN, "Drum and Bugle Corps," p. 1492.

98   Class of 1867. Benjamin, p. 276.

98   Benjamin explained. *Ibid.*

98   "writing to the mama's." West, p. 313.

99   Porter to Mrs. Yorke. Ford, Ch. 20, Part II, notes.

99   a new naval academy. Benjamin, p. 283.

102   Congress accedes to Japanese request. *Ibid.*, p. 288.

102   Worden and Dewey. Admiral of the Navy George Dewey, *Autobiography*, p. 143.

102   purchase of Lockwoodsville. Soley, pp. 121–22.

102   Grant's inaugural parade. Benjamin, p. 295.

102   *America* and *Constitution* removed. *Ibid.*, p. 280.

103   *Constellation* attached. Commander Ralph Earle, USN, *Life at the U.S. Naval Academy: The Making of the American Naval Officer*, p. 241.

103   law of July 15, 1870. Benjamin, pp. 284–85.

104   sea duty set at two years. *Ibid.*, p. 286.

104   lieutenants until 1893. *Ibid.*, p. 255.

104   varieties of hazing. See *Fag Ends from the Naval Academy*, and George F. Gibbs, *Junk: A Collection of Songs and Poems by Cadets at the United States Naval Academy*.

104   a battle royal. Rear Admiral Bradley A. Fiske, USN, *From Midshipman to Rear-Admiral*, pp. 10–11.

104   the most ruthless hazers. Benjamin, pp. 288–89.

104   eleven offenders dismissed. *Ibid.*

104   hazing outbreak 1874; the Hazing Law. *Ibid.*, pp. 289–90.

104   Conyers appointed. *Ibid.*, p. 292.

104   "The place was in an uproar. . . ." Robley D. Evans, *A Sailor's Log: Recollections of Forty Years of Naval Life*, p. 156.

105   Conyers hazed. *Ibid.*, p. 157.

105   Conyers resigns. Benjamin, p. 292.

105   other black midshipmen. *Ibid.*, pp. 293–94; Lieutenant Commander R.L. Field, USN (Ret.), "The Black Midshipman at the U.S. Naval Academy," p. 31.

106   Michelson's background. Dorothy Michelson Livingston, "Michelson in the Navy; the Navy in Michelson," pp. 72–73.

106   Fiske's background. Fiske, p. 3.

106   Fiske wrote. *Ibid.*, p. 15.

107   Michelson's grades. Livingston, p. 75.

107   Worden to Michelson. *Ibid.*

107   Michelson's experiments, resignation, and World War One service. *Ibid.*, pp. 76–79.

107   James Russell Soley. Charles Oscar Paullin, *Paullin's History of Naval Administration, 1775–1911*, pp. 369–70, 372.

107   foundation of the U.S. Naval Institute. Captain Roy C. Smith III, USNR (Ret.), "The First Hundred Years Are. . . .", pp. 50–54, 62; Captain W.D. Puleston, *Mahan*, pp. 56–62.

108   Rodgers returns. Benjamin, pp. 298–99.

108–09   cadet engineers. *Ibid.*, p. 286; Ellicott, "The Passing of the Cadet Engineers," pp. 1125–27.

109   Rodgers revises curriculum. Benjamin, pp. 300–01; Soley, p. 113.

109   Rodgers and Secretary Thompson. Benjamin, pp. 301–02.

109   Rodgers not completely satisfied. *Ibid.*, pp. 302–03.

111   Parker and Balch. *Ibid.*, pp. 306–07; Ford, Ch. 23, pp. 2–13.

111   Cadet Bowles; study abroad. Benjamin, pp. 308–09.

CHAPTER SIX

113   Rodgers's reappointment. Park Benjamin, *The United States Naval Academy*, pp. 310–11; Chevalier Thomas G. Ford, "History of the United States Naval Academy," Ch. 24, Part I, Memorandum.

113   sketch of Ramsay. Richard S. West, Jr., "The Superintendents of the Naval Academy," p. 61.

113   curriculum revision. Benjamin, pp. 317–18.

113–14   military reorganization. *Ibid.*, pp. 318–19, 325.

115   Benjamin wrote. *Ibid.*, p. 305.

116   Rodgers suggested. *Ibid.*, p. 300.

116–17   Act of August 5, 1882; its effects. *Ibid.*, pp. 312–15.

117   graduates may enter Marine Corps. Colonel John E. Greenwood, "The Corps' Old School Tie," p. 49.

117   implementation of act devastating. *Register of Alumni*, Classes of 1881 through 1887.

117 Hawthorne wins Medal of Honor. Rudolf J. Friedrich, "The First USNA Medal of Honor," p. 17.

117 "To him discipline. . . ." Richard Harding Davis, *Real Soldiers of Fortune*, p. 122.

117 McGiffin at the academy. *Ibid.*, pp. 122–27; cf. Midshipman J.A. Bukauskas, "The Terror of Annapolis: Philo N. McGiffin."

118–19 McGiffin's subsequent career. Davis, pp. 129–44.

119 Woodruff posts answers; cheers in the mess hall. Ford, Ch. 24, pp. 50–52.

119 "mutineers" confined; dismissals. Benjamin, pp. 320–21.

119 "Ramsay's Kindergarten." *Ibid.*, p. 321.

120–21 newsman's account. *Army & Navy Journal*, June 16, 1883.

122 Ramsay's order explained. *Ibid.*

122 "anything else but good." *Ibid.*

122 a corporate catharsis. Benjamin, pp. 324–25.

123 Personnel Act of 1882 repealed. *Ibid.*, p. 326.

124 W.T. Sampson. Carroll Storrs Alden and Rear Admiral Ralph Earle, *Makers of Naval Tradition*, p. 290.

124 hazing offenses. Benjamin, pp. 332–33.

124–25 Sampson, applied science, and technical studies. West, "The Superintendents of the Naval Academy," p. 63.

125 line and engineer curricula. Benjamin, p. 334.

125 aptitude grade. West, "The Superintendents of the Naval Academy," pp. 62–63.

125 conduct grade refined. Benjamin, pp. 331–32.

125–26 beginning of Navy football; 1882–1886 seasons. Morris A. Bealle, *Gangway for Navy: The Story of Football at the United States Naval Academy, 1879 to 1950*, pp. 8–12.

126–27 "As the game. . . ." *Ibid.*, p. 17.

127 Naval Academy Graduates Association. Benjamin, p. 414.

127 Colonel Thompson; formation of Naval Academy Athletic Association. *Ibid.*, pp. 336–37; Commander Ralph Earle, USN, *Life at the U.S. Naval Academy: The Making of the American Naval Officer*, p. 200; Walter Aamold, "Athletic Training at the Naval Academy," p. 1564.

127 athletic letter introduced. Captain Frank V. Rigler, USN (Ret.), "Superintendents of the Naval Academy," p. 21.

127–28 Cadet Michie and the first Army-Navy game. Stephen E. Ambrose, *Duty, Honor, Country: A History of West Point*, pp. 304–05; Aamold, "Athletic Training at the Naval Academy," p. 1564.

128 General Palmer recalled. Bealle, p. 26.

128–29 Navy goat. Aamold, "Naval Academy Athletics—1845 to 1945," pp. 112–13.

129 Army-Navy games of 1891–1893. Bealle, pp. 29–40.

129 Blue and Gold. Aamold, "Naval Academy Athletics," p. 112.

129 Reeves's helmet. Bealle, p. 39.

129–30 suppression of Army-Navy games. *Ibid.*, p. 41; Ambrose, p. 308.

130 other athletics. Benjamin, pp. 337–38.

130 Phythian and academy life. *Ibid.*, p. 335.

130 no changes to make. *Ibid.*

130 Cooper equally conservative. *Ibid.*, p. 339.

130 "institutional impulsion." Admiral James L. Holloway, Jr., USN (Ret.), to the author, 1976.

133 cruise ships. Benjamin, p. 338; Captain W.D. Puleston, *Annapolis: Gangway to the Quarterdeck*, p. 77; Midshipman K.W. Patrick, USN, "Midshipman Cruises," p. 1546.

133 Marine detachment on Porter Row. Midshipman Barton D. Strong, USN, "A History of the Marine Barracks, Annapolis," p. 3.

133 Sampson's purchase. Benjamin, p. 334.

133 Upshur Row. Earle, p. 281.

135 condition of New Quarters. West, "The Superintendents of the Naval Academy," p. 62.

135 "a reconstruction. . . ." Earle, pp. 282–83.

135 Thompson engages Flagg; Matthews Board. *Ibid.*, pp. 282–84; Benjamin, p. 409.

138 Spanish-American War graduations. *Ibid.*, pp. 339–40.

139 Clark exclaimed. Rear Admiral Charles E. Clark, *My Fifty Years in the Navy*, p. 294.

139 Cadet Boardman. *Lucky Bag*, 1900.

139 Spanish prisoners at Annapolis. P.H. Magruder, "The Spanish Naval Prisoners of War at Annapolis, 1898," pp. 489–95.

CHAPTER SEVEN

141 Naval Academy crest. Park Benjamin, *The United States Naval Academy*, p. 349.

142 1898 Board of Visitors; Secretary Long; appropriations. Commander Ralph Earle, USN, *Life at the U.S. Naval Academy: The Making of the American Naval Officer*, pp. 284–85; Benjamin, pp. 410–15.

142 Bancroft Hall. Captain W.D. Puleston, *Annapolis: Gangway to the Quarterdeck*, p. 119; Earle, p. 287.

143 Macdonough and Dahlgren halls. Benjamin, pp. 410–11.

143 chapel dimensions. Earle, p. 293.

143 halls officially opened. Margaret Horton Edsall, *A Place Called the Yard: Guide to the United States Naval Academy*, pp. 20–21.

144 grey brick. Earle, p. 290.

144 northeast wing of Bancroft ready. Puleston, *Annapolis*, p. 119.

144 completion dates. Earle, p. 293.

144 chapel doors. Edsall, p. 66.

144 construction completed: statistics. Earle, pp. 280, 285–86.

147 Roosevelt at graduations. Lieutenant C.T. Houpt, USNR, "Graduation Exercises at the Naval Academy," pp. 136–37.

147 Roosevelt and Midshipman Land. *Ibid.*; Captain Damon E. Cummings, USN (Ret.), *Admiral Richard Wainwright and the United States Fleet*, p. 126.

147 discovery and return of the remains of John Paul Jones. Samuel Eliot Morison, *John Paul Jones: A Sailor's Biography*, pp. 407–08.

148 John Paul Jones commemoration ceremony. Charles W. Stewart, editor, *John Paul Jones Commemoration at Annapolis, April 24, 1906*.

149 a prolonged anticlimax. Morison, *John Paul Jones*, pp. 408–09.

149 "It seemed a sacrilege. . . ." Rear Admiral Robert E. Coontz, USN (Ret.), *From the Mississippi to the Sea*, p. 308.

149 parodied a popular song. Morison, *John Paul Jones*, p. 409.

149 John Paul Jones crypt. Coontz, p. 307; Morison, *John Paul Jones*, p. 409; Commander David W. Plank, CHC, USN, *The Chapel of the United States Naval Academy, Annapolis*, p. 24.

149 reinstated the title "midshipman." Earle, p. 24.

149 Class of 1907. Houpt, "Graduation Exercises at the Naval Academy," p. 137.

149 commissioned ensigns immediately. *Ibid.*

150 King's origins. Ernest J. King and Walter Muir Whitehill, *Fleet Admiral King: A Naval Record*, p. 11.

150 Nimitz's origins. E.B. Potter, *Nimitz*, p. 27.

150 *Youth's Companion*. King and Whitehill, p. 14.

150 Nimitz's appointment. Potter, pp. 29–30.

150 Halsey's origins. Fleet Admiral William F. Halsey and Lieutenant Commander J. Bryan III, *Admiral Halsey's Story*, pp. 3–4.

151 Spruance's origins. Commander Thomas B. Buell, *The Quiet Warrior: A Biography of Admiral Raymond A. Spruance*, pp. 4–8.

151 Mitscher's origins. Theodore Taylor, *The Magnificent Mitscher*, pp. 18–19.

151 King at the academy. King and Whitehill, pp. 31–34.

151 King and the midshipman. *Ibid.*, p. 74.

152 the poorest fullback. Halsey and Bryan, p. 8.

152 their two-year record. Morris A. Bealle, *Gangway for Navy: The Story of Football at the United States Naval Academy*, pp. 60, 62.

152 Halsey at the academy. Halsey and Bryan, pp. 6–8.

152 "I wish you all the luck. . . ." *Ibid.*, p. 7.

152–53 Sampson-Schley controversy. Potter, pp. xi, 52–53; Rear Admiral Winfield Scott Schley, USN (Ret.), *Forty-five Years under the Flag*, pp. 408–28.

153 Nimitz at the academy. Potter, pp. 50–56.

154 "This escapade. . . ." *Ibid.*, p. 55.

154 Spruance at the academy. Buell, pp. 9–16.

154 Mitscher resigned. Taylor, pp. 21–22.

154–55 Meriwether-Branch fight. Baltimore *Sun*, November 7–9, 16, 18, 22, and 23, December 12, 1905; clippings in Academy Scrapbooks.

155 hazing scandal; Meriwether involved. Newspaper clippings, December 1905 through March 1906, in Academy Scrapbooks.

155 "Champ" Clark declared. *Ibid.*

155 dismissals; Roosevelt pardons Meriwether; Meriwether resigns. *Ibid.*, January through March 1906.

156 Mitscher at the academy. Taylor, pp. 21–26.

156 "more like a private. . . ." *Ibid.*, p. 22.

156–58 Japanese midshipmen. Captain J.M. Ellicott, USN (Ret.), "Japanese Students at the United States Naval Academy," pp. 303–07.

158 quotations. H. Irving Hancock, *Dave Darin's Second Year at Annapolis*, pp. 194–200.

158 esoteric terms. Many of these are defined in the *Lucky Bag* issues of the period.

159 "The tradition in those days. . . ." Admiral James L. Holloway, Jr., USN (Ret.), to the author.

159 Hancock advised. H. Irving Hancock, *Dave Darin's First Year at Annapolis*, p. 60.

160 no upper classman ever touched a plebe. Admiral James L. Holloway, Jr., to the author.

160 end of plebe year. *Ibid.*

160 midshipmen's schedule. Earle, pp. 99, 111–12.

160 "a very busy life. . . ." Commander Joseph P. Norfleet to the author.

160 Army-Navy game revived. Stephen E. Ambrose, *Duty, Honor, Country: A History of West Point*, pp. 309–10.

160 games of 1899–1901. *Ibid.*; Bealle, pp. 53–57.

160–62 "Skinny Paul" Dashiell. Professor J.C. Gray, U.S. Naval Academy, "Paul Joseph Dashiell, Ph.D."; Bealle, pp. 65–74; Captain Roy C. Smith III, USNR (Ret.), to the author.

162–63 "Anchor's Aweigh." Commander Leland P. Lovette, USN, *School of the Sea: The Annapolis Tradition in American Life*, pp. 111, 366.

163 football's future in doubt. Bealle, pp. 84–85; Ambrose, pp. 311–12.

163 academy sports multiplied. Aamold, "Naval Academy Athletics—1845–1945," pp. 113–16; Earle, pp. 178, 202.

163 extracurricular activities. Sarah Corbin Robert, "Extracurricula—Midshipmen Organizations and Activities," pp. 50, 55.

163 *Lucky Bag.* Captain Frank V. Rigler, USN (Ret.), "The Lucky Bag," pp. 19–22.

163–64 Naval Academy dairy. Earle, pp. 192–94.

164–65   practice ships and cruises. *Ibid.*, pp. 241–43; Puleston, *Annapolis*, p. 79; Midshipman K.W. Patrick, USN, "Midshipman Cruises," p. 1546; Lovette, p. 112.

165   the *Holland.* Puleston, *Annapolis*, p. 83.

165–66   aviation comes to Annapolis. Rear Admiral George Van Deurs, USN (Ret.), *Wings for the Fleet: A Narrative of Naval Aviation's Early Development, 1910–1916*, pp. 23, 69–70, 82, 99; Thomas Ray, "The First Three."

166–67   *Santee* and *Reina Mercedes.* Carroll Storrs Alden, "The *Santee*: An Appreciation."

167   Naval Postgraduate School. Earle, pp. 260–77.

167   the regiment reorganized. "The Departments," p. 1416.

167   strength increased. Earle, pp. 29–31.

167   "a navy second to none." E.B. Potter and Fleet Admiral Chester W. Nimitz, editors, *Sea Power: A Naval History*, pp. 464–65.

168   sketch of Admiral Eberle. Richard S. West, Jr., "The Superintendents of the Naval Academy," p. 64; Rear Admiral Daniel V. Gallery, USN (Ret.), *Eight Bells, and All's Well*, p. 30; Lieutenant Charles M. Todorich, "Citizen Sailors at Annapolis: The Story of the Reserve Officers Classes at the Naval Academy during World War I," pp. 6–7.

168   1,240 midshipmen. Superintendent's Annual Report, October 11, 1916, U.S. Naval Academy Archives.

168–69   reserve officer training. Todorich, "Citizen Sailors at Annapolis," pp. 3, 7, 9, 14. Superintendent's annual reports, September 28, 1917 and October 14, 1919, U.S. Naval Academy Archives; Louis H. Bolander, "The Naval Academy in Five Wars," p. 43; Admiral James L. Holloway, Jr., to the author.

169   "callous young snobs." Todorich, "Citizen Sailors at Annapolis," p. 19.

169   "some very good friends. . . ." Admiral James L. Holloway, Jr., to the author; cf. Todorich, "Citizen Sailors at Annapolis," pp. 20–22.

169   new wings for Bancroft Hall. Superintendent's annual reports, September 28, 1917 and June 26, 1918, U.S. Naval Academy Archives.

169   plebe class of 1917. Earle, p. 106.

169   40 per cent increase. Superintendent's Annual Report, June 26, 1918, U.S. Naval Academy Archives.

CHAPTER EIGHT

171   Captain Scales; the academy in 1919. Richard S. West, Jr., "The Superintendents of the Naval Academy," p. 64.

171   Daniels-Gallery fight. Rear Admiral Daniel V. Gallery, *Eight Bells, and All's Well*, pp. 36–38.

172   segregation crisis of 1920. Rear Admiral Winston P. Folk, USN (Ret.), "The Great Segregation Imbroglio of 1920," pp. 17–18.

172   Postgraduate School reopens. Superintendent's Annual Report, October 14, 1919, U.S. Naval Academy Archives; Ernest J. King and Walter Muir Whitehill, *Fleet Admiral King: A Naval Record*, pp. 149–53.

172   Luce Hall. Superintendent's Annual Report, September 1, 1920, U.S. Naval Academy Archives.

172   radio station. *Ibid.*, June 26, 1918.

172   Prince of Wales. West, "The Superintendents of the Naval Academy," p. 64.

174   sketch of Admiral Wilson. Admiral James L. Holloway, Jr., USN (Ret.), and Captain Roy C. Smith III, USNR (Ret.), to the author.

174   "His oversize cap. . . ." Captain Frank V. Rigler, USN (Ret.), "Superintendents of the Naval Academy," p. 21.

175–76   "To mould the material. . . ." *Annual Report of the Superintendent*, 1922, p. 1.

176–77   "Physical condition. . . ." *Ibid.*, 1924, p. 1.

177 leadership course. *Ibid.*, 1922, p. 1; *ibid.*, 1924, p. 6.

177 museum and guidebook. *Ibid.*, 1924, p. 2.

177 return of the *America*. *Ibid.*, 1922, p. 11.

177 Macedonian Monument. Margaret Horton Edsall, *A Place Called the Yard: Guide to the United States Naval Academy*, p. 55.

178 "While the fear. . . ." *Annual Report of the Superintendent*, 1923, p. 5.

178 to the dismay. Captain W.D. Puleston, *Annapolis: Gangway to the Quarterdeck*, p. 123.

178 "more human. . . ." *Annual Report of the Superintendent*, 1924, p. 13.

178 Christmas and Easter leaves; first-class liberty privileges. Puleston, *Annapolis*, p. 123.

178 all classes allowed. *Ibid.*; *Annual Report of the Superintendent*, 1923, p. 7.

179 "for contributing the most. . . ." *Ibid.*, 1924, p. 2.

179 uniform change. *Ibid.*, 1923, pp. 12–13.

179 a stern disciplinarian. A distinguished officer who prefers anonymity (hereafter cited as X) to the author.

180 only six hours. Commander Leland P. Lovette, *School of the Sea: The Annapolis Tradition in American Life*, p. 113.

180 Letter to the Regiment. *Annual Report of the Superintendent*, 1922, p. 4.

180 rates. *Ibid.*, pp. 5–6.

180 "the laying of hands. . . ." *Ibid.*

180 no hazing cases reported in 1923. *Ibid.*, 1924, p. 3.

181 "He enjoyed keeping people. . . ." X to the author.

181 aptitude testing; "Tactics for Examinations." *Annual Report of the Superintendent*, 1923, p. 8.

181 abolished comprehensives. West, "The Superintendents of the Naval Academy," p. 65.

181 Friday night lectures. *Annual Report of the Superintendent*, 1923, p. 7.

181 detailed guides. *Ibid.*, 1924, p. 6.

181 soliciting parental support. *Ibid.*, 1923, p. 4.

181 Wilson supported athletic program. *Ibid.*, 1922, p. 7; *ibid.*, 1924, p. 11.

181 he brought the proceedings to a dead end. X to the author.

181 1923 athletic record. *Annual Report of the Superintendent*, 1923, p. 14.

181 Rose Bowl. Morris A. Bealle, *Gangway for Navy: The Story of Football at the United States Naval Academy*, pp. 130–31.

181 Department of Physical Training. "The Departments," p. 1433.

181–82 "Spike" Webb. Felix Riesenberg, *The Story of the Naval Academy*, pp. 119–22.

182–83 "Doc" Snyder. Captain W.S. Busik, USN (Ret.), " 'Doc' Snyder, 1878–1977," p. 41.

183 Ring Dance. Lovette, pp. 193–94.

184 Admiral Burke. Ken Jones and Hubert Kelly, Jr., *Admiral Arleigh (31-Knot) Burke: The Story of a Fighting Sailor*, pp. 30–43.

184 Admiral Rickover. Clay Blair, Jr., *The Atomic Submarine*, pp. 19–21.

184–85 "This is not my favorite anecdote. . . ." Admiral Burke to the author.

185 "In an era. . . ." X to the author.

185 "The objective. . . ." Commander Ralph Earle, USN, *Life at the U.S. Naval Academy: The Making of the American Naval Officer*, p. 167.

185 introduction of aeronautics. *Annual Report of the Superintendent*, 1925, pp. 3–4.

185 "Navy Blue and Gold." Lovette, p. 368; *Shipmate*, May 1977, p. 14 (obituary for Professor Joseph W. Crosley).

185–86   the most dramatic moment in Navy athletics. Bealle, pp. 146–48.

186   lecture and discussion. West, "The Superintendents of the Naval Academy," p. 65.

187   Rhodes scholarships. *Ibid.*

187   Hubbard Hall. *Ibid.*; Charles Lee Lewis, "Description of the United States Naval Academy," p. 1465.

187   the academy accredited. Lovette, p. 114.

187–88   Tecumseh. Tecumseh Folder, Special Collections, Nimitz Library, U.S. Naval Academy.

188   death of Colonel Thompson. Walter Aamold, "Naval Academy Athletics—1845 to 1945," p. 116.

188   Thompson Stadium. *Annual Report of the Superintendent, 1931,* p. 7.

189   authorization of line officers. *Annual Report of the Navy Department, 1933,* p. 14.

189   Class of 1933. *Ibid.*; Superintendent's Annual Report, July 1, 1933.

189   Class of 1934 commissioned; commissions offered to 1933. Superintendent's Annual Report, July 10, 1934.

189   sketch of Admiral Hart. Puleston, *Annapolis,* p. 126; Dr. John T. Mason to the author.

189   "During the past year. . . ." *Annual Report of the Superintendent, 1931,* p. 2.

189   "of any economics. . . ." *Report of the Board of Visitors, 1931,* p. 6.

189   Hart's reforms. West, "The Superintendents of the Naval Academy," p. 66; "The Departments," pp. 1429, 1432; *Annual Report of the Superintendent, 1932,* pp. 7–8.

189–90   "the naval officer's education. . . ." Rear Admiral David F. Sellers, USN, "The United States Naval Academy: It Belongs to the Fleet," p. 1431.

191   "one justification for existence. . . ." *Ibid.,* p. 1428.

191   "I can say without hesitation. . . ." Lovette, p. 212.

191   hours restored to professional subjects. Superintendent's Annual Report, June 29, 1936.

191   Department of English, History and Government. West, "The Superintendents of the Naval Academy," p. 66.

191–92   great books. Lovette, pp. 217–18.

192   more time to cultural studies. *Ibid.,* p. 213.

192   Gate Three. *Annual Report of the Superintendent, 1932,* p. 5.

192–93   new construction. Puleston, *Annapolis,* p. 137; West, "The Superintendents of the Naval Academy," p. 67; Lovette, p. 115.

193   Preble Hall. Roy C. Smith III, "The First Hundred Years. . . ," p. 69; Captain Harry Baldridge, "Naval Academy Museum—The First Hundred Years," p. 84.

193   Navy sailing. Lieutenant Frances C. Lane, USN, "History of the Naval Academy Sailing Squadron," pp. 1–4, 6n, 9–10, 19; West, "The Superintendents of the Naval Academy," p. 66; *Lucky Bag,* 1945, xxvi–vii.

CHAPTER NINE

195   "We went to Germany. . . ." *Lucky Bag,* 1940, p. 63.

195–96   wartime schedule. Superintendent's Annual Report, 9 July 1941.

196   reserve midshipmen. *Ibid.*; Louis H. Bolander, "The Naval Academy in Five Wars," p. 43.

196   Pear Harbor day. Bolander, p. 44.

196   "the academy went wild. . . ." *Lucky Bag,* 1943, p. 156.

196–98   the academy at war. Richard S. West, Jr., "The Superintendents of the Naval Academy," p. 67; Professor Emeritus Neville T. Kirk and Captain James L. Anderson, USN (Ret.), to the author.

197   wartime graduates. Bolander, p. 45.

198 "Of course, we read. . . ." Captain James L. Anderson to the author.

198 members of fifty-four classes. *Register of Alumni*, Classes of 1890 through 1946.

198 losses. Rear Admiral James L. Holloway, Jr., "The Holloway Plan— A Summary View and Commentary," p. 1301.

198 Medals of Honor. *Register of Alumni* 1977, pp. A24–A26.

199 McCool's citation. Subcommittee on Veterans Affairs of the Committee on Labor and Public Welfare, U.S. Senate, *Medal of Honor Recipients 1863–1963*, p. 180.

200 "Six days we waited. . . ." *Lucky Bag*, 1947, p. 349.

200 "We were especially envious. . . ." Jimmy Carter, *Why Not the Best?* p. 49.

201 "a lifetime commitment. . . ." *Ibid.*, p. 44.

201 "We never ate a peaceful meal. . . ." *Ibid.*

201 The president recalled his first cruise. *Ibid.*, pp. 47–48.

201 Department of Aviation. *Report of the Board of Visitors*, 1946, p. 11.

202 memorial service. Felix Riesenberg, *The Story of the Naval Academy*, p. 149.

202–03 *Lucky Bag*, 1947, pp. 254–55.

203 *Time* closed its account. "One Hundred Years," *Time*, 8 October 1945, p. 27.

203 Holloway Board. Holloway, pp. 1295–96; John W. Masland and Laurence I. Radway, *Soldiers and Scholars: Military Education and National Policy*, pp. 106–10.

203 Holloway wrote. Holloway, p. 1296.

203–04 Holloway Plan. *Ibid.*

204 postwar turbulence. Admiral James L. Holloway, Jr., USN (Ret.), to the author.

205 two books. *Ibid.*

205 "an ever-increasing load. . . ." *Report of the Board of Visitors*, 1950, pp. 2–3.

205 "Adherence to fundamentals. . . ." *Ibid.*

205 a balanced, basic curriculum. *Ibid.*, p. 9.

205 academic time for the humanities. *Ibid.*, 1948, pp. 49–50.

205 "It is not profitable. . . ." *Ibid.*, 1950, p. 6.

205 academy accredited. *Annapolis: Unofficial Directory and Guide* [c. 1970], p. 9.

205 "Open letter to the First Class." *Report of the Board of Visitors*, 1947, p. 58.

205 outmoded regulations revoked. Admiral James L. Holloway, Jr., to the author.

205–06 academy sailing. Lieutenant Frances C. Lane, USN, "History of the Naval Academy Sailing Squadron," pp. 15, 18, 23; U.S. Naval Station Annapolis *Newsletter*, 10 May 1977; Admiral James L. Holloway, Jr., to the author.

206 Truman privately favored. Walter Millis, editor, *The Forrestal Diaries*, pp. 88–89.

206 Stearns-Eisenhower Board. Masland and Radway, p. 118.

206 board supported combined academy concept. *Ibid.*, p. 119.

206–07 Holloway recalled. Admiral James L. Holloway, Jr., to the author.

207 preliminary report. *Ibid.*; Masland and Radway, p. 119.

207 Secretary Johnson; final report. Admiral James L. Holloway, Jr., to the author; Masland and Radway, p. 121.

207 Johnson and Trivers. Lieutenant Commander R.L. Field, USN (Ret.), "The Black Midshipman at the U.S. Naval Academy," p. 31.

207–08 Brown at the academy. Ensign Wesley A. Brown, USN, "The First Negro Graduate of Annapolis Tells His Story," pp. 26–27, 111–13.

208 Admiral Hill. Professor Emeritus E.B. Potter to the author; Vice

217   poem. Copy furnished by Admiral Davidson, quoted by permission of Rear Admiral James W. Kelly, CHC, USN (Ret.).

217   marching to class eliminated. Admiral John F. Davidson to the author.

217   subcritical nuclear reactor. Associate Professor Wayne F. Eckley, "USNA's Subcritical Nuclear Reactor," pp. 29–31.

217–18   NAFAC. *Report of the Board of Visitors*, 1960, p. 16; *ibid.*, 1961, p. 15.

218   seventh and eighth wings. *Ibid.*, 1961, p. 16.

218   Moreell Commission. *Ibid.*, p. 5; *ibid.*, 1963, p. 18.

218–19   report leaked; Mahan Hall meeting. Admiral John F. Davidson and others to the author.

219   Kirkpatrick's war record. Clay Blair, Jr., *Silent Victory: The U.S. Submarine War against Japan*, pp. 201–02, 210, 246, 308.

219   McNamara told Kirkpatrick. Vice Admiral Charles S. Minter, Jr., USN (Ret.), to the author.

219   Warnecke and Associates. *Report of the Board of Visitors*, 1964, p. 18.

219   Warnecke told academy authorities. Admiral Charles S. Minter to the author.

219   appointment of academic dean under discussion. Admiral Robert W. McNitt to the author.

219   Secretary Korth's letter. McNitt, "Challenge and Change," p. 4.

219   "educationally imperative." *Report of the Board of Visitors*, 1963, p. 13.

219–20   "He recognized that Annapolis. . . ." McNitt, "Challenge and Change," pp. 4–5.

220   Drought appointed pro tem. *Report of the Board of Visitors*, 1964, p. 1.

220   towards a minors program. McNitt, "Challenge and Change," p. 5.

220   officers' academic credentials upgraded. *Report of the Board of Visitors*, May 1965, p. 14.

220   grading system revised. McNitt, "Challenge and Change," p. 5.

220   Trident Scholars. *Ibid.*; *Report of the Board of Visitors*, 1964, p. 11; Admiral Charles S. Minter to the author.

220–21   interservice transfers ended. Rear Admiral Charles C. Kirkpatrick to the author.

222–23   football. *Navy*, 1952–1965.

223   Bellino. *Navy*, 1959, p. 42; "Joe Bellino . . . The Return of No. 27," *Navy vs. William & Mary* Program, October 22, 1977, p. 45.

223   Staubach. *Navy*, 1964, pp. 41–42; Roger Staubach, with Sam Blair and Bob St. Clair, *Staubach: First Down, Lifetime to Go*, passim.

223   Father Ryan remembered. Staubach, p. 57.

223   Bellino said. "Joe Bellino . . . The Return of No. 27," p. 45.

223   Minter's appointment. Admiral Charles S. Minter to the author.

224   master plan completed. *Report of the Board of Visitors*, May 1965, p. 4.

224   the two buildings. *Ibid.*, May 1968, pp. 36–37.

224   Ricketts Hall. *Ibid.*, 1963, p. 18.

224   rehabilitation of Mahan, Sampson, and Maury halls. *Ibid.*, 1964, p. 3.

224   Congress authorizes construction. *Ibid.*, November 1965, p. 11.

224   minors program put into effect. *Ibid.*, May 1965, p. 11.

224   number of companies increased. McNitt, "Challenge and Change," p. 6.

224   squad leader system. *Ibid.*

225   Admiral Kauffman's career. Captain Frank V. Rigler, USN (Ret.), "Superintendents of the Naval Academy," p. 22.

226   "academic revolution." *Report of the Board of Visitors*, 1966, p. 19.

226   number of courses. *Ibid.*; *ibid.*, May 1968, p. 39.

226   postgraduate scholarships. *Ibid.*, 1966, p. 24.

226   Smedberg's experience. McNitt, "Challenge and Change," p. 6.

226   Kauffman became convinced. *Ibid.*

226   "professional revolution." *Report of the Board of Visitors*, April 1967, p. 18.

226   Professional Training Board; program strengthened. McNitt, "Challenge and Change," p. 6; *Report of the Board of Visitors*, April 1967, p. 19.

226–27   midshipman life. Lieutenant Commander George L. Breeden II, USN, to the author.

229   "Sir, sir is. . . ." *Reef Points*, 1967.

229   Middle States evaluation team. *Report of the Board of Visitors*, 1966, pp. 3, 17–18.

230   library plans. *Ibid.*, p. 17.

230   revision of the master plan. *Ibid.*, April 1967, pp. 3–8, 12.

230–31   administrative reforms. *Ibid.*, p. 25.

231   Admiral Calvert's career. *Annapolis: Unofficial Directory and Guide.* [c. 1970], p. 2.

231   "the Navy [to] have firm roots. . . ." Vice Admiral James Calvert, USN, "Thoughts upon the Conclusion of a Four-Year Tour," p. 7.

231   "a sense of self-confidence. . . ." *Ibid.*, p. 9.

231   "The balance between Athens and Sparta. . . ." Rear Admiral James Calvert, USN, "The Fine Line at the Naval Academy," p. 67.

231   Calvert realized. Calvert, "Thoughts upon the Conclusion of a Four-Year Tour," p. 8.

231   Kauffman expressed three concerns. Calvert, "The Fine Line at the Naval Academy," p. 65.

231   a fourth problem. *Ibid.*

231   10 per cent drop; continued downward. *Report of the Board of Visitors*, November 1965, p. 14; *ibid.*, 1966, p. 9; *ibid.*, May 1968, p. 31.

231–32   "How could we both. . . ." Calvert, "The Fine Line at the Naval Academy," p. 66.

232   "We had to stop asking. . . ." *Ibid.*

232   majors program in effect. *Ibid.*, p. 67.

232   twenty-four majors offered. *Report of the Board of Visitors*, May 1969, p. 20.

232–33   course requirements. Calvert, "The Fine Line at the Naval Academy," p. 66.

233   eighteen departments. *Report of the Board of Visitors*, 1970, p. 22.

233   majors' distribution fixed. *Ibid.*, 1972, pp. 12–13.

233   7,065 young men. *Ibid.*, 1970, p. 12.

234   strength of the brigade exceeds 4,000. *Ibid.*, 1971, p. 16.

234   upward trend continued. *Ibid.*, 1972, p. 2; *ibid.*, July 1975, p. 6; *ibid.*, May 1976, p. 7.

234   Chauvenet and Michelson halls completed. *Ibid.*, 1968, p. 6.

234   library and science buildings; rehabilitation of academic group; plans for new buildings. *Ibid.*; *ibid.*, May 1969, pp. 12, 30.

234   Congressional appropriations of 1970 and 1971. *Ibid.*, 1971, p. 20.

234   Zumwalt's instructions. Vice Admiral William P. Mack, USN (Ret.), to the author.

234   to make himself accessible. *Ibid.*

234   emphasis on professional training. *Ibid.*

234   professional-readiness examination. *Report of the Board of Visitors*, 1973, p. 11.

234   "stretch" program. Admiral William P. Mack to the author.

235   Clemens Committee. *Report of the Board of Visitors*, 1975, p. 2.

235–36   Navy Football. *Navy*, 1965–1972.

236   George Welsh. *Navy*, 1976, pp. 10–11.

236   "Football can be simple." *Navy*, 1977, p. 10.

237   Robert Crown Sailing Center. Lieutenant Frances C. Lane, USN, "History of the Naval Academy Sailing Squadron," p. 39.

237   Marine officers at the academy. Colonel John E. Greenwood, USMC, "The Corps' Old School Tie," p. 51.

237–38   Dr. Massie. "There have been changes; academy professor looks back," Annapolis *Evening Capital*, January 10, 1978.

238   hazing problem overcome. Admiral William P. Mack to the author; conversations with midshipmen, past and present.

238   black midshipmen in 1965. *Report of the Board of Visitors*, November 1965, p. 15.

238   minorities' enrollment climbed. *Ibid.*, December 1974, p. 4.

238–39   "The Junior Officer and the Human Person." *Ibid.*, April 1973, p. 14; Admiral William P. Mack to the author.

239   Secretary Chafee announced. McNitt, "Challenge and Change," p. 4.

239   the academy's argument. Admiral William P. Mack to the author.

239   admission of women. Captain Paul Schratz, USN (Ret.), "Sea Breezes: An Officer and a Gentlewoman," pp. 4–5.

244   first girls sworn in. *Report of the Board of Visitors*, 1976, p. 7; *U.S. Naval Academy Catalogue*, 1977, p. 17.

244–45   performance of female midshipmen. Schratz, p. 4.

245   eighty-three girls in Class of 1981. "All Hands: Induction Day," *Shipmate*, September 1977, p. 15.

Bibliography

Sources Directly Relating to the Naval Academy

Official Records

The two basic documentary sources are the annual reports of the Board of Visitors and of the superintendent of the Naval Academy, copies of which are in the Naval Academy Archives, Annapolis. Since 1863, the *Report of the Board of Visitors* has been published by the Government Printing Office, Washington, D.C. From 1922 to 1933 the *Annual Report of the Superintendent, United States Naval Academy*, was published by the Naval Academy Press. Preceding and subsequent reports were not published. This report was discontinued in 1945, since which time a "Statement of the Superintendent" has been included in the reports of the Board of Visitors. Successive volumes of the nineteenth-century *Journal of the Naval Academy*, written ship's-log style by the midshipman officer of the watch and primarily concerned with weather conditions and institutional minutiae, are also in the Naval Academy Archives. Most other nineteenth-century materials are in the National Archives, Washington, D.C. The most valuable of them, the superintendents' letter books, are filed in Record Group 45.

Unpublished Materials

Academy Scrapbooks. Seven large books, apparently maintained by the library staff, containing numerous newspaper cuttings concerning the academy, circa 1900-1938. Special Collections, Nimitz Library, U.S. Naval Academy.

Bukauskas, John A., Midshipman, USN. "The Terror of Annapolis: Philo N. McGiffin." U.S. Naval Academy course paper, 1977. Author's files.

Dempsey, George, Midshipman, USN. "Navy's Greatest Sport." U.S. Naval Academy course paper, 1957. Copy in the possession of Professor Anthony J. Rubino.

Ford, Thomas G., Chevalier. "History of the United States Naval Academy." Unpublished manuscript, 1887. Special Collections, Nimitz Library, U.S. Naval Academy.

Hart, Casper P. "Founding of the United States Naval Academy." Master's thesis, Columbia University, 1937. Copy in Special Collections, Nimitz Library, U.S. Naval Academy.

Lane, Frances C., Lieutenant, USN. "History of the Naval Academy Sailing Squadron." Monograph in draft state, 1977. Author's files.

Sabo, W.J., Lieutenant, USN. "The United States Naval Academy in Popular Magazines and Fiction, 1900-1950." University of Maryland Graduate School paper, 1977. Author's files.

Strong, Barton D., Midshipman, USN. "A History of the Marine Barracks, Annapolis, Maryland." U.S. Naval Academy course paper, 1964. Copy in U.S. Naval Academy Archives.

Todorich, Charles M., Lieutenant, USN. "Citizen Sailors at Annapolis: The Story

of the Reserve Officers Classes at the Naval Academy during World War I."
University of Maryland Graduate School paper, 1976. Author's files.

————. "The Naval Academy in the Pre-Civil War Era: 1845-61." University of
Maryland Graduate School paper, 1975. Author's files.

Histories and Descriptions

Note: The United States Naval Institute *Proceedings* is abbreviated *USNIP*.

Annapolis: The United States Naval Academy Catalog. Washington, D.C.: U.S.
Government Printing Office, various editions.

Annapolis: Unofficial Directory and Guide. San Diego, Cal.: Military Publishers,
n.d. [c. 1970 and 1973].

"The Departments." *USNIP*, October 1935.

Fag Ends from the Naval Academy. New York: Homer Lee & Company, 1877.
(A second edition appeared in 1881.)

"The Hell Cats: The Naval Academy's Drum and Bugle Corps." *Shipmate*, June
1976.

Lucky Bag. Annapolis, Md.: 1894 to date.

Navy: United States Naval Academy Football Handbook. Annapolis, Md.: The
Naval Academy Athletic Association, 1948 to date.

Reef Points. Annapolis, Md.: various editions, 1905 to date.

The United States Naval Academy. New York: E.A. Hart, editions of 1887, 1890,
and 1894.

Aamold, Walter. "Athletic Training at the Naval Academy." *USNIP*, October
1935.

————. "Early Days of the Telephone at the U.S. Naval Academy." *USNIP*, July
1975.

————. "Naval Academy Athletics—1845 to 1945." *USNIP*, April 1946.

Alden, Carroll Storrs. "The *Santee*: An Appreciation." *USNIP*, June 1913.

Alden, Carroll Storrs, and Rear Admiral Ralph Earle, USN (Ret.). *Makers of
Naval Tradition*. Boston: Ginn & Co., 1942.

Baldridge, Harry A., Captain, USN (Ret.). "Naval Academy Museum: The First
Hundred Years." *USNIP*, April 1946.

Bealle, Morris A. *Gangway for Navy: The Story of Football at the United States
Naval Academy, 1879 to 1950*. Washington, D.C.: Columbia Publishing, 1951.

[Benjamin, Park.] *Shakings*, by a Member of the Class of 1867. Boston: Lee &
Shepard, [1868].

Benjamin, Park. *The United States Naval Academy*. New York: G.P. Putnam's
Sons, 1900.

Bolander, Louis H. "Civil War Annapolis." *USNIP*, November 1937.

————. "The Naval Academy in Five Wars." *USNIP*, April 1946.

Brown, F.M., Lieutenant, USAF. "A Half Century of Frustration: A Study of
the Failure of Naval Academy Legislation between 1800 and 1845." *USNIP*,
May 1954.

Bruzek, Joseph C. "The U.S. Schooner Yacht *America*." *USNIP*, September 1967.

Calvert, James, Vice Admiral, USN. "The Fine Line at the Naval Academy."
USNIP, October 1970.

————. "Thoughts upon the Conclusion of a Four-Year Tour." *Shipmate*, April
1972.

Chauvenet, William. *History of the Origin of the United States Naval Academy:
A Letter from Prof. William Chauvenet to Mr. T.G. Ford*. St. Louis, Mo.:
Nixon-Jones Printing Company, [1910?]. Original in Chevalier Thomas G.
Ford, "History of the United States Naval Academy." Unpublished manu-
script.

Crane, John, and Lieutenant James F. Keiley, USNR. *United States Naval
Academy: The First Hundred Years*. New York: Whittlesey House, 1945.

Dukeshire, T.S., Captain, USN. "The Confederate Midshipmen and the Treasure
Train." *USNIP*, June 1957.

Duval, Ruby R. "The Naval Academy Cemetery on 'Strawberry Hill.'" *USNIP*, April 1946.

Earle, Ralph, Commander, USN. *Life at the U.S. Naval Academy: The Making of the American Naval Officer*. New York: G.P. Putnam's Sons, 1917.

Eckley, Wayne, Associate Professor Emeritus. "USNA's Subcritical Nuclear Reactor." *Shipmate*, June 1973.

Edsall, Margaret Horton. *A Place Called the Yard: Guide to the United States Naval Academy*. [Annapolis, Md.]: The Douglas W. Edsall Company, 1976.

Ellicott, J.M., Captain, USN (Ret.) "Japanese Students at the United States Naval Academy." *USNIP*, March 1947.

Field, R.L., Lieutenant Commander, USN (Ret.). "The Black Midshipman at the U.S. Naval Academy." *USNIP*, April 1973.

Flagg, Ernest. "New Buildings for the U.S. Naval Academy, Annapolis, Maryland." *The American Architect and Building News*, July 1 and 8, 1908.

Folk, Winston, Lieutenant, USN. "The Confederate States Naval Academy." *USNIP*, September 1934.

Folk, Winston P., Rear Admiral, USN (Ret.). "The Great Segregation Imbroglio of 1920." *Shipmate*, March 1976.

Gibbs, George F. *Junk: A Collection of Songs and Poems by Cadets at the United States Naval Academy*. Washington, D.C.: The Patentee Publishing Company, 1889.

Grantham, E.A., Midshipman, USN. "Drum and Bugle Corps." *USNIP*, October 1935.

———. "Extra-Curricular Activities." *USNIP*, October 1935.

Greenwood, John E., Colonel, USMC. "The Corps' Old School Tie." *USNIP*, November 1975.

Hatch, Alden. *Heroes of Annapolis*. New York: Julian Messner, 1943.

Heise, J. Arthur. *The Brass Factories: A Frank Appraisal of West Point, Annapolis, and the Air Force Academy*. Washington, D.C.: Public Affairs Press, 1969.

Herndon, G. Melville. "The Confederate States Naval Academy." *Virginia Magazine of History and Biography*, July 1961.

Holloway, James L., Jr., Rear Admiral, USN. "The Holloway Plan—A Summary View and Commentary." *USNIP*, November 1947.

Holloway, J.L. III, Admiral, USN. "Naval Academy Education and Training: A New Directive from the Chief of Naval Operations." *Shipmate*, March 1976.

Houpt, C.T., Lieutenant, USNR. "Graduation Exercises at the Naval Academy, 1854-1914." *USNIP*, April 1946.

Karsten, Peter. *The Naval Aristocracy: The Golden Age of Annapolis and the Emergence of Modern American Navalism*. New York: The Free Press, 1972.

Lewis, Charles Lee. "Description of the United States Naval Academy." *USNIP*, October 1935.

Lovette, Leland P., Commander, USN. *School of the Sea: The Annapolis Tradition in American Life*. New York: Frederick A. Stokes, 1941.

[Lull, Edward P., Lieutenant Commander, USN.] *Description and History of the Naval Academy from its Origin to the Present Time*, N.P.: 1869.

Maersch, Rosemary. "Who's Who . . . in Navy Goats." [Annapolis, Md.: Naval Academy Athletic Association], 1976. Copy in the files of the Naval Academy Athletic Association.

Magruder, P.H. "The Colonial Government House of Maryland." *USNIP*, October 1935.

———. "Naval Academy Practice Ships 1845-1909." *USNIP*, May 1934.

———. "The Spanish Naval Prisoners of War at Annapolis, 1898." *USNIP*, June 1930.

———. "The U.S. Naval Academy and Annapolis during the Civil War 1861-1865." *USNIP*, April 1946.

———. "A Walk through Annapolis in Bygone Days." *USNIP*, June 1929.

Magruder, P.H. "A Walk through the Naval Academy in Bygone Days and To-day." *USNIP*, May 1932.

Marshall, Edward Chauncey. *History of the Naval Academy*. New York: D. Van Nostrand, 1862.

Masland, John W., and Laurence I. Radway. *Soldiers and Scholars: Military Education and National Policy*. Princeton, N.J.: Princeton University Press, 1957.

McNitt, Robert W., Rear Admiral, USN (Ret.) "Challenge and Change: The Naval Academy—1959-1969." *Shipmate*, April 1972.

Patrick, K.W., Midshipman, USN. "Midshipman Cruises." *USNIP*, October 1935.

Pesses, Michael, CWO, USN. ". . . 'And the Band Played On': History of the Naval Academy Band." [Annapolis, Md.: U.S. Naval Academy, c. 1975.] Copy in the files of the Naval Academy Athletic Association.

Plank, David W., Chaplain, USN. *The Chapel of the United States Naval Academy, Annapolis*. Annapolis, Md.: U.S. Naval Academy, 1969.

Puleston, W.D., Captain, USN. *Annapolis: Gangway to the Quarterdeck*. New York: D. Appleton-Century, 1942.

Riesenberg, Felix. *The Story of the Naval Academy*. New York: Random House, 1958.

Rigler, Frank V., Captain, USN (Ret.). "Commandants of Midshipmen." *Shipmate*, June 1976.

———. "The Lucky Bag." *Shipmate*, June 1975.

———. "The Naval Academy: The First Quarter Century." *Shipmate*, September-October 1970.

———. "Superintendents of the Naval Academy." *Shipmate*, April 1972.

Robert, Sarah Corbin. "Extracurricula—Midshipmen Organizations and Activities." *USNIP*, April 1946.

———. "The Naval Academy Chapel—Cathedral of the Navy." *USNIP*, April 1946.

Rogers, Lane, Lieutenant Colonel, USMC. "The Marine Corps and the U.S. Naval Academy." *Shipmate*, November 1975.

Schratz, Paul, Captain, USN (Ret.). "Sea Breezes: An Officer and a Gentlewoman." *Shipmate*, October 1977.

Sellers, David F., Rear Admiral, USN. "The United States Naval Academy: It Belongs to the Fleet." *USNIP*, October 1936.

Smith, Dody W. "The Tripoli Monument." *USNIP*, January 1972.

Smith, Roy C., III, Captain, USNR (Ret.) "The First Hundred Years Are . . ." *USNIP*, October 1973.

Soley, James Russell. *Historical Sketch of the United States Naval Academy*. Washington, D.C.: U.S. Government Printing Office, 1876.

Stevens, William O., and Carroll S. Alden. *A Guide to Annapolis and the Naval Academy*. Baltimore: Lord Baltimore Press, 1920.

Stevens, William Oliver. *Annapolis: Anne Arundel's Town*. New York: Dodd, Mead & Co., 1937.

Stewart, Charles W., editor. *John Paul Jones Commemoration at Annapolis, April 24, 1906*. Washington, D.C.: U.S. Government Printing Office, 1907.

Sturdy, Henry Francis. "The Establishment of the Naval School at Annapolis." *USNIP*, April 1946.

———. "The Founding of the Naval Academy by Bancroft and Buchanan." *USNIP*, October 1935.

Thomson, Earl Wentworth. "The Naval Academy as an Undergraduate College." *USNIP*, March 1948.

U.S. Naval Institute and the U.S. Naval Academy Foundation, Inc. "The United States Naval Academy In The World of Tomorrow." Special Supplement, *The New York Times*, October 24, 1965.

West, Richard S., Jr. "The Superintendents of the Naval Academy." *USNIP*, April 1946.

Works Project Administration. *A Guide to the United States Naval Academy.* New York: Devin-Adair, 1941.

Autobiographies, Papers, Memoirs

Allen, Gardner W., editor. *The Papers of Francis Gregory Dallas, United States Navy.* New York: Naval History Society, 1917.

Baldwin, Hanson W., U.S. Navy (Ret.). "Reminiscences of Hanson Weightman Baldwin." U.S. Naval Institute Oral History Program, 1976.

Brady, Cyrus T. *Under Tops'ls and Tents.* New York: Charles Scribner's Sons, 1901.

Brown, Wesley A., Ensign, USN. "The First Negro Graduate of Annapolis Tells His Story." *The Saturday Evening Post,* June 25, 1949.

Butler, Benjamin F. *Butler's Book: Autobiography and Personal Reminiscences of Major-General Benj. F. Butler.* Boston: A.M. Thayer & Co., 1892.

Carter, Jimmy. *Why Not the Best?* New York: Bantam Books, 1976.

Clark, Charles E., Rear Admiral, USN (Ret.). *My Fifty Years in the Navy.* Boston: Little, Brown & Co., 1917.

Clemens, A.B. "Forty Years After." *USNIP,* January 1920.

Coontz, Robert E., Rear Admiral, USN (Ret.). *From the Mississippi to the Sea.* Philadelphia: Dorrance & Co., 1930.

Dewey, George, Admiral of the Navy. *Autobiography.* New York: Charles Scribner's Sons, 1913.

Ellicott, J.M., Captain, USN (Ret.). "The Passing of the Cadet Engineers." *USNIP,* August 1938.

Evans, Holden A. *One Man's Fight for a Better Navy.* New York: Dodd, Mead & Co., 1940.

Evans, Robley D., Rear Admiral, USN. *A Sailor's Log: Recollections of Forty Years of Naval Life.* New York: D. Appleton & Co., 1901.

Fiske, Bradley A., Rear Admiral, USN (Ret.). *From Midshipman to Rear-Admiral.* New York: The Century Company, 1919.

Franklin, Samuel R., Rear Admiral, USN (Ret.). *Memories of a Rear Admiral.* New York: Harper Brothers, 1898.

Gallery, Daniel V., Rear Admiral, USN (Ret.). *Eight Bells, and All's Well.* New York: W.W. Norton, 1965.

Goodrich, Caspar F., Rear Admiral, USN (Ret.). *Rope Yarns from the Old Navy.* New York: The Naval History Society, 1931.

Halsey, William F., Fleet Admiral, USN, and Lieutenant Commander J. Bryan III, USNR, *Admiral Halsey's Story.* New York: Whittlesey House, 1947.

Hart, Thomas C., Admiral, USN (Ret.). "The Reminiscences of Thomas C. Hart." Columbia University Oral History Research Office, 1962. Transcript at U.S. Naval Institute.

Horan, James D., editor. *C.S.S.* Shenandoah: *The Memoirs of Lieutenant Commanding James I. Waddell.* New York: Crown Publishers, Inc., 1960.

Kell, John McIntosh. *Recollections of a Naval Life.* Washington, D.C.: Neale, 1900.

Kimball, H.S. "The Naval Academy Crew Sixty Years Ago." *USNIP,* September 1954.

King, Ernest J., and Walter Muir Whitehill. *Fleet Admiral King: A Naval Record.* New York: W.W. Norton, 1952.

Lejeune, John A., Major General, USMC (Ret.). *The Reminiscences of a Marine.* Philadelphia: Dorrance & Co. [c. 1930].

Mahan, Alfred T., Captain, USN (Ret.). *From Sail to Steam.* New York: Harper Brothers, 1907.

Melson, Charles L., Vice Admiral, USN (Ret.). "Reminiscences of Vice Admiral Charles L. Melson, United States Navy." U.S. Naval Institute Oral History Program, 1974.

Morgan, James Morris. *Recollections of a Rebel Reefer*. Boston: Houghton Mifflin Co., 1917.

Parker, William Harwar, Captain. *Recollections of a Naval Officer, 1841-1865*. New York: Charles Scribner's Sons, 1883.

Rodman, Hugh, Rear Admiral, USN (Ret.). *Yarns of a Kentucky Admiral*. Indianapolis: Bobbs-Merrill Co., 1928.

Schley, Winfield Scott, Rear Admiral, USN (Ret.). *Forty-Five Years under the Flag*. New York: D. Appleton & Co., 1904.

Schroeder, Seaton, Rear Admiral, USN (Ret.). *A Half-Century of Naval Service*. New York: D. Appleton & Co., 1922.

Seager, Robert, II, and Doris D. Maguire, editors. *Letters and Papers of Alfred Thayer Mahan*. 3 vols. Annapolis, Md.: Naval Institute Press, 1975.

Selfridge, Thomas O. *Memoirs of Thomas O. Selfridge, Jr., Rear Admiral, USN*. New York: G.P. Putnam's Sons, 1924.

Spencer, Julian M. "The Academy Fifty Years Ago." *Lucky Bag*, 1911.

Staubach, Roger, with Sam Blair and Bob St. John. *Staubach: First Down, Lifetime to Go*. Waco, Texas: World Books, 1974.

Stirling, Yates, Rear Admiral, USN (Ret.). *Sea Duty: The Memoirs of a Fighting Admiral*. New York: G.P. Putnam's Sons, 1939.

Wiley, Henry A., Rear Admiral, USN (Ret.). *An Admiral from Texas*. Garden City, N.Y.: Doubleday, Doran & Co., 1934.

Zogbaum, Rufus F., Rear Admiral, USN (Ret.). *From Sail to Saratoga: A Naval Autobiography*. Privately printed, [Rome, n.d.].

Zumwalt, Elmo R., Jr., Admiral, USN (Ret.). *On Watch: A Memoir*. New York: Quadrangle/New York Times Book Co., 1976.

Biographies

"The First Academic Staff." *USNIP*, October 1935.

Blair, Clay, Jr. *The Atomic Submarine*. London: Odhams Press, Ltd.: 1955. (A slightly different American edition appeared as *The Atomic Submarine and Admiral Rickover*. New York: Holt [1954]).

Buell, Thomas B. *The Quiet Warrior: A Biography of Admiral Raymond A. Spruance*. Boston: Little, Brown & Co., 1974.

Busik, S.W., Captain, USN (Ret.). " 'Doc' Snyder, 1878-1977." *Shipmate*, September 1977.

Cummings, Damon E., Captain, USN (Ret.). *Admiral Richard Wainwright and the United States Fleet*. Washington, D.C.: U.S. Government Printing Office, 1962.

Davis, Richard Harding. *Real Soldiers of Fortune*. New York: Charles Scribner's Sons, 1906.

Delaney, Norman C. *John McIntosh Kell of the Raider* Alabama. University, Ala.: The University of Alabama Press, 1973.

Edwards, E.M.H. *Commander William Barker Cushing of the United States Navy*. New York: F. Tennyson Neely, 1898.

Frank, Bemis M. *Halsey*. New York: Ballantine Books, 1974.

Friedrich, Rudolf J. "The First USNA Medal of Honor." *Shipmate*, July-August 1973.

Gleaves, Albert, Rear Admiral, USN (Ret.). *Life and Letters of Rear Admiral Stephen B. Luce*. New York: G.P. Putnam's Sons, 1925.

Gray, J.C. "Paul Joseph Dashiell, Ph.D." *USNIP*, August 1938.

Hart, Caroline Benson, and Louise Powers Benesch. *From Frigate to Dreadnaught: William Herbert Brownson, USN*. Sharon, Conn.: King House, 1973.

Jones, Ken, and Hubert Kelly, Jr. *Admiral Arleigh (31-Knot) Burke: The Story of a Fighting Sailor*. Philadelphia: Chilton Books, 1962.

Lewis, Charles Lee. *Admiral Franklin Buchanan: Fearless Man of Action*. Baltimore: Norman, Remington, 1929.

Littlehales, G.W. "William Chauvenet and the United States Naval Academy." *USNIP*, September 1905.

Livingston, Dorothy Michelson. "Michelson in the Navy; the Navy in Michelson." *USNIP*, June 1969.

Maclay, Edgar S., editor. *The Life and Adventures of Jack Philip, Rear Admiral, USN*. New York: The Illustrated Navy, 1903.

Morison, Elting E. *Admiral Sims and the Modern American Navy*. Boston: Houghton Mifflin Co., 1942.

Nye, Russel B. *George Bancroft: Brahmin Rebel*. New York: Alfred A. Knopf, 1944.

Potter, E.B. *Nimitz*. Annapolis, Md.: Naval Institute Press, 1976.

Puleston, W.D., Captain, USN. *Mahan*. New Haven, Conn.: Yale University Press, 1939.

Reardon, K.J., Midshipman, USN. "Dean Drought: Leader of USNA's Academic Revolution." *Trident* Magazine, April 1966.

Roske, Ralph J., and Charles Van Doren. *Lincoln's Commando: The Biography of Commander W.B. Cushing, U.S.N.* New York: Harper Brothers, 1957.

Seager, Robert, II. *Alfred Thayer Mahan: The Man and His Letters*. Annapolis, Md.: Naval Institute Press, 1977.

Spector, Ronald. *Admiral of the New Empire: The Life and Career of George Dewey*. Baton Rouge, La.: Louisiana State University Press, 1974.

Taylor, Theodore. *The Magnificent Mitscher*. New York: W.W. Norton & Co., 1954.

Walker, Jeanie Mort. *Life of Captain Joseph Fry*. Hartford, Conn.: The J.B. Burr Publishing Company, 1875.

West, Richard S., Jr. *The Second Admiral: A Life of David Dixon Porter 1813-1891*. New York: Coward-McCann, 1937.

Wilson, William E., Lieutenant, USNR. "Graduates of the U.S. Naval Academy." *USNIP*, April 1946.

Fiction

Beach, Edward L., Lieutenant Commander, USN. *An Annapolis Plebe*. Philadelphia: Penn Publishing Company, 1907.

———. *An Annapolis Youngster*. Philadelphia: Penn Publishing Company, 1908.

———. *An Annapolis Second Classman*. Philadelphia: Penn Publishing Company, 1909.

———. *An Annapolis First Classman*. Philadelphia: Penn Publishing Company, 1910.

Clark, H.H. *Midshipman Stanford*. Boston: Lothrop, Lee and Shepard, 1916.

Hamil, Thomas A., Midshipman, USN, and Midshipman J. Kendrick Noble, USN. *Ploob: A Midshipman's First Year at Annapolis*. New York: Noble and Noble, [1949].

Hancock, H. Irving. *Dave Darin's First Year at Annapolis*. Philadelphia: Henry Artemus, 1910.

———. *Dave Darin's Second Year at Annapolis*. New York: Saalfeld Publishing Company, 1911.

———. *Dave Darin's Third Year at Annapolis*. New York: Saalfeld Publishing Company, 1911.

———. *Dan Darin's Fourth Year at Annapolis*. Philadelphia: Henry Artemus, 1911.

Hobson, Richmond P. *Buck Jones at Annapolis*. New York: D. Appleton & Co., 1907.

Schmidt, Kurt. *Annapolis Misfit*. New York: Crown Publishers, Inc., 1974.

West, Roger [Virginia Watson]. *Midshipman Days*. Boston: Houghton Mifflin Co., 1913.

General Sources

Ambrose, Stephen E. *Duty, Honor, Country: A History of West Point*. Baltimore, Md.: The Johns Hopkins University Press, 1966.

Blair, Clay, Jr. *Silent Victory: The U.S. Submarine War against Japan*. Philadelphia: J.B. Lippincott Co., 1975.

Boatner, Mark Mayo, III, Lieutenant Colonel, USA. *The Civil War Dictionary*. New York: David McKay Co., 1959.

Coletta, Paolo E. *The American Naval Heritage in Brief*. Washington, D.C.: University Press of America, 1978.

Hagan, Kenneth J., editor. *In Peace and War: Interpretations of American Naval History 1775-1978*. Westport, Conn.: Greenwood Press, 1978.

Hayford, Harrison, editor. *The Somers Mutiny Affair*. Englewood Cliffs, N.J.: Prentice-Hall Inc., 1960.

Hesseltine, William B., and Hazel C. Wolf. *The Blue and The Grey on the Nile*. Chicago: The University of Chicago Press, 1961.

Miller, Nathan. *The U.S. Navy: An Illustrated History*. New York and Annapolis: American Heritage Publishing Co., Inc., and Naval Institute Press, 1977.

Millis, Walter, editor. *The Forrestal Diaries*. New York: Viking, 1951.

Morison, Samuel Eliot. *John Paul Jones: A Sailor's Biography*. Boston: Little, Brown & Co., 1959.

―――. *"Old Bruin": Commodore Matthew Calbraith Perry*. Boston: Little, Brown & Co., 1967.

Paullin, Charles Oscar. *Paullin's History of Naval Administration 1775-1911*. Annapolis, Md.: U.S. Naval Institute, 1968.

Potter, E.B. *The Naval Academy Illustrated History of the United States Navy*. New York: Thomas Y. Crowell, 1971.

Potter, E.B., and Fleet Admiral Chester W. Nimitz, USN, editors. *Sea Power: A Naval History*. Englewood Cliffs, N.J.: Prentice-Hall, Inc., 1960.

Ray, Thomas. "The First Three." *USNIP*, January, July, October 1971.

Rhodes, James Ford. *History of the United States from the Compromise of 1850*. New York: Harper Brothers, 1900.

Rudolph, Frederick. *The American College and University*. New York: Alfred A. Knopf, Inc., 1962.

Scharf, J.T. *History of the Confederate States Navy*. New York: Rogers and Sherwood, 1887.

Tily, James C. *The Uniforms of the United States Navy*. New York: Thomas Yoseloff, 1964.

United States Senate, Subcommittee on Veterans' Affairs of the Committee on Labor and Public Welfare. *Medal of Honor Recipients 1863-1963*. Washington, D.C.: U.S. Government Printing Office, 1964.

Van De Water, Frederic F. *The Captain Called It Mutiny*. New York: Ives Washburn, 1954.

Van Deurs, George, Rear Admiral, USN (Ret.). *Wings for the Fleet: A Narrative of Naval Aviation's Early Development, 1910-1916*. Annapolis, Md.: U.S. Naval Institute, 1966.

Index

Note: Numbers in italic refer to illustrations.

Note: Unless otherwise specified, all academic and geographical entries refer to the U.S. Naval Academy or the city of Annapolis, Maryland. Ranks indicated are those held by the individual when first mentioned in the text and are not necessarily the highest achieved. Those for which no other service is stated are U.S. Navy.